Illustrated H
of APPLEDORE

Its Life and People

2

John & Janie Carter

David Carter

Published by David Carter
Docton Court, 2 Myrtle Street
Appledore, Bideford, EX39 1PH

First published 2009

British Library Cataloguing in Publication Data
A catalogue record for this book is available from the British Library

ISBN 978-0-9538524-1-3

Line illustrations by Bill Wright, Appledore, Devon
Designed and produced by Collum Design, Westward Ho! Devon
Printed and bound in the UK by Kingfisher Print & Design, Totnes, Devon

CONTENTS

"Appledore is my favourite village in Britain. In spite of all the changes and the tarmac that has replaced the cobbles, the zest is still there. Appledore is too down-to-earth to be a tourist attraction like Clovelly. With Westward Ho! as the invaluable buffer nearby, it is isolated, on the way to nowhere."

(Daniel Farson: 'A Window on the Sea', 1977)

INTRODUCTION

APPLEDORE- the *little* village with the **BIG** history

This small peninsula jutting into the Torridge is what this book is all about.

When I wrote my first book on the history of Appledore, I put everything I had into it - time, energy, enthusiasm, and above all - information. I was only going to do it once, so I made it as complete as I could. I was pleased with the result, and as the book is heading for its fourth printing, it appears that other people liked it too. That did leave me with a bit of a problem for the often-requested sequel, but in the intervening years a lot has happened.

Firstly I have moved to Appledore. This had been a long-term ambition, but Jenny and I eventually found a way to make it happen, and to earn a living here at the same time. We bought and restored one of Appledore's most historic buildings, which is now our home and workplace. The restoration of Docton Court was very satisfying, and we also relish living in a building with such a long history – but more of that later. I have been able to discover much more detailed information about Appledore, plus many more old photographs, but I needed to find a good way of presenting all this, otherwise it would be just a meaningless jumble of bits.

After having lived in Appledore for a couple of years, and walking round the village pondering its layout and buildings, the idea came to me of producing an extended historical tour of the village. This tour would concentrate on the history of individual buildings, on the people who lived in each one and what they did. The idea grew, and after having talked to many people in Appledore, each of whom had a small piece of the finished picture, I have now been able to piece together this new history book. I hope that you will enjoy it as much as the last one.

START
HERE

BACKGROUND AND EARLY HISTORY:

North Devon may seem quite remote and isolated from the rest of England, but historically the lack of roads hasn't prevented it from being a major player in terms of trade with the rest of the world. Mention the name of Appledore in many ports round the globe, and you'd be identified as a 'Bar-man', and guaranteed respect from anyone that knew the sailing industry and the men that undertook long and dangerous voyages. But when did men come to settle into the mouth of this sheltered estuary…?

PRE-HISTORY:

The evidence for early settlements in North Devon is generally more subtle than in other parts of the Country. At Westward Ho! the receding tide sometimes reveals a Mesolithic petrified forest exposed in the shifting sands. Amongst this has been found a kitchen-midden (rubbish pit) of waste discarded by prehistoric people. It was found to contain burned animal and fish bones, hazelnut husks, acorn cups, seeds, fresh-water shells and flakes from flint instruments. It has been dated to 4,200 BC. Other wooden stakes have been dated to 2,850 BC, and later bones of cattle, sheep and goats were dated to Roman times.

EARLY VISITORS:

Despite its appearance as a quiet backwater, many travellers from overseas made their way to North Devon. According to Ptolomy, writing in AD 100, Hercules supposedly sailed around the Devon coast in a golden bowl, when undertaking the tenth of his twelve labours. He landed at Hartland Point, allegedly staying there for several years, ruling his country from that location.

A little later, St Brennan, a 6th century Welsh monk, is supposed to have made the voyage across the Bristol Channel from South Wales in a stone coffin. He entered the Taw & Torridge estuary, but by-passed Appledore and founded a monastery at Braunton - which he presumably felt was more sheltered.

In the post-Roman period, most of the South West was inhabited by the Dumnonii tribe, but they didn't use coins, or have large settlements. These were self-sufficient people, although they did all share the same type of decorated pottery.

Roman olive-oil amphora discovered in the bed of the Torridge at Appledore. (Devon Notes and Queries)

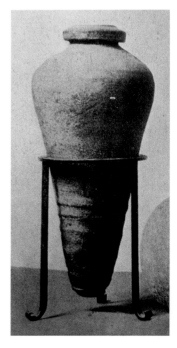

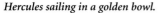

Hercules sailing in a golden bowl.

These people seemed to accept the Roman Conquest with little resistance, and so very few Roman garrison forts were placed in their territory. In consequence, the Roman way of life was never fully adopted here, which probably explains why Cornwall and Devon have culturally been somewhat distant from the rest of England.

SAINT KILLERS:

A book of Saints written in the 12th century, described how the blessed martyr John crossed the river Thorich (Torridge), after having been beheaded, and placed his head on the other bank, where a church was founded in his honour. He gave Instow its name (a contraction of Johns-town), and became its patron saint. However, this incident can only lead to the conclusion that the people of Appledore were not only barbaric enough to behead a Celtic saint, but also stupid enough to let him escape afterwards!

The beheaded St John crossing the river Torridge.

HISTORIC BATTLES:

We can attribute a number of battles to the area around Appledore. In 878, a Danish army lead by King Ubba, landed here and were defeated by the brave men of Devon. Legend has it that this battle ended near Bloody Corner, between Appledore and Northam, and an inscribed plaque was erected on the spot in 1890 to commemorate the event. This monument replaced an earlier stone known as the 'Bloody Stone', because when it became wet, it was supposed to bleed. This was no miracle, just a stone on which a red-coloured moss grew, which became more visible when

made wet. However, the tradition of a battle on this site can be inferred from such traditional tales, but if this stone did commemorate a battle, it is more likely to have been one in 1069.

Three years after the Battle of Hastings, there were still rumblings of discontent from the supporters of the defeated Harold Godwinson. Harold's sons mounted various counter-attacks from their exile in Ireland, and in 1069 their final attempt to overthrow William the Conqueror came when they sailed from Ireland with an army of about 3,000 men, in sixty-four ships. They landed at 'Tawmutha' – now generally identified as Tomouth, or Appledore - but they were met with resistance from the newly installed Norman military regime. Many were killed, and the others were driven back to their ships, where Harold's sons eventually admitted defeat, and settled in Flanders. The Norman invasion of 1066 was finally settled – and it ended here in Appledore.

DOMESDAY:

Written sources from the 11th century are mostly limited to the Anglo-Saxon Chronicles and the Domesday Book, so we have precious little information upon which to base our understanding of these times. The Domesday Book of 1086 does not mention Appledore's name, but it does mention Northam. It gives a description of the fishery and salt-works contained within the manorial lands, so we can tell that this must be Appledore - being the part of Northam parish that was by the sea.

A WOMAN SCORNED:

The Manor of Northam plus about a dozen other manors were held by the Saxon noble Beorhtric. The story is that in his youth

Beorhtric was sent as ambassador to the Court of Flanders, where the Count's daughter Matilda fell in love with him, but he rebuffed her advances and declined to marry her. After longing for him for several years Matilda found another suitable husband in the form of her illegitimate cousin 'William the Bastard' (although he probably wasn't called that to his face!).

Beorhtric returned to Devon to look after his lands, whereas Matilda's husband William rose in social standing and in 1066 led an army to invade England. After his victory at Hastings, William was thereafter known as 'William - the Conqueror' - a much grander title for the new King of England. Matilda became Queen and exerted her powers - she seized all of Beorhtric's lands in revenge and gave them to the Abbott of St Stephen's at Caen, who had helped finance the 1066 invasion. Beorhtric was taken to Winchester, and put in prison where he subsequently died (beware a woman scorned!).

LORD OF THE MANOR:

Ownership of the Northam Manorial lands remained with the Abbott of Caen until 1539 when Henry VIII seized them and gave them to the Arundel family. After the dissolution these were given to the Dean of Windsor in 1547. Manorial lands & titles were granted to various nobles who could in turn lease or sell these rights to others, so the question of who actually owns the Manorial Lands is not easy to answer. However, I will just briefly mention the people who had control of the rights at any time and who shaped the history of Appledore.

Historically, the Lord-of-the-Manor had control over all his subjects, could tax them, and make them work for him, but he was also responsible for the economic well-being of the community. He held local Courts concerning land rights, tenants, and law-breaking - indeed he had the power of capital punishment. His

powers were wide-ranging. In 1584, the manor appears to have been sold to Sir Walter Raleigh, who then sold it to the Borough family in 1596 – they lived at Borough House at Northam. In 1616 it became the property of the Berry family (Sir Thomas Berry built the almshouses in 1682), but he then sold it to his cousin Thomas Melhuish of Watertown. In 1770 William Melhuish leased the manor for 200 years to the Clevelands of Tapeley Estate, who sub-let it to Thomas Burnard Chanter of Knapp House in the mid-19th century (see, I told you it was complicated!). Manorial powers have now devolved to the local Council, who thankfully no longer have power of capital punishment!

ORIGIN OF THE NAME:

It is possible that the name 'Appledore' did not exist in the 11th century, and that any settlement here was called 'Tawmouth', this being the name mentioned in the Anglo Saxon Chronicles. The name 'Appledore' first appears in the early 14th century, and is supposed to come from Old English, meaning 'Apple Tree'.

The name 'Affpeldorford' appearing in a document from the 1320s. (National Archives)

In my first book, I indicated that the earliest reference to the name 'Appledore' was in 1335. Since then I have discovered a possible earlier reference to Appledore in a Petition document dating from the 1320s, in which the Devon village of 'Affpeldorford' is mentioned.

Does this perhaps come from 'Aber-Taw-Ford' – ie: the Ford (river-crossing) at the Mouth of the Taw? If so, then the earlier name of 'Tawmouth' (Mouth of the Taw) equates better with the Welsh 'Aber-Taw', which has the same meaning. However, there is no definitive answer, it's all just interesting speculation.

Our Appledore ancestors were far from being uncultured - this music was being sung in Northam Parish Church in the 14th century. This Kyrie was discarded after Henry VIII dismissed the Catholic Church. It only survived by being used as a cover for the church accounts book. (North Devon Record Office).

GROWTH AND DECLINE:

Appledore in the 1340s must have been quite lively and prosperous. In 1346, seven ships and 120 men were sent from the Torridge to help Edward III's blockade of the port of Calais. However, three years later, the Black Death hit England, wiping out half its population, and there is a period of a couple of hundred years when there is no news of Appledore, but we can assume that it entered a deep decline with a much reduced population.

PIONEER EXPLORER:

The early pioneering explorers' names are well known to us – Columbus, Magellan, Vasco da Gama – they all forged links with other parts of the world through their adventurous ocean voyages. However there is another un-sung hero whose voyages in far more dangerous territory seem to have largely gone unnoticed in our history books.

Stephen Borough was born in Northam in 1525, and learned his sea-faring abilities at Appledore, becoming one of Britain's greatest navigators, and a pioneer of English exploration. At that time, it was thought that there might be a shorter route to the Far East, across the top of Russia, instead of going all the way around South Africa. Stephen Borough was recruited by London merchants to go and find this route. He made the first of two voyages in 1553, and although he failed to find it, he did set up trading links with Ivan the Terrible, and founded an overseas trading company, called the Muscovy Company. If he had succeeded in finding a new route, no doubt his name would be far more celebrated. He went on to become the Chief Pilot of England, and one of the Masters of Ordnance for the Navy. He is buried at Chatham, where a plaque in the church records his North Devon origins.

Borough House, Northam.

BOROUGH HOUSE:

Stephen Borough's ancestral home was Borough House in Northam, on the road that led to the Burrows. The house was later to be immortalised by Charles Kingsley, as the home of his Westward Ho! hero Amyas Leigh. The history of the house could be traced back to the 13th century, and was passed down through continual family ownership for six hundred years (the Borough family, the Leighs, the Berrys, the Melhuishes, the Downes and the Bartons). Then in the 1860s, the house and lands were bought by William Yeo of Appledore, who succeeded in ending the life of this great and historic house, by pulling it down, and replacing it with new houses.

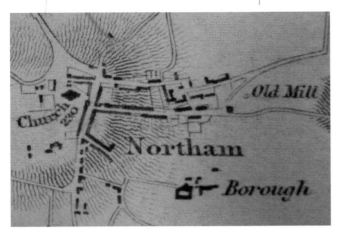

1855 map showing the extent of Northam, including the location of Borough House. (UK Hydrographic Office).

TUDOR PROSPERITY:

England's maritime empire prospered again under the Tudors, and by 1582 there were 115 mariners registered here (compared to 39 at Bideford). At that time Appledore was part of the port of Barnstaple, which was ruled by a Corporation for the benefit of its merchants, making them, and the town, very wealthy.

However, its harbour was too shallow for large vessels, so most vessels were unloaded at Appledore, and the goods shipped up-river in smaller barges. In this way, most of the wealth by-passed Appledore, but it did keep our mariners in continual work, building and manning ships for these merchants. Most of the trade was with France and Spain, and a typical list of goods imported through Appledore at that time would be: wine, dried fruits, oil, salt, vinegar, prunes, pitch, iron, and wool.

THE SPANISH ARMADA:

Things were hotting up with the Spanish though, and in 1586, just two years before the Spanish Armada, the 'Zeraphen' sailed from Appledore to Spain on a trading voyage. However, upon arrival the crew were charged with piracy, threatened with the impressment of their ship, and narrowly escaped trial for heresy. They had to flee Spain in secret, abandoning all their goods. This was too much for England to bear, and with a rumoured Spanish invasion of England in the offing, the maritime community prepared for war.

In 1588, five ships were sent from the Torridge, full of mariners under the command of Sir Richard Grenville. They joined Francis Drake at Plymouth, and together the fleet sailed off to fight the Spanish Armada. Most of the crew of these vessels would have come from Appledore, and they played a vital part in defending our nation at this time of conflict. Whilst their names are unknown, their heroism is legendary, and their actions changed the course of our nation's history.

THE AFRICAN TRADE:

With trade to Spain and Portugal curtailed, Britain looked for other parts of the World with which to do business. In 1588 (the same year as the Armada), Elizabeth I granted eight licences to permit trading to the coast of Guinea in West Africa, and this included one trader from Barnstaple, called Richard Dodderidge. Given the size of ships needed for such a voyage, these expeditions would have departed from Appledore rather than Barnstaple. Trading links were established, and ships were soon bringing back an even greater assortment of cargoes.

Amongst these were some native Africans, whose arrival on our shores can be seen from the Parish Registers of Barnstaple, where there are a number of baptisms or burials for a 'nyger' or 'nigor', such as this one – the first recorded such baptism of a black person in this town:

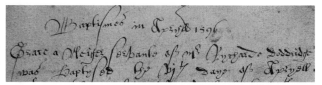

1596: Grace, a neiger servant of Rychard Doddridge was baptised the 6th day of Apryll. (North Devon Record Office).

TREASURE:

Richard Dodderidge came to Barnstaple from South Molton in 1565, a move which proved to be a good one for him. His trade with Africa made him immensely rich. On Boxing Day 1590, one of his ships arrived back carrying a different kind of cargo - treasure. Whilst in the harbour at Guinea, Dodderidge's ship encountered a Portuguese vessel in the harbour. We don't know if any fighting took place, but this enemy vessel was seized and brought back as booty. The 'Lost Chronicle' of Barnstaple described its contents: *"Four chests of gold to the value of £16,000, chains of gold with civet, ambergris, elephant tooths, and other things of great price."*

The gold chests were later weighed and found to be about 320 lbs in weight. That one capture was worth about five million pounds

for Richard Dodderidge in today's terms. It must have been quite a celebration when this booty was unloaded. In 1596 the link with Appledore was strengthened when Appledore merchant John Darracott married Richard Dodderidge's daughter.

BLACK SLAVES:

Although Dodderidge is known to have brought black Africans to Devon in the 1590s, it must be pointed out that the word 'slave' never appears at this time - the main purpose of these trading voyages was to bring back a varied range of new cargoes. Indeed we had no need for slaves, as Britain had no plantations, and there were plenty of other people in this Country who were willing to be servants. The status of these immigrants is therefore uncertain, but there is no evidence to show that they were not as free as any other servants. Apart from Dodderidge, other local merchants acquired black servants, and these must have created quite a talking point in a provincial town like Barnstaple. However, it is doubtful whether any Appledore merchants were rich enough to acquire such a luxury.

WHITE SLAVES:

Slavery is usually seen as a black issue - with the transportation of black Africans to the New World generally starting in the 1620s. However, at the same time, there was also a reverse people-trade, going in the other direction. Between the 1620s and the 1820s, English men and women were captured by North Africans, and taken to Morocco, Algeria, Libya and Tunisia, and sold as slaves. These 'Barbary Corsairs' mostly captured Englishmen from ships at sea, rather than undertaking raiding parties on land, and given that Devon is a sea-going county, a large number of its inhabitants were taken in this way. Evidence actually suggests that the number of Devonians enslaved in North Africa

exceeded the number of Africans taken by Devonians to the New World. Thousands of Devon sailors were at risk on the seas, and in 1637 the British Navy used force to release three-hundred captives. Of these, almost a third were from Devon, including a Richard Knollman from Bideford, and a Philip Strange from Barnstaple.

So next time some ancestors go missing from your family tree, just think that they might have ended up in Africa, and that slavery is an issue in which Devon people are just as much victims as perpetrators.

THE NEW WORLD:

In 1586, the Lord-of-the-Manor at Bideford, Sir Richard Grenville (a cousin of both Sir Walter Raleigh and Sir Francis Drake), was even more aggressive in his quest for booty, and gathered an expeditionary force of six ships, filled with 600 sailors and soldiers. Officially it was supposed to take men and supplies to found the first-ever American colony at Roanoke Island in Virginia, but somehow they also managed to return laden with sugar, ginger and hides. The Roanoke Colonists disappeared two years later, and to this day no-one knows exactly what happened to them. Were any Appledore men part of this, trying to make a new life for themselves with a spirit of adventure? We will never know, but it

would be surprising if there weren't.

Over the next few years, Richard Grenville brought back many other prizes to Bideford, and was instrumental in turning it into the third largest port in the country. He died in 1591 fighting the Spanish in the Azores. Grenville had put forward the idea of planting English colonists in the New World, ten years before Raleigh, but is not often credited with his foresight in this matter. North America was at that time on the minds of many people, helped in part by some native Americans being brought back and seen walking the streets here. The first successful American colony was established in 1607 at Jamestown, followed by a larger settlement at Boston in 1630, which Appledore emigrants no doubt helped to found. Our trade with the New World grew and flourished, but ended in 1775 when the American colonies eventually won their Independence.

Tombstone in the ancient Copps Hill Burying Ground at Boston Massachusetts. Nathaniel Brewer, Ellis Cook and George Darracott – and surnames don't come much more 'Appledore' than Darracott.

EXPANSION:

Appledore expanded at this time of great trade and prosperity. The parish church at Northam was extended in 1593, and again in 1623. By 1630, a visitor reported that Appledore had *"many fair buildings the equal of most market towns, and was furnished with good and skilful mariners"*.

Trade and emigration across the Atlantic

continued. In 1633, Richard Collacott from Barnstaple acquired land on Cape Cod in Massachusetts, which by 1639 had become known as 'Barnstable'. Biddeford in Maine was established by settlers from Bideford in Devon, although this name doesn't seem to have been used until 1718. Appledore Island off the coast of Maine was also probably settled in the 1630s, but the settlers left in the early 1700s as Maine wanted to tax them, so they moved to Gosport in New Hampshire.

COD FISHING:

One of the significant historical trades of Appledore is generally stated to be 'Newfoundland Cod Fishing' - but what does this mean? Certainly this sounds far more serious than a day-trip out to sea with a rod and a line. Why did we have to go all the way to Newfoundland to catch fish, and how did we do it? This seems like an awfully long way to go for a few baskets of cod!

Cod fishing in the Grand Banks off Newfoundland started in the mid 1500s, although such voyages are not recorded in detail as this cargo did not have to be taxed, but from 1588 there are records of fish-oil being imported here. This was more like an industrial process than a fishing trip. It generally started in January, with young men being recruited at local taverns and fairs. A couple of months was spent preparing the ships for the voyage, which then crossed the Atlantic arriving at a sheltered Newfoundland bay around April time. A further two months was spent setting up a shoreline fish-processing 'factory'. The shoals

of cod arrived off the shores in June and July, and were caught from smaller boats stored permanently in Newfoundland. The fish were drained of oil, then salted, dried, and packed ready for shipping back home.

A typical vessel carried a crew of forty, from which eight crews of three men would each catch about 25,000 cod, giving a total of 200,000 fish - about 100 tons, plus about 12 tons of fish-oil. So how did an 80-ton ship bring back well over its own weight in fish products – well the simple answer is that it didn't. A fleet of 'sac ships' were sent over, arriving in July or August, carrying supplies for the fishermen and bringing back the processed cod, which was largely sold to France and Spain. England got the fish-oil, which was mostly turned into soap.

Often the fishermen stayed in Newfoundland for two summers and a winter, and while some settled there permanently, most returned to Devon on a regular basis. By 1775, about 20,000 men were going to these fishing banks each summer, but the trade had seriously diminished by 1815 as so many men were taken for Napoleonic war duties. Cod fishing off Newfoundland finally ceased in the 1840s.

CUSTOMS OFFICE:

The Customs Offices were located at Bideford and Barnstaple where the merchants lived. In 1765, there were calls for Appledore to be made a legal quay for dutiable goods, but Officers at Barnstaple refused, describing it as "a place as lawless as any in this kingdom".

Nevertheless, traders who found it 'inconvenient' to declare their goods, often landed them at Appledore and took the risk. Cargoes were brought in by small coasters, but vanished once they were on shore. Little is recorded on the business of smuggling, as it was only when people were caught that records were made. Appledore was a great place to smuggle, and possibly still is?

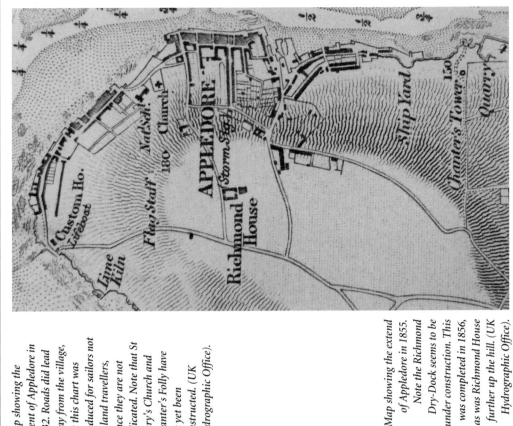

Map showing the extent of Appledore in 1832. Roads did lead away from the village, but this chart was produced for sailors not for land travellers, hence they are not indicated. Note that St Mary's Church and Chanter's Folly have not yet been constructed. (UK Hydrographic Office).

Map showing the extend of Appledore in 1855. Note the Richmond Dry-Dock seems to be under construction. This was completed in 1856, as was Richmond House further up the hill. (UK Hydrographic Office).

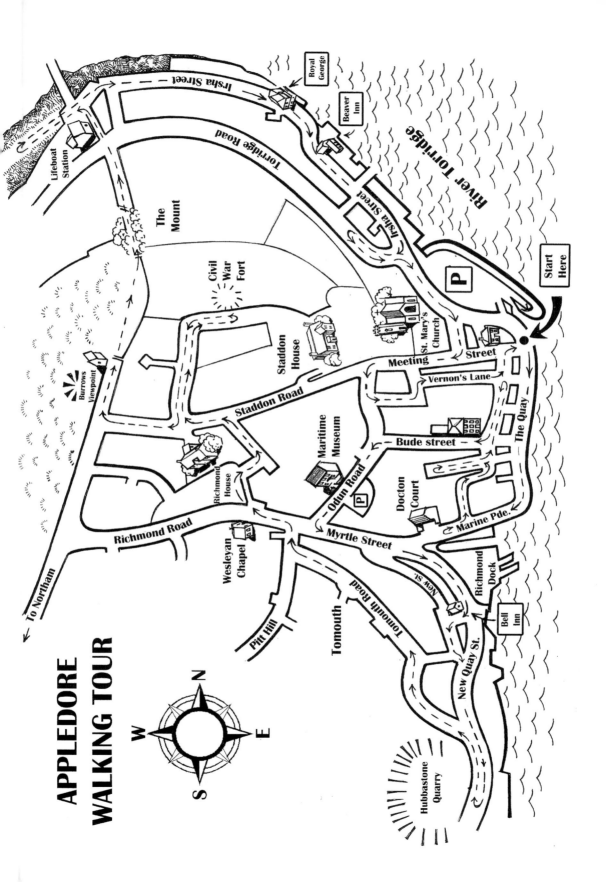

APPLEDORE WALKING TOUR

Royal George

Beaver Inn

Irsha Street

Lifeboat Station

Torridge Road

River Torridge

The Mount

Civil War Fort

Start Here

Burrows Viewpoint

Staddon House

St. Mary's Church

Meeting Street

Vernon's Lane

Staddon Road

Maritime Museum

Bude street

The Quay

Richmond House

Odun Road

Docton Court

Marine Pde.

Richmond Road

Wesleyan Chapel

Myrtle Street

New St.

Richmond Dock

Bell Inn

Pitt Hill

Tomouth

Tomouth Road

New Quay St.

To Northam

Hubbastone Quarry

N
S
E
W

Benjamin Donn's map showing Appledore in 1765. Note the disused Chapel and the Parish Workhouse at Marshford crossroads.

IS APPLEDORE A TOWN OR A VILLAGE?

Most Appledorians would probably plump for Appledore being a village, albeit quite a large one. Historically though, Appledore has always been considered to be the poor relation of Northam. From the time of Domesday until the early Victorian period, the church (and therefore the source of power) was at Northam. However, in 1850 a local directory described the parish as "the little seaport <u>town</u> of Appledore, and the ridge <u>hamlet</u> of Northam". This puts a slightly different slant on things, and elevates Appledore up the scale of importance. Generally a town was considered to be self-sufficient for shops and services. This was certainly the case for Appledore a hundred years ago, but no longer. So even though Appledore's population hasn't changed much, for this reason alone I think we can now accept that Appledore is a village.

EARTHQUAKE:

Appledore was shaken in 1883, when earthquake tremors were felt in the village. The local papers reported that a severe shock and loud rumblings were experienced. Some houses literally rocked, and a noise like a heavy goods train approaching was heard.

VISITORS:

Some might say that Appledore is plagued by visitors. However, we are now a tourist village – no longer can we rely on shipbuilding, fishing, or seafaring for our income. We welcome all visitors, whether for a few hours, or a few months. Generally it is the village character and history that they come to see, so we must strive hard to preserve this.

Visitors are not a modern trend though. A directory from 1830 noted that Appledore was frequented by "genteel individuals from distant parts", who came to inhale its breezes, bathe in its waters, and stay in its lodging houses (ie: holiday cottages). Some gentry came here for longer periods, investing in houses in which they would stay (ie: second-home owners). This is not a modern phenomenon, although today we do have more 'gentry' who can afford to do this.

With the growth of Westward Ho!, sea-bathing and golf, more nobility came here for the season. In 1871, amongst the list of fashionable arrivals to Westward Ho! was the Marquis of Sligo, who made the journey by train from London to Bideford in five & a half hours (it's not much quicker today!).

In August 1901, the papers reported that Appledore had had a record day for visitors, the lodging houses were all full, and every train brought even more crowds who kept the ferry boats busy crossing and re-crossing the river. A visitor sending a postcard home at this time wrote: *"the houses here are irregular and pressed together, as though they wish to keep the secrets that the years have given them."*

I hope to be able to unlock some of these secrets for you in this book – Appledore has a fascinating history, much of which is still around us. You just have to know where to look, and have someone to guide you though the narrow streets and cobbled courts. So sit back and enjoy the journey…

BEFORE THE QUAY:

Now that we've got the early history over with, we can start looking at the history that is still around us. First, let's have a bit of history about the Quay itself.

In the early 1800s, there was no public quay here. The waterfront may have partly resembled the way Irsha Street is today, with the back gardens of the waterside properties facing towards the river. In this case, it was the back gardens of the commercial properties in Market Street - Appledore's original Main Street – which faced the river. These properties would each have had landing places for vessels, ranging in size from fishing boats to small trading coasters, and some properties had riverfront warehouses for storage. However, Appledore mostly faced inwards for protection against the gales and elements.

FLOODING:

Pigs and chickens were kept in these back gardens. The quay area has always been prone to flooding with spring tides, and at times like this the livestock would be taken up Bude Street, Vernons Lane or Meeting Street, where they were kept in small fenced areas until the flooding subsided.

In 1896, the newspapers reported that a fishing boat could be taken down Market Street - the water in some of the houses being up to two feet deep. This was not an unusual event, and at other times baulks of timber bumped through the streets and had to be removed to prevent damage to the houses.

Flooding was not always caused by high tides - there are also records of freak events. In 1851, two houses in Irsha Street were demolished by a heavy swell. Twelve years later, the waters were reported as having risen ten feet higher than they should, caused by a 'strong gale from the west'. Sea walls in Marine Parade and West Appledore were washed away, and the North Devon Journal said that the houses on the Quay were flooded, 'much to the annoyance of the inmates' (a rather curious description of the residents, making Appledore sound rather like an asylum!).

Flooding still occurred into the 1990s, but this was solved in 1997 with the construction of an extended raised quay and promenade. It's not often we are appreciative of late 20th century development, but this quay is a great improvement over the previous wartime structure, and gives Appledore an outside space which is now used for a variety of leisure events.

EARLY QUAYS:

When Queen Victoria came to the throne in 1837 the central part of Appledore consisted of a collection of buildings backing onto the river, which individual owners used for their own commercial purposes.

Lord-of-the-Manor, Thomas Chanter, is credited with persuading the land-owners here to join their individual properties together and construct one large quay for everyone. However, I think that greater credit should be given to the land-owners themselves, who in 1838 called a meeting to agree what measures should be undertaken to construct a new quay. These owners were: John Beara, Edward Hodges, William Haynes, Richard Limbery, Richard Dart, Thomas Chappell, Thomas Cook, and William Parnell. Like most grand schemes it took a while to happen, and Thomas Chanter probably gave it his financial support. Seven years later in 1845 an 800-foot long quay was formally opened and was free to be used by everyone.

This is the quay seen on the early black & white photos of the village, gracefully curving to follow the line of the buildings behind. Originally it was called 'Victoria Quay' after the new Queen, but it was also called 'Market Quay' or 'Manor Quay' - today it is just known as 'The Quay'. It soon became the new centre of town, where all the shipping activity took place.

The Market Quay opened with ceremonial cannon fire, marching bands, a grand public tea, speeches, and fireworks. What a great occasion!

This quay was still owned by the individual people who provided the land. However, as it was now a public area, the owners were reluctant to spend money on keeping it maintained, and fifty years later it had got into a bit of a state - you can see the pot-holed surface on some of the old photographs. There were calls for the quay to be formally adopted and repaired by the Council, but local councillor Harold Moody was opposed to this, as he didn't want to see it 'laid out with municipal seats and trees'.

By 1895 only the central part of the quay was said to be in good condition - the rest was in a pretty awful state, but eventually everyone relented and the Council took ownership and responsibility for this quay.

This early curved quay continued to be used throughout the 1930s. In 1914 there had been plans to widen it which were shelved when the 1st World War broke out. With the onset of the 2nd World War in 1939 however, it was quickly realised that the quay was of strategic importance, and it was quickly extended. A huge concrete retaining wall was built further out in the river, giving a greater working area on the quay. The work cost £27,000. A similar development was repeated in 1997 when the promenade, quay and flood-defence was built, with more of the river being filched for development. This is now a great space for Appledore - even if it is laid out with seats and trees!

Quite where the original shoreline was we don't know, but it is likely that earlier generations also pushed the boundaries out. There is evidence that houses further inland were originally facing the sea, but I will describe these later. In the meanwhile, who knows what will happen in the future - one day we might be shaking hands across the river with Instow.

Anyway, let's now start looking at some of the individual buildings in a little more detail:

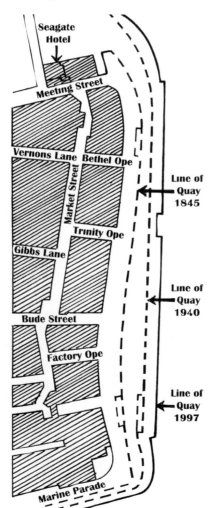

Plan showing how
Appledore Quay has increased in size over the years.

A view of a flooded Appledore Quay in the 1930s. Flooding continued until 1997 when the new raised quay was constructed.

Appledore Quay being constructed in 1940 when it was realised that this would be of strategic importance to the war effort.

SEAGATE HOTEL:

Originally known as 'The Tavern', it is first mentioned in a deed of 1717 when the building was sold by William Browning to John Jeffery, both local merchants. However, these deeds suggest existence back to the mid-1600s, when mariner Richard Kemp was in ownership. When the Inn was sold in 1824, the lands were described as being Glebe & Tithe lands, owned by the Parish of Northam, and included three acres of pasture (presumably the land leading up the hill where the churchyard now lies). At that time the landlords were Robert & Grace Luxton.

In 1828 it was taken by William Cock whose family continued to run the Tavern for another fifty years. During this time Thomas Chanter held his Manorial Court here, and after one Court in 1850, it was said that 'this was followed by an excellent dinner'.

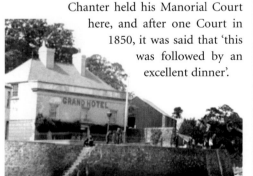

The creeper-clad frontage of the Grand Hotel in about 1910. Note the set of steps leading to the beach, and also the huge trees behind, which are actually at the bottom of the churchyard. On the right are the sheds of Blackmore's Shipbuilding Yard, which operated here until 1928.

In 1898 the inn's name changed to 'Quay House', and again in 1908 to the 'Grand Hotel' – the railway had just arrived at Appledore, and it was going up-market.

Cashing in on the new breed of visitors arriving by train, in 1908 the Grand Hotel offered the chance of an afternoon stroll through its Pleasure Grounds - although actually this was the path from the Station anyway.

SECRET SOCIETIES:

The Seagate Hotel was also used as the meeting place for various organisations based on principles similar to Freemasonry. The 'Royal Antediluvian Order of Buffaloes' was founded in 1822 as a philanthropic and charitable body. The last meeting of the 'Appledore Lodge' was held in the back room of the Seagate Hotel. The Buffaloes had other local lodges called 'Amyas Leigh Lodge', 'Hubbastone Lodge', 'Sailors Anchor Lodge', 'Rose of Torridge Lodge', 'Penhorwood Lodge', Friendship Lodge, Taw Valley Lodge, and 'Rose Salterne Lodge'.

Key to names for faces on page 21.

Seen here in this meeting of 'Buffaloes' at the Seagate Hotel around 1960, are:
(1) Stafford Cawsey, (2) Dennis Lesslie, (3) 'Fairy' Harris, (4) Billy Harris, (5) Not known, (6) Tim Schiller,
(7) Billy Eastman, (8) Albert Cawsey, (9) Eddie Kitto, (10) 'Toggo' Moyce, (11) Bill Bowden,
(12) 'Ossie' Williams, (13) Johnson Bignell, (14) 'Bomber' Harris, (15) Charles Clark, (16) Mervin Harris,
(17) Unknown, (18) Sid Eastman, (19) Unknown (20), 'Penny' Hookway, (21) Harold Hutley, (22) Arthur Stoner.

This view from the 1940s, shows the Seagate Hotel and the shop at 22 the Quay. In the 1920s this was a
bakery with bread ovens in the back. Appledore children were told that these ovens were used as a hiding
place by sailors when the press-gangs came round. Whilst this does seem a little anachronistic, there may be a
remnant of truth somewhere here.

In the 1870s Appledore also had two lodges of 'Good Templars' (a temperance masonic-type organisation founded in New York, and brought to England in 1868). In 1877 their 500 members mounted a grand parade through the town, supported by members from Northam and Bideford. Headed by two large flags, their regalia-draped members were hailed as benefactors of the town and cheered by hundreds of people crowding the streets. They had some success in their cause: in 1874, it was reported that three pubs 'cursed by strong drink' had recently closed.

This wasn't the first 'secret' society formed here. In 1763 a lodge of Freemasonry was formed in Appledore, meeting in the house of one of their members. It lasted for about twelve years, before the lodge moved to Bideford.

THE WILD WEST:

The Seagate Hotel used to mark the end of civilisation as most Appledore people knew it. Beyond here was somewhere they didn't go – West Appledore. Also known as the hamlet of 'Irsha', West Appledore was a wild lawless place, and any stranger spotted walking down the street would be lucky to escape with just verbal abuse. In 1854 the North Devon Journal recounts that a poor Cornish woman was stoned by a rabble of children of both sexes.

The quay ended at this point, and anyone brave enough to venture into West Appledore had to either pick their way across the beach, or follow the path from the Seagate below the church - there being no usable road here until about 1939.

Locals still talk about going 'over Point', ie: going past Tavern Corner to West Appledore. Originally known as Gribble's Point – it was probably named after an 18th century landowner. In 1749, mariner Philip Gribble stood as surety for 47 of the 52 licensed victuallers in the parish of Northam. He was

therefore obviously a man of some standing and could well be the man after whom this Point was named. After all anyone who supports 47 landlords is worthy of being remembered in a place name.

During the summer, the Appledore Silver Band can be found playing on the Quay here in the evenings.

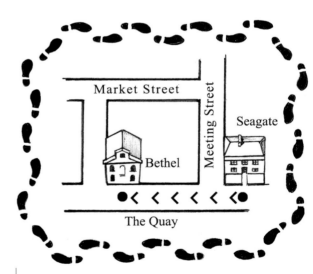

CONTINUE SOUTH ALONG THE QUAY TOWARDS THE BETHEL CHAPEL

The Appledore band on board a ship off the quay in 1907.
This band evolved from the Appledore Town Band started in 1888, when ten men formed a group to play at social evening entertainments. At that time, the bandmaster (on harmonium) was Thomas Jordan, and the rest of the band were: Robert Parkhouse (cello); John Parkhouse, Charles Mills, George Beer and William Parkhouse (cornets), Richard Blackmore and Thomas Williams (violins); William Parkhouse (flute), and another John Parkhouse (drums).

All this beach has been long-buried under extensions to the original quay, and the main road now passes above where this Victorian photographer stood in about 1900. From this beach viewpoint, you can see the barber's shop on the corner and the Bethel slip-way. The large flag-pole was used to hoist warnings giving notice of pending storms - in 1863 Admiral Fitzroy telegraphed Appledore saying that 'the signal drum should be hoisted with the cone upwards', indicating that a strong gale was expected. Barometers were installed in the Lifeboat house and Harbour Office in the same year.

This view of the small quayfront shop in the 1950s shows 'Mac' Austin outside his newsagents and general provisions shop, which went right through into Market Street. Next to him is Ada Williams (nee Schillers), famed for her speciality sweets, apparently from a secret recipe handed down though her family. Afterwards this became a small café run by Mrs Peake.

This forest of masts shows just how busy Appledore was in times past. Today, just a few pleasure craft occupy the same space.

1 MEETING STREET:

On the opposite side of the road from the Seagate Hotel stands a building with a curved-frontage. In the early 20th century this was the barber's shop of Reuben Smith (see book 1, page 99), but was then taken over by Reginald Hearne. In a book that my father wrote about his boyhood memories he described the horrors of visiting the Appledore barber:

"I think I was about four when mother took me for my first hair cut. The barber got about half-way through the job, but by then I had experienced more than enough of this terrible ordeal of having my head pushed backwards and forwards, of hair getting in my eyes, up my nose and down my neck. I registered a very noisy protest and refused to be tortured any further. No coaxing on the part of the barber or mother was of any avail, and I was taken home in disgrace half done. I believe in the end my grandfather was allowed to finish me off with a pudding basin."
(*Appledore Boyhood Memories, by E R Carter*).

In the 1920s & 1930s this building was a fish and chip shop run by 'Pumpy' Bartlett – he also supplied you with paraffin, which he pumped from his tank (it gave his fish and chips a unique flavour!). After this it became a sweet shop run by the Lock family and then Lizzie White.

REMAINS OF THE RIVERFRONT:

In the space between this small shop and Missioner's Cottage, is the last remaining suggestion of how things were before the quay. Behind the wall, the back of this Market Street building faces the sea, with a small courtyard area indicating the ground level at this time.

THE BETHEL:

Still surviving as a Chapel, the Bethel was founded in 1827 to assist visiting sailors, hence its prominent position on the Quay. Little is known of its early history as a chapel, although much more is known of its later mission and secular activities in the community as the Seaman's Mission. In 1850, John Darracott was paying rent on behalf of the Bethel to Mrs Fishwick who owned the property in Market Street at the rear. It therefore appears that Mrs Fishwick's late husband allowed the Bethel to be built on his land.

TO THE GLORY OF GOD AND IN LOVING MEMORY OF CAPTAIN THOMAS HUTCHINGS MASTER MARINER OF APPLEDORE WHO DIED 21st JULY 1949. THIS WINDOW WAS ERECTED BY HIS WIFE & CHILDREN. R.I.P.

The memorial window in the Bethel for Thomas Hutchings.

THOMAS HUTCHINGS:

A notable memorial inside the Bethel is a window to Thomas Hutchings. In 1894, Thomas was aged 27 and employed as first mate on the barque 'Dovenby' which was en-route to Australia carrying five miles of cable for the new tramways being built in Melbourne and Sydney. Whilst rounding the Cape of Good Hope during a storm, a huge timber struck him severely crushing his arm. Thomas refused for the ship to be diverted so that he could get medical help, as this would have meant danger to the rest of the crew (mostly all Appledore men) in the severe stormy conditions. Instead the ship sailed on to Sydney, and arrived there thirty days later, too late to save his now withered and useless arm. This injury gave him pain for the rest of his life and he was never able to earn a living at sea again, but his great sacrifice ensured that the rest of the crew was not put into unnecessary danger. The window was erected after his death in 1949 and shows the 'Ulida', another barque on which he sailed. A true Appledore hero.

SEAMEN'S MISSION:

The Bethel also operated a 'Seamen's Mission' next door at number 20. It had a bit of a rocky start though – in 1850 their secretary, Benjamin Herman, a schoolmaster from Pitt Hill, ran off with the previous six years' funds, said to be over £540 (almost £50,000 today). The North Devon Journal reported that he "left the neighbourhood in a very abrupt manner", which is probably an understatement. He was eventually caught and ended up in Exeter jail. Between 1850 and 1892, various lectures were held here for the Appledore 'Mutual Improvement Society'. In 1857 local minister John Darracott gave a lecture about the Pagan Temples of Ancient Britain – although presumably he was not in favour of these.

In 1888, the property was bought by 65-year-old Bideford magistrate William Hanson, into which he created a Temperance Hotel. The resident Missionary lived here in a flat at the top, and although this was a Christian Mission, it was designed to reach those who belonged to neither Church nor Chapel. However, the words 'FEAR GOD' emblazoned over the entrance door were probably not the friendliest welcome to any Christian or non-Christian. The Queen of Sweden and Norway is reported to have sent a donation of £5 towards this venture.

Compare this picture of the Bethel façade with how it looks today. Originally the upper room had large windows and the lower floor had small windows. Today it is the other way round.

Previously this Chapel had an upper gallery, reused from St Mary's Church, but the space was reconfigured in the late 1940s.

This Mission was a success which lasted for many years, providing books, games, sea-charts, bagatelle board and billiard table for the entertainment of sailors with time on their hands. Many chose to spend their leisure time here rather than in a pub – which was the whole idea.

In 1904 Mr Hanson's daughter sadly died, which the newspapers reported with great sadness and that she was 'well known to the sailors' (which I'm sure was far more innocent than it sounded!).

THE BETHEL STEPS:

Opposite the Bethel are steps leading down from the Quay to the river. Although the quay has been widened several times, there have always been steps in the same location, known locally as the 'Bethel Steps'. This painting of them is by Albert Lilley (1868-1954). A talented local artist, he married Blanche Heywood from West Farm in 1906.

THE GORRELL LIBRARY:

The Mission was still going strong in 1950, when a Mr Walter Gorrell, vice-president of a paint manufacturer from Baltimore, donated 150 books. He said that this was the first instalment towards a collection to be known as the 'Gorrell Library' in memory of his ancestors who emigrated from Appledore to America about 130 years ago. Does anyone know what happened to this Library?

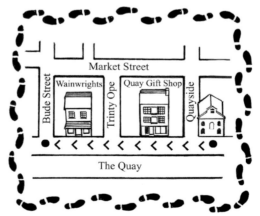

MOVE FURTHER ALONG THE QUAY TO THE JUNCTION WITH BUDE STREET

the Quay tasted to hungry boys like ambrosia, the food of the gods. Just round the corner up Trinity (or 'Heddon's') Ope was Meo Down's and at the bottom of Myrtle Street Yeo's shop, both offering similar satisfaction".
(Appledore Boyhood Memories, by E R Carter).

18 THE QUAY – KATHLEEN & MAY HOUSE:

This was originally a quay-side warehouse and coal merchant's store, which explains why the lower storey is twice as high as it needs to be. Coal was taken directly from the ships into the warehouse, run in the early 1900s by Arthur Cook and Alfred Galsworthy. The Harris family took over until the 1960s when the coal business declined, and it became a garage for W Harris Hauliers. In the late 1960s they ran a petrol station here, and it is said that the petrol storage tanks are still buried underneath the building. The Appledore Boys Brigade also used the upper floor as their meeting hall.

Trinity House crest.

TRINITY BUOY STORE:

The Buoy Store has been here since the Quay was formed. 'Trinity House' is the organisation responsible for Aids to Navigation in England and Wales. This consists not only of sixty-nine lighthouses, but over four-hundred buoys situated in places where vessels need to have reliable information about the channel to follow.

THE QUAY GIFT SHOP:

The façade of this building is obviously made to face onto a working quay. The large opening doors would enable goods to be winched directly into warehouse storage from the unloading wharf below. In the 20th century, the upper floor was Johnny Copp's sail-loft whilst the lower floor was a fish and chip shop run sequentially by the Bennett, Lamey, and Harris families. My father recalls this in his boyhood memories:

"A very favourite food with kids was chips and fish. I'm sure a pen'erth of chips eaten straight out of newspaper from Bennett's shop on

Bideford Bar is one of the most dangerous estuary entrances in the country, due to the shallow sand-bar that spans the mouth of the estuary lying in wait for unsuspecting ships. Anyone not knowing the right tidal conditions or position of the underwater banks was in grave danger of running aground – not advisable even in calm conditions, but undoubtedly fatal in stormy ones. A study of shipwreck records indicates that 520 known ships were wrecked in the Bideford Bay area in the last 380 years, most of these at the entrance to the estuary. How many unrecorded ships

The Seaman's Mission Men's Group in the early 1950s. They are: Back row: 'Cocky' Lamey, Mr Harris, J Taylor, W Taylor, Paddy Cox, Sidney Cann, 'Groves' Copp. Middle row: Tom Bailey, Bill Heddon, Mr Lamey, Tom Gregory, Mr Jenkins, Fred Lewis, [unknown], [unknown]. Front row: Mr Powe, [unknown], Mr Taylor, Alex Richards (resident missionary), Mrs Richards, Mr Hutchings, 'Daddy' Screech, Tommy Jewell; and the young man in the life-buoy: George Moyse.

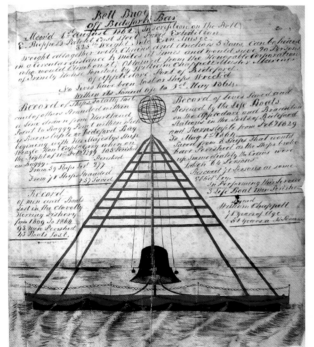

The first buoy you encounter when approaching the estuary is the Bell Buoy. This has been the saviour of many sailors lost in poor visibility, not knowing if deadly rocks were twenty yards away or twenty miles away. Its sound would have made their hearts leap, when all seemed lost. The bell could be heard from a distance of four miles and the structure was designed to allow twenty shipwrecked sailors to climb onto it. It was exhibited at the Paris Exhibition of 1855. The five-ton buoy was obtained from Trinity House by William Chappell, 51-years a seaman at Appledore, and moored in August 1862. (North Devon Museum Trust Collection).

foundered there and how many thousands of lives this represents, we can only imagine.

For this reason, in 1820 the Bideford Bar was the first estuary in the Country to be fitted with navigation buoys.

There are now seven buoys marking the safe route across the Bar and into the Estuary. The buoys used to be brought to this store for routine maintenance, but in 2000 the site was no longer needed and was sold. The buoys in the river are still maintained by Trinity House, the only river in Britain for which they are still directly responsible.

Just out of interest: 'Trinity House' evolved from a fraternity of seamen set up as long ago as the 14th century to provide welfare to sailors. These fraternities were dedicated to the Holy Trinity, hence the later name of 'Trinity House'.

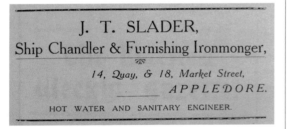

J. T. SLADER,
Ship Chandler & Furnishing Ironmonger,

14, Quay, & 18, Market Street,
APPLEDORE.

HOT WATER AND SANITARY ENGINEER.

14 THE QUAY:

Currently 'Uncle Wainwright's Charity Shop', raising funds for St Mary's Church.

Between 1880 and 1926, this was the chandler's shop of John Thomas Slader, Parish Clerk in Appledore for fifty years. He was certainly a stalwart of Appledore. After he died, the business continued until 1939. The premises went right through to Market Street, where another shop sold china and other household goods.

Members of the Down family outside their shop on the Quay in 1944. The three sisters are Bertha Down, Sarah Down and Annie Down. Children: Valerie Owen, John Yeo and Shirley Yeo.

My father remembers buying his first bike here:

"I cycled every day regardless of weather, even going home for dinner, as I did not really fancy school meals - they had no hope of competing with mother's cooking. I purchased my first bicycle from Reggie Down's shop on the Quay when I was 12, having saved for a long while for the deposit, and then paying so much a week to clear the outstanding balance. I didn't realise the 'never-never' system had been going so long!"

(Appledore Boyhood Memories, by E R Carter).

After the War, the shop continued as a hardware shop run by the Down family, and since has been a wool-shop, DIY shop, fishing-tackle and gift shop, and now the Church Charity Shop.

Note the three monkeys on the shop front. No-one knows their significance, but these are generally called 'Hear no evil, Speak no evil, and See no evil'.

(Bideford Gazette: 26th April 1892).

The inside of Appledore Market shown above in working condition, and shown below looking very dilapidated just prior to demolition in 1961.

THE MARKET, APPLEDORE.

WEDNESDAY, MAY 4TH, 1892.

MESSRS. J. J. BRADDICK & SONS have received instructions to sell by public auction, on the above date, about 200 Pairs

BOOTS AND SHOES,

Mostly Men's and Boys' strong Nailed, Ladies' Elastic, &c. Sale to commence at 11 o'clock.

(National Monuments Record Centre).

OPES, COURTS AND DRANGS:

What is an Ope?

There are a few Opes leading off Appledore Quay, basically these are 'openings between buildings'. Apart from 'Factory Ope' their names have now disappeared from maps and street signs – but it would be good to have these reinstated. 'Trinity Ope' and 'Bethel Ope' are such great names.

What is a Court?

A 'Court' is a semi-enclosed yard or courtyard, surrounded by houses. Generally the yard itself does not have specific ownership, but is equally owned by all the surrounding houses. This derived from the time when there was a central well to which all householders had rights. The wells have now all disappeared, which is a shame – can we have some of these features back too?

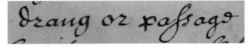

The first written evidence of the 'drang' word is in this document from 1688, referring to a passageway in Barnstaple.

What is a Drang?

The 'Drang' word is used quite widely in the south-west to describe a narrow alleyway. Its origins are unknown, although it has been suggested that it may come from an old Saxon verb 'drengen' meaning to press or push through, used in leatherwork, but in this case driving a narrow path between buildings.

CONTINUE ALONG THE QUAY AND TURN RIGHT INTO MARINE PARADE

APPLEDORE MARKET:

A market was probably held near this spot for as long as people have lived here. In 1822 a market took place every Wednesday and Saturday, but in 1828 a new Market Place for Appledore was built on the corner of Bude Street and Market Street. It was paid for by Richard Dart, built by Alexander Beara from Instow, and stretched down to the riverfront. It consisted of an inward-looking courtyard, within which anyone could hire a stall and bring their wares for sale.

The main entrance was off Market Street (see book 1, page 73), but there was a warehouse at the river end where goods could be unloaded. In its heyday over a dozen butchers occupied stalls here and many traders came from outlying farms, bringing their produce in ponies and carts, with some also coming over on the ferry. They sold their wares from panniers, full to the brim with dairy and garden produce.

> **APPLEDORE.**
> MARKET.—Beef, 7d to 9d; Mutton, 9d to 10d; Lamb, 9s quarter; Pork, 7d to 9d; Eggs, 16 for 1s; Lard, 10d; Butter, 1s 10d; Fowls, 5s to 7s couple; Ducks, 7s to 8s couple; Potatoes, white rocks, 5s 6d per bag, red Regent's, 7s.

A few of the items on offer at the Market. (Bideford Gazette: 27th March 1877).

Appledore Quay and its salmon boats in the 1940s. The building to the top left was a coal store, and then housed Dave Hocking's 'Ensign' bus. Behind it was Appledore Market.

Appledore Quay in the 1920s.

In 1858 the annual rent for a small stand was a very reasonable four shillings. The market was privately owned by the Beara family throughout its life, but its use had declined by the 1950s and it was demolished in 1961.

THE COLLAR FACTORY:

In 1876 a collar and cuff factory was established in Appledore. It occupied the upper floors of a former malting house at number 10 the Quay, and extended as far back as the present newsagents shop in Market Street. The entrance was from Factory Ope at the side - from which the street gets its name. The factory was owned by Mr A Duncan from Manchester and Mr G Vincent from Ilminster, who found that establishing collar works in different parts of the country enabled them to find willing workers. They had already opened a mechanised factory in Bideford, but the Appledore factory concentrated on hand-production and by 1891 was employing 113 Appledore ladies and girls.

FACTORY . OPE

They used linen from Ireland and calico from Manchester. This was given to the cutters, who used wooden templates to cut the materials to the right shape. It passed through various processes: stamping, clipping, creasing, stitching, button-holing, washing, starching, ironing, dressing, and finishing. The works also needed box-makers, packers and general labourers.

The factory despatched their finished goods twice a day to Bideford, which then sent them on to the wholesale houses in London and Manchester.

VINCENT & DUNCAN,
Linen Collar Manufacturers
BIDEFORD.
DEVON.

CHILD LABOUR:

Annie White from Market Street was one of their first employees. Although aged only 7, she found that her nimble fingers were much better at sewing than the older girls. As the girls were paid by piecework, she often managed to earn more than the older workers, but being under age she was quickly hidden away in a convenient cupboard when the inspectors came round.

In 1911 fire broke out in a hamper on the ground floor and smoke spread upwards. The exit was blocked and the thirty girls in the building became panic-stricken. They managed to break a window and some of them jumped to the ground below, sustaining minor injuries. 28-year-old Emma Yeo tried to get out of a top window, but was eventually reached on a ladder by Walter Jenkins, although she fainted with fright as she was brought down. The fire was finally put out using buckets of water by William Jenkins, John Rowe, John Lemon, and the Police. The factory closed in 1923 due to changes in fashion and the building was put up for sale.

WILLIAM NEALE ELLIS:

William Neale Ellis ran a lock-up chemist's shop in Bude Street until he moved his business into bigger premises at 10 the Quay in 1927. In recent years, these premises have been used as a gallery, gift-shop, tea-shop and restaurant.

A DANGEROUS PLACE AT NIGHT:

What could possibly be dangerous at night in Appledore? Gang of marauding hooligans? Wild animals? Actually the most dangerous thing was the darkness itself – and an unprotected quay edge. There are many tales of people accidentally encountering the quay edge in the darkness - and not all lived to tell the tale.

In 1863 Sarah Beara mistook her way home and walked over the quay edge. Luckily the tide was out, or she would have drowned. As it was she just smashed both her ankles - so that was

ok! Later the same year, John Prance was found dead lying in the water - the night having been very dark, he was understood to have fallen over the edge.

There were letters to the papers deploring the lack of street lighting, and why a civilised town like Appledore didn't have this. The only light in the early evenings were a few rays shed from the windows. Gas lighting eventually came to Appledore in 1875, too late for these unfortunate people.

That didn't stop others from falling off the edge, even in daylight. In 1890 Charles Schiller stepped back and mistook his footing. He landed on the beach below and died from his injuries a couple of days later.

During the 2nd World War when blackouts were in force, perhaps the most poignant accident occurred. It was a stormy night when Sarah Bates from 5 New Quay Street went into the Post Office where May Cann served her - she was the last person to see Sarah alive. Sarah Bates failed to return home to her sister and in the morning a search was undertaken. The search lasted over a week but there was no sign of her and it seemed certain that the wind blew her over the quay in the darkness. The mystery was solved a few months later when the quay development works were underway and her false teeth were found lying in the silt.

Beware dark and stormy nights!

FACTORY OPE:

In 1890, there were dwellings behind the library building, described as 'unfit for habitation', and the owner Mr Haynes was instructed to repair these, or they would be demolished by the Council. We're not sure if he did, but the property is no longer there.

Slightly luckier was Percy Reed, of 'Beachside', Factory Ope, who in 1930 won a car in a national lottery draw. For the purchase of a one-shilling ticket, he beat all competition and was presented with a brand new Morris Cowley. I bet he never got it up Factory Ope!

1906: the ground floor of the Library was used as a coal store by Arthur Cook, and later by Mervin Harris.

THE LIBRARY:

The building which houses our library was one of the warehouse and workshop buildings which fronted onto the river. Between the 1820s and the 1850s it housed the block-making workshop of William Haynes.

The building began its literary use in 1859, when local boot-maker Samuel Fursey provided an alternative social activity to the drinking of alcohol, and opened the Working Men's Reading Rooms. Newspapers such as the North Devon Journal, Mercantile Gazette, Daily News, Bristol Mercury, and Cassell's Illustrated Family Paper were supplied by Francis Bligh in Marine Parade, and books arrived soon afterwards.

Later, part of the building was being used as living accommodation, and there is a story that the biggest and heaviest postman in England lived there. Johnny Cawsey was so big that when his cap measurements were sent to headquarters, the postal authorities wrote back saying: "a cap of such size had never been made before". He was also a splendid musician and used to play the harp and accordion so the women in the neighbouring collar factory could dance on the quay during their work breaks.

The building was badly damaged by a fire in 1901 and the interior was rebuilt to provide two floors inside, instead of the original three. The original window openings from the three-story interior can be seen on the side elevation.

Meetings and debates were then held in this building. In 1903 Dr Valentine gave a lecture on the 'Uses and Mis-uses of Tobacco'. He suggested "Do not smoke to excess, and if you don't smoke, never commence the habit" (and this was decades before the tobacco companies were still saying the smoking was probably good for you!).

During the 2nd World War, the building was used as the offices of the Harbour Patrol, but it was formerly opened as a Devon County Library on 15th July 1952, with Rev. Alfred Green formally issuing the first reader's ticket.

As often seemed to be the case with libraries, there are memories from the village children of the librarian being a formidable woman (Mrs Minchell's name gets mentioned here), which probably scared many a young boy from borrowing books - not today of course, our librarians are much friendlier.

THEVENARD:

Next to the library is a house called 'Thevenard'. From 1938 this was the dentist's practice of Thomas Satchwell, and in the 1950s and 1960s it was Mr Powe's decorator's shop, the serving counter being just inside the french windows.

REGATTAS:

A few words at this point about regattas - which have been held in Appledore for generations. However, don't let me bore you about these, this is my father's description of them in the 1930s:

Gig and Punt chase at the regatta in 1956.

"The outstanding red letter day of the year was Regatta day held in early August. The Quay, furnished with stalls and decorations, was lined with crowds four or five deep to watch the races, and all barges, vessels and steamers moored off or alongside were similarly decorated and beflagged to make a really exciting scene. Very popular were the novel or comedy events, such as the Gig and Punt chase. One man in a small punt, usually with a shovel for propulsion, weaved in and out of the crowd of moored boats, pursued by a team in the gig, which was a large four-oared rowing boat. The gig crew, which also had a fifth member to steer by means of an oar over the stern, did their best to catch and capsize the single man, but as the punt was more manoeuvrable, he was often more than a match for the larger boat. More serious, although still a novel form of entertainment was the Elopement race. The males lined up to row their boats the length of the course to where their spouses were waiting to join them and help row the boat back down the course, striving to be first across the finishing line."

(Appledore Boyhood Memories, by E R Carter).

OTHER CELEBRATIONS:

There were also annual land-based events. In 1850, the papers reported that the Guy Fawkes night celebrations had been revived. Many tar barrels and other flammable substances were to be seen on the streets. This sounds similar to the celebrations carried out today in Ottery St Mary, where flaming tar barrels are carried through the streets - thankfully not done in the confined Appledore streets. Opinions differ as to the origin of this festival of fire which seems to pre-date anything that Guy Fawkes started, but the most widely accepted version is that it began as a pagan ritual to cleanse the streets of evil spirits.

HOOLIGANS:

Rowdyism and hooliganism are also perceived to be modern problems, but not so - kids have always been kids, and always will be. A letter to the papers in 1910 bemoaned that: *"Appledore street corners are now the centres of hooliganism. The language and behaviour by boys and girls, especially in Market Street, calls for prompt action. Their only playground is the streets, there are no home lessons, and no home influence."* Times have changed - and probably for the better.

Earlier in 1867, six Appledore boys aged about sixteen, were convicted of causing a nuisance by hanging around in front of the shops in Market Street and blocking the path. William Sage, Henry Popham, Thomas Lamey, George Norman, Samuel Booms, and William Tamlyn (there we are – they are now named and shamed – that will teach them!).

WANTED, Respectable Young MAN as IMPROVER to the Boot and Shoe Making. Must be able to sew and stitch. Indoors or out. —Apply, C. HUXTABLE, Quay, Appledore.

(Bideford Gazette: 18th Oct 1892).

This image from about 1905 shows the bootmaking shop of Charles Huxtable
- the awning providing some welcome shade for the sailors. Further to the right is the Library / Reading
Rooms can be seen, with large adverts for the 'Western Morning News' and the 'Daily Mercury'. At this time
the ground floor was used a warehouse by coal merchant Arthur Cook, and the large building next to it was
operating as a collar factory. Note that there is no entrance from this collar factory onto the quay itself.

The shoemaking family of Charles and Elizabeth Huxtable in 1904 with their children Charles, George, Richard, Frederick Arthur, Adeline and baby Nell. Also in the photo are Elizabeth's parents, George and Grace Galsworthy.

Appledore Quay looking south in about 1920.
During a cruise along the Torridge in 1925 the author Hillaire Belloc perceived this about Appledore:
"Another pleasing thing about the Bideford River is the startling contrast between Appledore, on the business side of the harbour, and Instow, all so genteel upon the further shore: Appledore frankly a lair, and Instow a desirable resort. Appledore for beer, Instow for wine; and the English talked in one, almost incomprehensible to the other." (The Cruise of the 'Nona', by Hillaire Belloc).

Appledore Quay looking north in the 1890s. Note the early gas-lamp installed in 1875.

POST OFFICE:

Thankfully we still have a Post Office on the Quay, which re-opened in April 2008 after an 18-month absence. Our Post Office has had a number of locations over the years: Market Street, Bude Street, Myrtle Street, etc. It moved to the Quay during the 2nd World War and is now run by the Johns family from Instow.

The building itself appears in the earliest known photo of Appledore Quay (book 1, page 7), with a plain windowed frontage on the ground floor and a single central door. In 1892, a shopfront was installed by Charles Huxtable, a boot & shoemaker from Fremington. He started his business in a temporary shop in Market Street and then moved into these larger premises on the Quay. He ran his boot-making business here until he died in 1934.

This long building leads back from the Quay some 125 feet and was built in 1770 by local merchant Thomas Chappell, on land previously owned by the Docton family. He constructed warehousing and upper-level workshops - the lifting beam can still be seen at the far end of the narrow cobbled drang. The building was sold in 1814 to Emanuel and Betsy Halls, who built a small quayside house for themselves on the right of this building – now replaced by a 20th century construction

called 'Ferriwais'. William Yeo bought the warehouse building in 1845, owning it until the time of his death in 1872.

In the early 20th century, the upper floor became the sailmakers' workshop of the Oatway family (see photo in book 1, page 97), whose sailmaking pitch buckets were still sitting here in 2008. The building also appears to be known as 'Popham House', named after a sailmaking family.

J. BEARA & CO.,

Ship & General Ironmongers, . .   Cutlers & Tool Merchants

Agent for Peacock and Buchan's Patent Compositions, and

Plumbers, Braziers, and Tin Plate Workers. . .   Halls' Sanitary Washable Distemper

Sanitary, Hotwater, and Electrical Engineers. . .   Competent Workmen sent and Estimates Given.

QUAY, APPLEDORE,

4 THE QUAY:

The Beara family owned the building until the 1970s when it became a mini-supermarket, currently run by The Co-operative. Generations of Bearas ran many businesses in Appledore, so to mention them all would need a separate book. The family originally came from Instow about 200 years ago and ran tailors, drapers, chandlers, ironmongery, and grocery shops in Appledore. John Beara born in 1829, is rumoured to have invented and patented the process of oil-skinning, which enabled manufacturers to produce waterproof clothing for sailors. However, oil-skins were around

From this shop the Beara family ran a chandlery business, with a boat repair workshop behind. In the main shop was a central staircase leading up to a balcony. Messrs Beara and Cook had a considerable export trade with Newfoundland and Prince Edward Island, supplying ships-blocks, sails, clothing, boots, rope, etc. Like most quayside properties, Bearas also owned the land in front of their properties right up to the river edge, including the slipway known as 'Beara's Slip'

During the 2nd World War, number 4 the Quay was requisitioned as the NAAFI, Officers' Quarters, and Harbour Office of HMS Appledore. The upper floors were used to billet Royal Navy sailors, who were also housed in the Seagate Hotel. Very few Americans were seen in Appledore during the War, even though they had a base just across the river. Appledore housed the Royal Marines, who were tasked with assisting the training of frogmen at West Appledore and other special operations.

prior to his birth so this seems to be wishful Appledore thinking, although he did produce his own oil-skins in his works at 2 Bude Street.

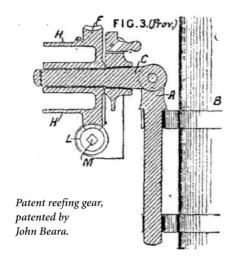

Patent reefing gear, patented by John Beara.

John Beara and George Williams patented a reefing appliance for sailing vessels in 1904, so this family are not without credit in this inventive respect.

The house to the left of this building set back from the quay (Devonia) was the Beara family home.

FERRY BOATS:

Before we leave the Quay and continue round to Marine Parade, we need to mention the ferries. A map of the Torridge Estuary, produced in 1754, stated that there was a ferry between Appledore and Instow at "all times of the tide, cost 1d per man". Seeing as the river virtually disappears for about half the day, this 24-hour service does seem quite remarkable. However, ferrymen used to lay planks down for passengers to use, and in some cases actually carried people to the boats.

The earliest mention of a ferry is in 1634, when Edward Berryman was granted a licence for running a ferry, not only for passengers, but also horses, cattle, sheep, and pigs.

There used to be an Appledore-Braunton ferry but this stopped working before the 2nd World War. The earliest reference to this is in 1797, and the landing point was close to the site of the ancient Chapel of St Anne on the Braunton Burrows, suggesting the antiquity of this route. The crossing was arduous and risky, with a distance of about a mile and with swirling currents of up to seven knots.

THE MAIL BOAT:

In 1848, the villagers got fed up waiting for their post to arrive via Bideford, so they arranged for their mail to be delivered to a shop in Instow, and brought across the river by ferryman Samuel Fishley. When the G.P.O. heard about this, they suspected tampering of the mail was taking place and sent an inspector to find out what was going on. They explained to him that the mail had been delivered legitimately to an agreed address in Instow, and that what happened to it afterwards was only the concern of Appledore people, not the G.P.O. The inspector agreed that the ferry was a better way of transporting the mail and so they made the delivery route official, appointing an approved ferryman to undertake this task.

My father remembers the ferry in the late 1920s whilst waiting for his father to return from one of his long sea voyages:

"I treasured my father's short holidays between voyages, although they only lasted two or three weeks. He used to travel by train from Liverpool and get off at the little station at Instow. I always went down on the Quay to meet him, standing on the slip-way opposite Beara's shop or on the big rock at the water's edge when the tide was low. The ferry was an open 18-foot clinker-built boat with a tan lug-sail, and I always wondered why it zig-zagged across the river, taking so long to reach the Quay on my side, but skimmed over the water when taking him back. Usually the ferryman was Bill Bailey in his boat called 'Mona'. I was always intrigued

Ferryman 'Daddy' Johns carrying two lady passengers across the river in the early 1900s.

Overloaded ferry boats in the 1930s. It's not surprising that there were many ferry accidents. In 1829 William Oatway's ferry was carrying passengers back from Barnstaple when a squall hit the boat and it overturned. Although a nearby boat got to them within a couple of minutes it was early January and by the time they pulled them from the water ferryman Philip Green, passenger Maria Pile, and 2 boys William Oatway and John Keena had all drowned.

that he had long bobbed hair like a lady, but I later understood that he had a permanently deformed ear."
(Appledore Boyhood Memories, by E R Carter).

Ferryman Bill Bailey (1876-1955).

In the 20th century, the ferry was an important link, transporting mail, newspapers, shipyard workers to the docks, Customs Officers visiting ships, plus anyone who needed to catch the Instow train. When the Yelland Power Station was being constructed between 1951 and 1956, about eighty workmen were being taken across the river on a daily basis.

The Appledore-Instow ferry stopped running at the end of 2006, probably for the first time in many hundreds of years. Lack of use and high running costs were blamed, but these days, journeys by land are quicker and more reliable. However, there have always been complaints, as found by this correspondent writing to the papers in 1855:

"Exorbitant charges are now enforced. A few days ago I had to pay one shilling for crossing in a boat from Appledore to Instow. Surely something should at once be done to prevent a continuance of such extortion, and it is hoped that the

inhabitants of Appledore will soon stir themselves in the matter." (Exeter Flying Post, 22nd Nov 1855).

FERRY DISASTERS:

The river can be deceptive, and the ferryman's job dangerous. In 1910, ferryman 41-year-old Tom Fishwick was drowned when his lug-sail boat 'Dora' was swamped by a heavy gale. He vainly tried to save his three passengers, but was hampered by his oilskin coat and boots and quickly became exhausted. Hundreds of people witnessed this from the shore but were powerless to help. He left a wife and eight children unprovided for.

Tom Fishwick's son John later followed his father, running a ferry business until he retired in 1952. Johns of Instow have also operated ferries here since 1870. Four generations of Johns were involved, starting with 'Daddy' Johns, then Dicky, Freddie, and Norman.

ROCK HOUSE AND ROCK COTTAGE:

On the corner of the Quay and Marine Parade we have Rock House and Rock Cottage, named after 'Rock Point', which was at this end of the quay. Originally this was one complete grand house, home of the Chappell family until 1846, and probably built for them. They also owned about 150 feet of the adjacent quay. 'Rock House' was the home of Appledore's doctor in the 1930s, Dr Desmond Sedgley Valentine, son of Dr William Valentine, who was also Appledore's doctor from 1899 to 1932. After William's retirement, his son Desmond took over and ran the surgery from Rock House, and is still fondly remembered by many elderly Appledore residents, who still refer to this as 'Doctor's Corner'.

Next door in 'Rock Cottage' was Charles Stuart's dental surgery from 1918 to 1938. My father 'fondly' recalls a visit to him:

"The dentist, Mr Stuart, lived on the Quay. Patients went into the front parlour, sat in one chair of a three-piece suite, while Mr Stuart, usually wearing a tweed jacket and golfing plus-fours, removed an instrument from a small glass-fronted cabinet and without any injection nonsense, set to work poking and pulling. He managed to abstract a troublesome back tooth, and I bled rather profusely."
(Appledore Boyhood Memories, by E R Carter).

CUSTOMS HOUSE:

The Customs House for Appledore was on this corner from about 1900 until the end of the 1st World War. A Customs watch-house had been at the other end of the village since the 1820s, keeping an eye on the comings and goings of vessels in the estuary. As you can see in the above picture, this three-story Customs House has been tacked-on to the end of the Marine Parade terrace, there being no entrance from Marine Parade itself. It has since been demolished and replaced with a single-story garage.

THE PARLOUR:

As we round the corner of the quay and turn into Marine Parade, we get a good view of the sheltered inlet here, known as 'The Parlour'. This inlet has been largely filled-in by the Richmond Dry-Dock – of which more in a moment. Until the 1850s, this was a sandy inlet where ships could shelter and be maintained. The origin of the name 'Parlour' is unknown, but this is an obvious place where ships can be protected, so it would be surprising if sailors

hadn't been making use of this place for a thousand years or more.

There are no photographs of the Parlour before Richmond Dock was built, but we do have a view of it by the celebrated painter Thomas Girton in 1798. Girton was a talented artist, but he died in 1802, aged just 27. He was a friend of J.M.W. Turner who said of him: "If Girton had lived, I would have starved". Luckily Girton's brief life brought him to North Devon where he painted this view of Appledore from across the river. In it you can see Marine Parade and its Quayside, with several sets of steps leading down to the beach.
(Courtauld Institute).

The quay-edge wall facing the Parlour was much taller a century ago, and formed a shield against the winds cutting around this corner. The height was reduced when the Marine Parade road was formed in 1933. During the 2nd World War, a look-out post was erected at the point where the quay turns the corner. This temporary six-sided structure was removed when the war ended (see book 1, page 137).

BUS STOP:

Where the Bus Stop now stands used to be some run-down public toilets, but these were removed in 2002. A small fire-station with roof-top siren stood here until 1961. During the 2nd World War, there was a large underground air-raid shelter here for the Richmond Dock workers. A dry-dock of this size was of strategic importance and worked around the clock during the War, so it was important to give its workers some protection in the event of an air raid. Thankfully this shelter was never used in anger, and this underground room now appears to have been filled in, although the structure is probably still buried here.

Bus services in the 1920s ran to Bideford every 30 minutes, exactly the same as today. Prior to buses, in the 1850s there was a passage boat service to Bideford running three times a day.

The view held by people further up-river was not always complimentary though. Up until the 1930s, Bideford schoolchildren still chanted:

> *"Appledore rats,*
> *Northam cats,*
> *Bideford ladies and gentlemen".*

Another Bideford School Playground chant, bemoaning the perceived parasites from Appledore was:

> *"Appledore folks,*
> *Come down in boats,*
> *To take away Bideford butter.*
> *It I were mayor,*
> *I vow and declare,*
> *I'd shove their noses in the gutter."*

Marine Parade:

The houses in Marine Parade were mostly constructed in the mid to late 1700s - built for gentry rather than the working people of Appledore. However, this road actually indicates the line of Appledore's first quay. Being in a sheltered inlet, this was a good location to build a wharf where ships could unload. Called the 'Narrow Quay' or 'Docton's Quay' it is first recorded as belonging to the Docton family in 1758, although a rough wooden quay would have been here several hundred years before

that. All traces of it have now disappeared under the street.

Although these houses faced onto a roadway, it was not a thoroughfare for anything more than pedestrians as the road leading towards the hill was blocked by buildings, and only a narrow tunnel underneath a house allowed people to pass. When the Richmond Dock was built in 1856, the householders in Marine Parade adopted the land by the dock wall as their front gardens.

The Road-widening Saga:

In 1865 there were calls during a meeting of the Northam Council for Marine Parade to be widened, but nothing was done. In 1896 it was agreed that the land should be taken for a roadway, but again nothing happened. In 1909 the Pophams agreed to give up some of their land and to remove their building which was blocking the proposed road. Even though this building was demolished in 1911 still no road

Early views of Marine Parade showing the cobbled pathway and the gardens opposite. These were the houses for the gentry of Appledore, in a secluded location with a grand view of the river.

was forthcoming, although Mr Tuplin suggested that a drinking fountain should be put on the new roadway in honour of the Coronation. In 1914 improvements to the sewers were carried out here, and the gardens were bought from the owners of the houses, but still no road. A boathouse on the corner of Marine Parade belonging to Mr Mead was also demolished ready for this scheme, but still the road scheme failed to happen.

Eventually in 1923 the Council agreed to drop the scheme completely, after a petition against it signed by 71 people. Ah - democracy in action!

Ten years later in 1933, and over seventy years after it was first suggested, Marine Parade eventually got its road. A three-storey sail-loft warehouse was demolished at the landward end of Richmond Dock, the space was made, and the road could get through. The uniform appearance of the Marine Parade houses was created at this time by tidying their front gardens behind a continuous low-wall. Look above this and you will see that the houses are not as similar as they first appear.

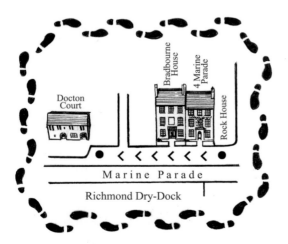

STOP AT THE END OF MARINE PARADE JUST BEFORE THE ROADWAY NARROWS

1 MARINE PARADE:

In Dec 1842, Thomas Fursey moved here from his former position as Master of an orphanage in Indonesia. His wife's health had deteriorated in the tropical climate, so they returned to England and set up a private boarding school in his house. He offered to teach the boys: reading, orthography, arithmetic, merchant's accounts and ancient history, all at a cost of £25 per annum for the over-10s. The girls were offered other subjects including music and ornamental needlework. He also stressed that pupils would receive 'kind treatment, wholesome food, and single beds'. This was one of many such Appledore schools that existed in the days before more formal education was provided.

In the 1870s, surgeon Dr Frederick Pratt lived here. He seemed to have a curious hobby of collecting dolls and in 1875 staged his 3rd annual exhibition of them in this house. He also displayed various birds, fish, insects, reptiles and worms, in what he called the Appledore Natural History Museum. Later between 1912 and 1935 this house was the home of sailmaker John Popham.

These properties also had rights of ownership across the road and onto the foreshore. When numbers 1 and 2 Marine Parade were sold in 1856, with walled gardens and fruit trees, they also got an extensive piece of beach below the road called the 'Limestone Ground'.

THE LIMESTONE GROUND:

The foreshore below the quay-edge at the Parlour is marked as the 'Limestone Ground' on William Yeo's 1853 plan for the construction of Richmond Dock. This was an area where vessels bringing in limestone for the lime-kilns could dump piles of stone, ready for onward transportation up the river by smaller barges. Whilst this seems a strange way to double-handle heavy cargoes, there was probably a

Marine Parade being widened in 1933 and the householders losing their front gardens.

Tidal flooding still occurred in Appledore until 1997 when the quay defence wall was completed. This view shows Marine Parade under a few inches of water in 1990. 'Joints' the butchers is seen on the left, and next door is the 'West of England' Building Society office.

tax-dodge involved here. Appledore, being a free-port, was able to receive cargoes without paying tax, unlike the opposite side of the river where tax would have to be paid – and heavy manual labour was cheaper than paying tax!

4 MARINE PARADE:

The deeds of this house give ownership details back to 1771 when Miles Hammett bought it from the previous owner James Cook, so it would seem logical to assume that the date of construction is possibly sometime around the 1740s.

Mr Hammett retains ownership until 1818 until it comes into the Bligh family. Francis Bligh was a Lieutenant in the Royal Navy retiring on a pension, although he was only 31 years old. Given his name and background it would have been interesting for him to be a descendant of William Bligh of the 'Bounty' fame, but I regret that is not the case. No infamous connections for Appledore this time!

Francis Bligh seemed set for a long and happy retirement, and his new wife gave him three children, but unfortunately Francis died after five years here, leaving her a widow. She did however get to keep the house, which was handed down through various generations of the Bligh family for nearly 100 years, until it was eventually sold to the Lawdays.

 The ghost of a young girl has often been seen and felt here.

Some children staying in the house in the 1980s were playing in the garden. When later asked what they had been doing, they replied "playing with the little girl dressed in funny clothes". They described a girl in old-fashioned costume. Another guest independently identified the presence of a young girl in the house, and also the exact spot in the house with which she has often been associated. Who she was is still a mystery.

5 MARINE PARADE:

'Bradbourne House' was the birthplace of one of Appledore's boys-made-good. William James Tatem, the son of Thomas and Louisa was born here in 1868. However, before we find out about him, let's tell you about the bust-up that his father Thomas Tatem had with William Yeo – after all, it is quite a good story…

TATEM V. YEO:

Thomas Tatem owned a brigantine called the 'Georgina'. In 1865, she had just arrived at Appledore for repairs and 24-year-old Tatem moored her against the quay opposite his house. He wanted to put her in the Dry-Dock, but William Yeo refused as the Dock was already fully booked. The position of the moored vessel upset Yeo, as he thought that Tatem had left her there maliciously to block the entrance to the Dock. To counter this, Yeo moored one of his own ships alongside the 'Georgina' and wedged her tight with heavy chains and large padlocks. Tatem was verbally warned by Yeo's thugs not to touch the chains or he would meet with a nasty accident!

Neither party would budge, and the stalemate continued for five months, after which time Yeo's ship was finally moved. Tatem then sued Yeo for damages and loss of earnings in a case that kept their respective lawyers busy for a long time. The jury at Exeter finally awarded Tatem damages of £200. Whether the two men shook hands afterwards is not recorded, but I think we can probably guess the answer to that one.

Memorial to Thomas Tatem in Appledore Church, erected by his son William.

The victory was short-lived though, as Thomas Tatem died of typhoid three years later - aged just twenty-seven. His wife Louisa lived for another forty-four years as a widow.

William Tatem (Amgueddfa Cymru – National Maritime Museum Wales).

WILLIAM TATEM:

Anyway, back to Thomas's more famous son. Like many boys after leaving school William Tatem went to sea with his first voyage taking him around Cape Horn where he was shipwrecked. At the age of 18 he found more stable employment with a shipping company in Cardiff, eventually setting up his own shipping business, which by 1910 was running sixteen modern steamers. It was called the 'Tatem Steam Navigation Company', and was one of the foremost shipping companies in Cardiff. During the 1st World War, Tatem co-operated with the Government and allowed his ships to be requisitioned, after which he was well known in Government circles, and had the ear of Prime Minister Lloyd George. Allegedly Tatem is said to have made Lloyd George an offer: 'If you honour me with a peerage, I'll let you have £50,000 for your party'. Lloyd George was resistant, but Tatem wrote him a cheque and signed it 'Lord Glanely', so that it could only be cashed after he was honoured. The ruse worked, and in 1918 he was given a peerage as 'Lord Glanely of St Fagans', in respect of his war services. He never forgot his roots though, and in 1911 presented a peal of bells to the church to go into the newly completed tower.

Later he donated a stained-glass window to the church commemorating the men of Appledore who died in the 1st World War.

One of the memorial windows in St Mary's Church in memory of those who died in the War.

Tatem became a successful racehorse owner, bought himself a huge mansion in Newmarket, and in 1919 his horse 'Grand Parade' won the Derby at 33-1. He eventually retired to Weston-super-Mare, where he was killed in an air raid during the 2nd World War.

9 MARINE PARADE:

This shop was built in 1901 as a bakery by the Popham family. Early photographs show the sign 'Marine Steam Bakery' over the door. Earlier buildings on this site and across the roadway were owned by the same family, but were demolished to make space for the road widening. The Popham family gained their

wealth when Thomas Popham won a 16th share in a Government Lottery syndicate in 1818 worth £20,000 (about £14 million in today's money based on average earnings). He invested this money in shipping and properties in Marine Parade and Bude Street. George Popham ran the bakery here until the 1950s. The building later became a butcher's, and is currently trading as an antique shop.

LISTED BUILDINGS:

Appledore contains about 180 listed buildings, plus two special ones which are graded II*. These stand near to each other on either side of Marine Parade. The first of these is the Richmond Dry-Dock.

RICHMOND DRY-DOCK:

No history of Appledore would be complete without the history of the Richmond Dock. It is an important Victorian industrial structure, which brought prosperity to Appledore and wealth to the man who built it. In 2007, Dr Mark Horton gave a guided tour of the village as part of Appledore's first Book Festival and said, *"The Richmond Dock should be Appledore's most treasured possession, it is fundamental to the character of Appledore".*

We have already heard how this area was a sandy creek upon which boats were moored and repaired, but this work could only be done when the tide was out. Previously, local shipbuilders Thomas Geen and William

Clibbett had used this beach as a shipbuilding yard, but what was needed was a controlled area in which work could be undertaken at all times of the day. In 1853 William Yeo, a merchant living in Bude Street, put forward the idea of a dry-dock at a public meeting at which Rev. Jerome Clapp offered his approval. Some of the land had to be bought from its owners, but most of it was foreshore and owned by the Crown. Yeo negotiated to buy this part of the river from the Crown, and eventually paid £76 for the privilege

1840 tithe map showing the sandy inlet of the Parlour, prior to the Richmond Dock. At the time, this was owned by James Chappell and let to Thomas Geen for use as a shipbuilder's yard. (Devon Record Office).

Construction of the dock started the following year. This involved filling in the sides of the creek and leaving the central space enclosed with retaining walls, using stone taken from the Hubbastone Quarry. Two years later, a space had been created that was 330 feet long, 36 feet wide, and could hold two large vessels at once. A large removable caisson was used to seal the end of the dock from the river. The works also involved the construction of outbuildings, rigging lofts, saw mills and smith shops. The total cost was about £20,000 which is about £3 million in today's terms. When finished the dock brought work and prosperity to Appledore, not only in ship repairing but in many other maritime trades from boat building & sail-making, to rope-making & chandlery.

OPENING OF THE DOCK:

The Richmond Dry-Dock was completed in 1856, and the first ship was received there on 17th July of that year. She was a barque of about 1,200 tons called the 'Elizabeth Yeo' after William's wife Elizabeth, and had been sailed over from Prince Edward Island to be fitted out.

The Bideford Gazette described the event: *"Flags were waving in all directions, guns firing and crowds of people striving for advantageous positions from which to behold the entrance of the splendid vessel, which was safely brought into the dock and secured amidst the hurrahs of the assembled multitudes."*

WILLIAM YEO:

William Yeo's involvement in various aspects of the shipping business, including the Richmond Dock, made him Appledore's main employer and elevated him to the position of local squire. He looked after his workers when times were bad, but of course he also made enemies, and anyone who questioned his methods found that few would do business with them. At the same time as building the Dock, Yeo also built a grand house near the top of Staddon Hill which we shall see later in this tour.

The peak year of James and William Yeo's achievement was in 1865, when eighteen vessels were built and sold through Appledore for at least £43,000 – that's over £6 million today. However, in 1870 William Yeo realised that his shipping business had reached its peak and he should diversify. Various investments were made in property and other interests, but these had little time to take effect before William's untimely death in 1872 at the age of 58.

William and Elizabeth Yeo had six daughters but only one son, and when this son died at the age of seven there was no-one left to carry on the business. After this, the work dried up, depression hit Appledore, and the prosperous years came to an end.

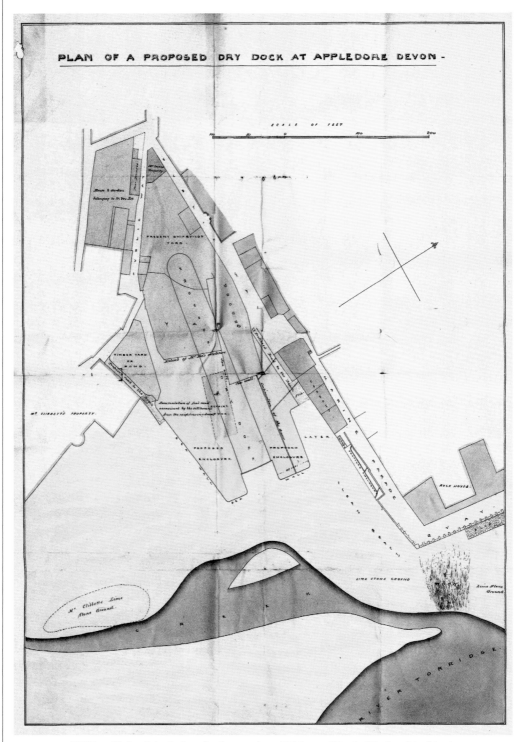

William Yeo's original plans for the creation of Richmond Dock. (National Archives).

ROBERT COCK:

The trustees of William Yeo's estate ran the dry-dock for over 20 years, but it was only a fraction of its former glory. In 1882 the dock was leased to Robert Cock who set about rebuilding the business. Over the next 18 months nearly forty vessels passed through the dock, having undergone various repairs. By 1889 work was back to a high level again, when the following first-hand account of a visit to the dock was written:

"Store buildings stretch to the left and right. Oakum-picking goes on amid the chat of old tars who are eking out a pension by reducing the rope ends to thread-like fibres, used in caulking of vessels. Up in the spacious stores – some 160ft long and 24 ft wide – we mount, first to the trunnel loft, then to the mould loft, next to the stores where paints and oils, skylights and companions, and ship's gear of all kind await the needy vessel. In the saw-pit, odorous pine-smells greet us, and nails and gear of all descriptions are in this store running parallel with the dock itself. Here is the pitch-house, with five large furnaces in which the black saturnine liquid is heated.

In the building yard adjoining the dry-dock, the storage of timber occupies the foreshore, whilst yellow pine, pitch-pine, oak, elm, green-heart, teak, and American elm, occupy the yard. Mr Cock's premises cover some 6 acres. Across the road from the dock gates is a substantial run of lofts. Rock salt is stored below, rigging above, and in the second storey sail-makers are at work with their needle and cotton.

Beyond the gear store, where pumps, winches, and the thousand & one items of a vessel's outfit, are in waiting, lies 'the steamer' – where the planks are steamed and given the pliable quality which bends them, when they take that flowing line on the ship. Then the smithy, where the swarthy smiths, stout sons of Vulcan, weld the metal to an endless variety of shapes and uses. There are four forges, drilling machines and iron stores. The glowing forge fires throw fantastic shadows on the walls, and we can imagine as we take a parting glance at the weird scene, that we are assisting at the great ceremonial of the forging of the anchor in the brave old days of old." (Strongs Industries of North Devon).

Robert Cock and his Sons continued to run the Richmond Dock until 1932 during which time the shipbuilding and repair business underwent drastic change, the greatest of which was the change from timber ships to iron ships. The first iron ship was launched here in 1902.

In 1909 the largest steamship ever docked at Appledore was brought into the dry-dock to have new floors and ceilings fitted. She was the 'Ragusa' from Cardiff, a vessel of 2,000 tons, and she filled the entire length of the dock.

DISASTER IN THE DOCK:

In 1899, disaster struck the dock, when the entrance gates holding back the water failed. It was high tide, there was a strong gale blowing, and the caisson which was firmly wedged in the entrance, was stoved-in by the force of the water, propelled into the dock ahead of a torrent of water, and smashed to pieces. Two vessels were in the dock at the time, which collided violently causing serious damage to

John Couch from Richmond Road, foreman in the Richmond Dock in March 1932.
(Basil Greenhill Collection in North Devon Record Office).

An aerial view of Richmond Dock and Marine Parade in 1918. Note the oval-shaped caisson wedged in the
entrance of the dock to keep out the water. It is evident that this whole area is formed on reclaimed land – the
houses around the edge originally being waterside properties.

both, and causing the bottom of the dock to be broken up. If this failure had happened during a normal working day, dozens of men would have stood no chance of survival and would have been drowned or crushed in this sudden onslaught.

Thankfully it happened just before 6:00am on a Sunday morning, and no-one was there apart from the night watchman – but he certainly had an eventful night! Hundreds of people visited the scene of the disaster during the day, but it was over seven months before a new caisson could be installed and ship-repair work could start again.

ACCIDENTS:

Shipbuilding is a dangerous business. There are more hazards than you can imagine, so it is not surprising that many accidents occurred here. Non-fatal accidents occurred to a few of my ancestors, so I include some of these purely for personal interest:

In 1860, a scaffold collapsed and Thomas Lock (my great great grandfather) and others fell to the bottom of the dock. He sustained a broken leg and other injuries, whilst other casualties had fractured skulls.

In 1887, carpenter William Slader fell from a scaffold stage whilst working on a schooner. He struck his shoulder and rebounded thirty-feet into the bottom of the dock. He broke his right leg, dislocated his shoulder, and remained unconscious for nearly a day.

In 1898, seven men & boys were on a stage at the side of a vessel when a rope broke, throwing them and the scaffold into the dock. Luckily there was water in the dock at the time and they escaped unscathed.

Deaths have also occurred in the dock: 1866 – William Eastman, a 51-year-old carpenter from New Street fell into the hold of a vessel, broke his legs and ribs, and died later in hospital. He left a wife and six children. 1870 – William Horrell, a 29-year-old rigger fell from the mast of a vessel when a fixing broke. He landed on deck and died a few hours later. He left a wife and three children.

1898 – Captain Aleston who slipped off a plank whilst boarding his vessel, fell 30-feet to the bottom. He died the next day. He left a wife and five children.

WARTIME:

In 1932 Robert Cock and Sons went into liquidation. The Richmond Dock and Yard was acquired by Philip Kelly Harris who mortgaged his New Quay and Hubbastone Yards to finance this expansion. It was a brave time to expand a business with the depression of the 1930s, but a boom time was just ahead for them - the 2nd World War. The Harris family ran it until 1963.

From 1939 onwards Appledore's ship-building industry had more work than it could cope with, as the demand for specialist vessels and repairs increased dramatically. Most of the able-bodied men had joined the forces so there were few people to undertake the work.

Women were therefore brought in as part of the workforce, May Cann being the first woman employed there. She worked on motor torpedo boats and launches, doing deck-laying, painting, and riveting. Twenty other women were also employed playing their vital part in the War effort. Wooden vessels were back in fashion, needed for mine-deploying work. Leading up to D-Day there were more landing

The steamer 'James Spier' undergoing repairs in Richmond Dock in July 1906.
(Basil Greenhill Collection in North Devon Record Office).

The 'Hoveringham 1' in Richmond Dock in 1965. She was built for the Hoveringham Sand and Gravel
Company. (Basil Greenhill Collection in North Devon Record Office).

On 31st May 1948, the large stone warehouse building on the Richmond Dock site caught fire. This photo was taken from Myrtle House, which was damaged by the ferocity of the flames even from over 100 yards away.

The next day the damage is obvious, and firemen are still damping down the smouldering ruins. The building was demolished shortly afterwards. (North Devon Athenaeum).

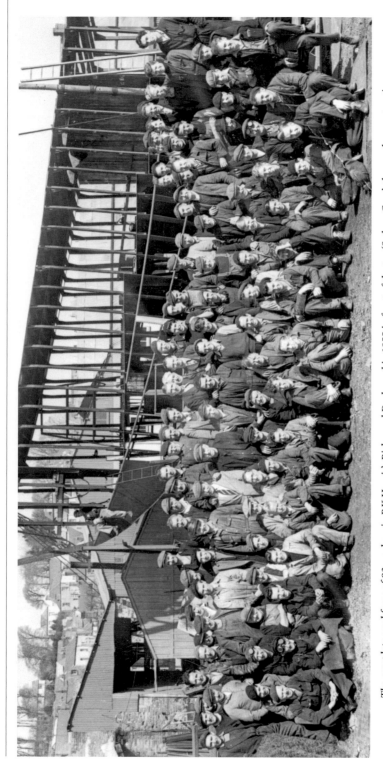

The complete workforce of 93 workers in P.K Harris's Richmond Dock yard in 1955 in front of the tug 'Sydney Cove', then under construction.

The men in the picture are: Bobby Lamey, Dick Curtis, Bobby Ross, Jack Eastman, John Lamey, Micky Pate, Jack Bowden, Archie Peake, 'Mac' Harris, Brian Jenkins, Billy Cann, Jack Moore, Leo Lamey, Bobby Lang, Charlie Edwards senr, 'Brummie' Bill, Bert Jewell, Charlie Stevens, Arthur Harris, Johnny Vikmanis, Wilfie Griffiths, Christopher Hughes, George Tonge, Bobby Nichols, Frankie Canteen, Walter Hoyle, Jack Guard, Wilfie Tanton, Ernest Forrester, Ted Sims, Sid Littlejohns, Bernard Carey, Richard Hocking, Jimmy Gray, Victor Keen, Studley Screech, Albert Cawsey, Sid Syms, John Kemp, 'Curley' Lamey, 'Taffy' Richards, Ernest Carter, Edwin Peake junr, Billy Hammett, 'Happy' Hutchings, Charlie Edwards junr, Tony Mounce, John 'Webber' Craner, Tommy Harding, Billy Kemp, Tony Powe, Joe Gifford, Terry Peake, Brian Sharrock, Dave Cherrett, Eddie Keron, Derek Kitto, Leslie Tithecott, Jack Fowler, Leonard Cann, George Ashton, Walter Cooke, Ivor Bettis, Richard Harris, Derek Godfrey, Kenneth Olde, Kenneth McDine, Peter Cann, Beresford Kitto, Graham Harris, Clifford Bartlett, Vernon Martin, Falkland Kivell, Harry Mountjoy, ~~~ Sheppard, Harold Stevens senr, John Brown, Jack Farthing, Harry Edwards, Peter Gist, Alfred Docherty, Dick Pickard, Trevor Jones, Jack Eastman, Jim Hallett, Ian Cox, Jack Mill, Freddie Palmer, Albert Cawsey senr, Billy Stoneman, 'Bunny' Newman, Jock Kidd, and Wally Lamphrey.

Two other men don't appear in the photo, as they had gone for lunch! They were Billy Cann and 'Nambo' Richards.

craft requiring attention than could be handled, so any mercantile repairs were halted by order of the Admiralty. Hours of work were 8:00am - 8:00pm Monday to Saturday, and on Sundays until noon. The P.K. Harris hooter sounded twice a day to mark beginning and end of work. My father mentions the hooters in his memoirs:

"There were actually two hooters in Appledore - one worked on compressed air in the lower Dock (Richmond) sited by the power/compressor house; and a mechanical hooter in the Upper Dock, sited by the gate, near to what we called 'Dripping Corner'. (The field below Chanters Folly drained over a high retaining wall here and it was rarely dry). The hooters sounded six times daily - early morning when work commenced; the start and finish of mid-morning break; the beginning and end of lunch hour, and finally for knocking off at the end of the day."
(Appledore Boyhood Memories, by E R Carter)

In spite of hard times after the War shipbuilding continued here, with tugs being the most common type of vessel ordered. In 1957, more tugs were being built here than in any other place in Britain. But by 1963 the yard was in financial difficulties, the bank refused to put more credit into the Company, and the yard closed overnight. A survival package was formed by local businessmen and their M.P. who created a new company called 'Appledore Shipbuilders Ltd', and work again resumed in the Richmond Dock. A 20-ton travelling crane was erected in 1968. However, expansion was necessary, and a new covered shipyard opened in 1970 built on Bidna Marsh just up the river. Richmond Dock and Yard were now only suitable for the construction and repair of tugs & small coasters, a market in which the new Shipbuilding Company was not interested. The

Dock soon fell into disuse, and has only occasionally been used since. Its future currently lies in doubt, the site having been subject to a number of housing development proposals. In 1987 an application to fill in the dock and build houses on the site was only narrowly defeated. We currently hope that a sensible solution will be found for preserving this important structure for the future.

DOCTON COURT:

Opposite the Richmond Dock stands Docton Court - the other of Appledore's Grade II* structures. Forgive me if I write more about Docton Court than other properties, but having poured a large part of my children's inheritance into restoring it, I think I'm allowed a little indulgence on this!

Firstly, many older Appledore residents will know the building as 'Docton House'. Historically Docton House was the living accommodation at the rear, and the front-range was known simply as 'Doctons'. As these are now two separate properties, the front part needed something a little more distinctive so I added the 'Court' to its name, in line with the many other courts which are in Appledore.

As we claim it to be Appledore's oldest building, I am often asked how old it is. Actually our insurance company asked me the same question when I rang them for a quote, but the tele-sales muppet I spoke to didn't like my answer of "about 14th century" and said "Don't you have an *exact* date then?"

Deed granting approval to build commercial premises in Appledore in 1334. (National Archives).

Although our deeds only go back to about 1900, as luck would have it I think we do now have an exact date, and we believe that the building may have been started in 1334. This isn't just invented to keep my insurance company's computer happy, we do have solid evidence for this. A document in the National Archives gives permission for Barnstaple merchant Geoffrey Fardel to build business premises here in 1334, and the described position matches the location of this property. It also suggests that the land between here and the main river frontage was quite a lot closer than it is today, and was also in the same ownership. The rent for this was one silver penny per year. As Geoffrey Fardel was heavily in debt at Exeter about eight years later, this seems likely, and also something I can identify with!

After that, and for the next 500 years or so, the history of this building is based on many assumptions. It is likely that the Black Death in 1349 put paid to Mr Fardel's business, and that the lands were afterwards obtained by the monks of Hartland Abbey. No records of this have survived, but land ownership after the dissolution by Henry VIII does infer this connection, and it would make sense having a Cistercian rest-house here. Travellers visiting the Abbey would have about one day's journey from Appledore, this being the nearest safest landing place for a ship.

A 19th century tradition also recounts that Docton House was the residence of a Spanish Don or Ambassador at the time of the Armada (1580s). He was supposed to be a merchant dealing in Spanish produce, so we can imagine his cellars here filled with Mediterranean choice wines and other goods. After this, the building came into the possession of the Docton family. No records survive, but 1588 would seem to be a good date for a Spaniard to disappear - that being the year of the Spanish Armada. The Doctons purchased land in Appledore in the early 1600s, so this cannot be coincidental. The Doctons were a prominent North Devon family, and appear in the parish records in Northam until the 18th century.

The cartouche over the doorway confirms the marriage between the Docton and Chantrell families in the 1540s. However, the carved crest was probably put here a couple of generations afterwards, by Thomas Docton who turned this old building into a grand house in the 1620s. An ornate barrel-vaulted ceiling filled the upper chambers, and the building was also extended to the rear at this time.

There are three early Tudor granite-framed doorways on the lower floor (the 3rd one is hidden within the neighbouring garage), indicating that this building originally had commercial use on this level. Although we have no records for this specific property, a contemporary record of a similar cellar at Instow was found to contain: butts of sherry, vinegar, Spanish iron, raisins, figs, salt, butter and coal.

On 10th July 1645, Prince Charles (the future Charles II) visited Appledore and possibly stayed here. Although aged only 15, he had been appointed commander of the Royalist forces in the south-west and was here to raise more forces to the cause, but more importantly to escape the threat of disease in Bristol.

In 1737, Dorothy Docton set up a charity to enable six poor children under the age of 11 to be taught to read until they could understand the Bible in English. This charity was based on the income gained from 'Jefferys Lands' near Benson's New Quay, bequeathed in 1724 by John Jeffery for charitable use. However in 1775, these lands were in the possession of the Benson family who argued that the land was not accurately described, and so they neglected to pay any further income to this charity. Given that the money from John Jefferies gift was to be used to provide bread to the parish poor four times a year, this does seem rather mean. Dorothy Docton died in 1744 after which this building left the ownership of the Docton family, and the surrounding lands which extended back as far as One-End Street were sold off. Nearly fifty years later though, it was still known as Docton's Mansion.

> ### DEVONSHIRE.
> TO be SOLD in a SURVEY to be held for that Purpose, at Docken's Mansion-House, in Appledore, within the Parish of Northam, in the County of Devon, on Thursday the 9th Day of April next, by Four o'Clock in the Afternoon, the Fee-simple and Inheritance of all that commodious Dwelling - House, called DOCKEN's MANSION HOUSE; together with a very good Malt-House, Brew-house, an excellent Brick-Kiln, several convenient Cellars, Stable, Coach-House, &c. &c. a remarkable fine walled Garden, about one Acre, with a large Quantity of all Sorts of Fruit Trees. The Premises are situate at the East End of the Town of Appledore, adjoining the River Torridge, about two Miles from Bideford, in good Repair, and well adapted for a Gentleman's Family, or a Person in the Mercantile Line.
> Apply to WILLIAM HENRY HATHERLEY, Attorney, in Bideford aforesaid, who has several large SUMS of MONEY to advance on good Freehold Security.
> Dated Bideford, March 24, 1789.

(Exeter Flying Post: 2nd April 1789)

In 1864 a sale notice for Doctons refers to 2 dwelling houses, malt-house, cellars, lofts, stable, enclosed yards, and walled garden, late in occupation of William Williams.

DOCTON HOUSE:

This house at the back of Docton Court was probably built in the 1620s by the Docton family as a service wing for their 'mansion' at the front. You will only see this house if you go up the steps at the side. My father recalls going there some eighty years ago:

"I remember the open courtyard at the top of the stairs had three boat swings, which took two children at a time sitting facing each other, each one pulling a rope to keep them going. The three swings had names painted on them - 'Why Not', 'Come Up', and 'Try Me', and I think we had to pay something like a half-penny for an hour's use."
(Appledore Boyhood Memories, by E R Carter).

The best feature of Docton House is a huge 11-foot-wide open-fireplace, which during recent renovation works showed that it contained a traditional cloam oven and an even earlier bread oven. When the sealed-up bread oven was opened, an old shoe was found dating to around 1620, several pieces of elaborate glassware including a jar still holding a pink powder, some bones, pottery, threads and hairs. It was once the custom to seal up a fire or oven by witchcraft, and it is believed that these finds were the result of such a practice. White-witchcraft of this sort would have been quite wide-spread in Appledore in the 1600s, although not practised for sinister reasons, just to counter superstitions. The hearth was seen as a vulnerable position in a house as it was always open to the sky, and any sinister forces could easily gain entrance down the chimney.

WITCHCRAFT:

Not all witchcraft practices had such innocent intents. In England between 1550 and

1660 there was a paranoid craze for witch-hunting, and in 1682 at Bideford three women were tried and convicted of witchcraft, and executed at Exeter. They were Mary Trembles, Susanna Edwards, and Temperance Lloyd, and they are believed to have been the last people hanged for witchcraft in England.

THE
Tryal, Condemnation, and
EXECUTION
OF THREE
WITCHES,
VIZ.
TEMPERACE FLOYD,
MARY FLOYD,
AND
SUSANNA EDWARDS.

Who were Arraigned at *Exeter* on the 18th, of *August*, 1682. And being prov'd Guilty of Witch-Craft, were Condemn'd to be Hang'd, which was according-ly Executed in the view of many Spectators, whose strange and much to be lamented Impudence, is never to be forgot-ten.

Also, how they Confessed what Mis-chiefs they had done, by the assistance of the Devil, who lay with the above-named *Temperance Floyd* Nine Nights toge-ther. Also, how they Squeezed one *Hannah Thomas* to death in their Arms; How they also caused several Ships to be cast away, causing a Boy to fall from the top of a Main-Mast into the Sea.

With many Wonderful Things, worth your Reading.

Printed for *J. Deacon*, at the sign of the *Rainbow*, a little be-yond St. *Andrews* Church, in *Holborn*. 1682.

Temperance Lloyd was found to have consorted with Satan, and had described meeting him in her house: a black man, two foot high, with huge staring eyes and a mouth like a toad – ah yes, that would be him! When the confused old woman was found unable to recite the Lord's Prayer, her fate was sealed, along with her equally confused friends.

Soon all three had been taken into custody and at Exeter Assizes the judge accepted the testimony from Bideford. He found them guilty and they were hanged within a week, all because of fear, and unfounded paranoia based on superstition. No wonder people buried things near fireplaces.

Meanwhile back at Docton House, another historical find was an elaborate ceramic fire-back, probably the finest ever found in North Devon. It was investigated by Devon Archaeology who published a report on this.

In later years Docton House was the home of Alfie Green, whom many older Appledore residents remember when they visited him here to have their photographs taken with a glass-plate camera. Apart from being a professional photographer, he was a part-time minister at the Northam Congregational Church, Chairman of the Council, Secretary of the football club, Secretary of the rowing club, Organiser of social events, President of the Regatta Committee, and much more besides. My father recalls him, as follows:

"Alfred Green was a well-known local character, a leading light in the social activities of the village. A block-maker by trade, he was a natural public speaker, and was always in great demand taking special services and acting as guest speaker throughout the district. He is well remembered too for his photography and magic lantern shows. I can certainly remember the time he took my photo. I was very reluctant to change from short to long trousers. Apart from thinking I would look stupid in them, I also believed they would restrict my movement running and jumping, and would be a nuisance messing about on the river. I must have been nearly 15 when I grudgingly submitted to wear long trousers. Mother wanted a photo taken right away to send to Dad, but I only agreed providing I could creep down to Alfie's studio after dark."
(Appledore Boyhood Memories, by E R Carter).

During the 2nd World War, Docton House was home for the Officers and Commander for HMS Appledore - of which more later.

Ghosts of hooded figures have been seen walking though the kitchen area of Docton House. The person witnessing these figures believed them to be women with shawls over their heads, not knowing that the building used to be a monastery. When told this, it became clear that these figures were actually the ghosts of hooded monks.

SPINDLEBERRY COTTAGE:

In front of Docton Court lies 'Spindleberry Cottage'. Originally called 'Johns Cottage', it being the home of William and Laura Johns. The house had an external porch facing Docton Courtyard in which garden the Johns grew all their own vegetables.

MAGOURNEY COTTAGE:

To the right of Docton Court lies 'Magourney Cottage', which contains late 17th century panelling and the remains of a barrel-vaulted ceiling within its roof space. It is of a later date than Docton Court, but would have originally been on the same lands and therefore had links with the Docton family.

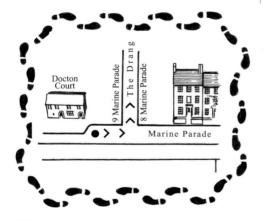

GO UP THE NARROW DRANG BETWEEN NUMBERS 8 AND 9 MARINE PARADE

Leaving Marine Parade now, we squeeze up 'The Drang' as it is known locally. Although just 3-foot wide, the Highways Agency have provided helpful signs here telling us that cars are not permitted, and just in case we try and sneak up here in a car after dark, the signs are

also illuminated – so we have no excuse about not seeing them!

Up the drang on the left is the 'Appletree Mews' development, tastefully built here in the late 1990s on the site of an old pear orchard - the trees supposedly belonging to the monks at Docton Court who brewed their own perry. On the right, an even narrower drang leads along the back of the Marine Parade houses. The 1840 tithe map shows this path continuing through to Market Street and the Quay, although it is not clear whether this was actually the case. There is a good example of a surviving cob wall just down this drang on the right-hand side.

The two-storey stone building on the corner was used as a store by Dr Desmond Valentine, and in which he used to mix his own medicines.

SILVER STREET:

Rounding the corner at the top of the drang, the street officially becomes 'Silver Street'. The houses here are probably of early 19th century construction, although only half of them show on the 1840 tithe map. These were some of the poorer houses for Appledore sailors and their families.

In 1882, John Taylor from number 1 Silver Street was summoned for neglecting his wife and seven children, and leaving them chargeable to the Union Workhouse.

As we turn the corner at the far end of Silver Street, note the small lock-up shop on the right. This was a betting shop before the 2nd World War (Jones & Joint), in the 1950s a greengrocers shop, and in the 1960s an electrical shop.

If you look down to Homeside Terrace below the shop, there is access to a small undercroft. There are stories of people actually living here in Victorian times. Obviously these were desperate times for some, but anywhere dry and out of the wind was more comfortable than life on board ship.

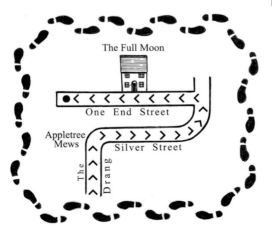

AT THE END OF SILVER STREET TURN LEFT UP ONE-END STREET

ONE END STREET
APPLEDORE

Turning left at the end of Silver Street, we come to the aptly-named 'One-End Street', which for those who haven't worked it out yet, only has one end! There is a path continuing upwards from the top end of this street which is worth exploring - it almost reaches Odun Road, but not quite. As far as we can tell it never did reach any further, as the gentry landowners in Odun Road would have no need of a quick route to visit the 'working peasants' further down the hill.

Actually 'One-End Street' is a fairly modern name, only appearing in about 1830. Prior to that it was known as 'Cock Street', some say because there used to be a cock-pit here, but it is more likely to have been named after a Mr Cock as this surname was quite common in the village. James Cock was an Appledore merchant in the late 1600s, and upon his death he endowed a charity to assist the widows and orphans of Appledore - so he's quite a good person to name a street after - let's attribute it to him!

One-End Street is a great place for a street party – we should have these more often. In 1911 for the Coronation of George V, it was planned that a thousand children in Appledore would be given a free tea and a Coronation Mug in memory of the event. The papers reported that every street was decked with flags and festoons, and never before was so much bunting displayed in Appledore. A patriotic address was given by postmaster William Land at Western Hill. The subsequent parade was said to be the longest procession of children ever seen in Appledore. They marched through the streets, passed through the grounds of The Holt, and then to a field at Staddon for an afternoon of sports.

No 1, One-End Street:

This house curving around the corner is surrounded on 3 sides by the street. It has a fine plastered dining room ceiling with mouldings typical of the 1740s.

If we imagine Appledore 250 years ago prior to any of the buildings that now tumble onto the quay, it is possible that this house had a river view from its end windows, and that the line of the river has been pushed out considerably over the years. This is pure speculation, but there is evidence to suggest this was the case.

The house contained a draper's shop between 1840 and 1880 run by Mary Grigg. By the 1980s it was being used as a café.

The Secret Tunnel:

There are so many tales of underground tunnels in Appledore that I have lost count of them. Tunnels down Market Street, tunnels along Irsha Street, even a tunnel leading up the river to Knapp House (and that's over a mile away). It's amazing that Appledore hasn't collapsed into all these tunnels! Many of these tunnel-rumours probably come from glimpses of lost cellars and the supposition that these must lead somewhere, so I am therefore very

sceptical about any alleged tunnel.

However, there is some good evidence for a tunnel leading from the cellar under number 1 One-End Street down to the river, although if there was an entrance here, it has since been blocked up and the cellar tanked. You can sometimes hear the sound of water in this cellar as if lapping onto a shingle beach. Lengths of timber were supposedly brought up through this tunnel for storage, and later up to a sawmills further up the hill.

Down on the quay, there is testimony from Tom Berry (now deceased) there was a brick-lined tunnel leading inland from the quay-edge, in which he had stood upright and could not touch the sides. At about 6'6", Tom Berry was said to have been the tallest man in Appledore, so this tunnel was not a small construction. There are also tales of a 'Watergate' opening onto Appledore Quay in Victorian times.

Joining these stories and tunnel-ends together, in the middle sits the Appledore library building, again with stories of a tunnel underneath. The deeds of the building give a description of the property which interestingly mentions a 'timber pond, store and workshop'. What is a 'timber pond' if not an underground area for seasoning timber?

So we now have two ends and a middle, which I think is fairly good evidence for a complete tunnel. Of course this wouldn't have been for smuggling or contraband, that would be dishonest - and secret!

The Family from One-End Street:

Readers of children's literature may be familiar with a series of books about 'The Family from One End Street', by Eve Garnett. It tells the story of the Ruggles family with seven children who live at number 1 One-End Street in the fictional village of Otwell-on-the-Ouse. It was groundbreaking for its portrayal of a working-class family and their battle against conditions in the slums.

Although not from Appledore, the author was educated in Devon and took the title of her book from this quirky house at the bottom of One-End Street. The book won the Carnegie Medal for best children's book of 1937, beating other classics including Tolkien's 'The Hobbit'.

BOWDEN'S GROCERY SHOP:

There were no shops in One-End Street apart from Louisa Bowden's Grocery & sweet shop at number 4. (See book 1, page 13, in which the two men standing have now been identified as Mr Guigan, left; and Capt. Griffiths, right).

APERIENT or ANTIBILIOUS PILLS, Prepared and Sold by ROBERT BOWDEN, Appledore.

Robert Bowden was an invalid, but he made medicines at his house at 2 One-End Street. (Bideford Gazette: 23rd April 1861).

THE FULL MOON:

One-End Street had its own pub at number 6, named the 'Full Moon'. The house has deeds going back to 1684 when mariner William Gording is selling it to tailor Anhillis Smale, although the building is believed to have been built around 1655. The Full Moon pub is first known to exist in 1817 run by Sarah King. Later it was owned by Elizabeth Evans who passed it to her son-in-law Arthur Day. He died in 1857, and his family kept the pub going until 1865 at which date it closed.

APPLEDORE, NORTH DEVON.
TO MALTSTERS, INNKEEPERS, AND OTHERS.
TO BE SOLD, by Auction, at the 'Royal Hotel,' Appledore, on Thursday, the 16th November inst.; at 6 o'clock in the Evening, all that old established Public-house known by the name of the 'FULL MOON,' situate in One End-street, Appledore aforesaid, now in the occupation of Mr. DAY.
The BREWING UTENSILS will be Sold with the Premises.

(North Devon Journal: 9th Nov 1865).

REDEVELOPMENT:

In 1970, the Northam Town Council commissioned a Conservation Area Study for Appledore to report on housing conditions and suggest improvements to preserve the environment of any areas of special architectural or historic interest. Their consultants noted that up to forty houses in Appledore were unfit for human habitation, and concluded that it would be better to get rid of some unfit properties and to provide new development, designed to be in keeping with the existing character.

It was recommended that Numbers 3 to 9 One-End Street should be demolished and replaced with a paved modern urban square. This would "bring more light to the front of the houses in Silver Street, and also enhance the environment of the street scene".

Not surprisingly the residents of Appledore made their feelings known on this appalling vandalism of our heritage, and the Appledore Conservation Society was born out of this which fought against bureaucratic decisions and unsympathetic schemes. However, don't let my judgement sway you, look at this artist's impression for yourself and make up your own mind.

Proposed urban square for One-End Street.

The above photograph from 1940 shows the wartime quay being constructed. We can see the old quay wall which appears to have a 7'0" high round hole in it, as though the construction works have caused an old blocked-up tunnel to become exposed. Could this be our secret tunnel?
The children looking at the works are Cynthia Reed (centre), Stuart Berry (left), and Lionel Cork (right).

Appledore Quay under construction in 1940.

No 5 One-End Street:

This small unassuming cottage on the left at number 5 (one of the houses due to be demolished in the 1970s) is the oldest surviving cottage in the street. Muriel Stanton wrote about being brought up there in the 1920s and 1930s.

"Electricity was brought to the house in 1930, before that we had paraffin lamps and candles. Cooking was done on black Bodley coal oven. The house had winding stairs and hidden cupboards. One day a doctor called on an old lady in one of these old cottages. He came in and shouted the lady's name. She told him to come upstairs to the bedroom. He had a good look round but couldn't find the stairs anywhere (they were hidden away behind a cupboard door). "Where are the stairs?" he shouted.

"If you can't find the stairs, how can you find out what's wrong with me!" came the reply." (Looking Back, by Muriel Stanton).

Muriel described that the house had deeds going back to the time of Elizabeth I, indeed others have suggested that the cottage is perhaps much older still, dating back to the mid-1400s, however no such ancient documents now seem to exist.

Prostitutes:

It's taken a little while, but we have finally found a reason to mention prostitution. Given the desperate conditions that some people were living in it's not surprising that women used whatever means they could to supplement their income. With a ready market of visiting sailors, business was probably quite good. The reports of prostitution are few and far between, but like smuggling, it only gets recorded when something goes wrong - and it certainly went wrong for Catherine Taylor at 7 One-End Street.

In 1891 she was described as a 'charwoman', but the following year the court described her as a 'common prostitute' and found that she had neglected her three children to go on the streets.

The visiting inspector found a baby in a cradle alone in a room, flea-bitten and dirty, lying on rags smelling strongly of urine. Catherine was reported as having continually been seen with strange seamen, and her cousin who lived in the same house admitted that Catherine often 'stayed out all night' although she could not say what for.

The children were all underweight, their clothes filthy and inadequate, and from different fathers. All of them slept in one bedstead which was in a foul condition, the straw mattress soaked with urine.

Catherine was sentenced to fourteen days in prison. The eldest girl (Blanche, 13) was taken away into care of the NSPCC and sent to their care home in Surrey. The other two children (Annie and Minnie) were sent to the workhouse whilst their mother was serving her sentence.

Members of the Bennett family outside 18 One-End Street in the 1930s.

THE BAKEHOUSE DANCES:

Night-life came to One-End Street in the 1920s and 1930s when dances were held at number 20, in a large garage building at the back of Alfred Reed's bakery shop in Bude Street. He used this rear entrance for the deliveries and storing his carts and van. His shop also had a back entrance so that One-End Street customers in a hurry could walk right though.

His daughters were very musical, so he started up the Saturday Night Dance Club for the young people of Appledore which ran between the 1st and 2nd World Wars. The space would be cleared up ready for Saturday night and the piano made ready, usually played by Audrey Reed. The entrance fee was 6d, and every Saturday night the young people of Appledore went to the Bakehouse and danced the two-step, circle dances, and the valletta. These Bakehouse dances were very popular and Rev. Muller, the vicar of the time, became quite jealous and later started organising his own dances on special occasions.

During the Queen's Coronation in 1953 a TV was installed here, and many people crowded in here to watch before joining their individual street parties.

17-21 ONE-END STREET:

Numbers 17 to 21, were all built in 1891 on the site of previous buildings.

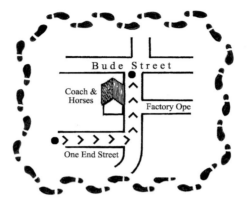

There are stories of a ghost appearing at the top of One-End Street, although these are rather confused. Some say that there is a ghost of a lady taking water from the pump that used to stand here. Others refer to the ghost of a white rabbit, which is supposed to jump out at you – hmmm, frightening!

RETURN DOWN ONE-END STREET & TURN LEFT INTO MARKET STREET

MARKET STREET SHOPS:

Returning back down One-End Street we now enter the heart of Appledore – Market Street. This was the original main street, its buildings following the line of the shore, and many properties along here have been a shop at one time or another.

Life was tough for a sailor, but it was sometimes tough for a shopkeeper. In 1858, all the shopkeepers agreed to reduce their opening hours and to close their shops at 8:00pm every evening (except Saturday) so that they could get a little rest. Given that these were all family businesses, these were quite long hours. In 1896 grocers gave themselves even more time off, with Wednesday 'half-days' when they closed at 4:00pm, except for ironmongers who had to stay open until 6:00pm. No – don't ask me why either!

There have been so many shops in Market Street over the years continually changing hands, it would be difficult (and rather tedious) to try and tell you where and when they all existed. However, I will give you some names and dates of shops that have been identified, as we go along. I have largely restricted this to prior to the 2nd World War.

COACH & HORSES:

At number 5 Market Street this ancient Appledore Inn is first mentioned by name in 1806, but was almost certainly serving visiting sailors a couple of hundred years before that, when it probably had a river-frontage, the buildings in front being constructed in later years.

In 1867, the legal battle between Thomas Tatem and William Yeo (see 5 Marine Parade) started here when a fight broke out between Tatem and William Knight (Yeo's agent). Tatem taunted that he could beat them in Court, backing up this assertion with his fist in Knight's face and some 'rough & tumble' then ensued between the two men. Punches, scratches and bites were traded before the fight was broken up, only to recommence later in Court.

For the record the known landlords of the Coach & Horses from 1822 up to the 2nd World War have been: Ann Bevan, Thomas Fieldew, William Burnicle, Robert Tatem, John Prout, Fanny Tatem, Hannah Prout, Hannah Short, Mr McConnell, John Hooper, Josiah Evans, John Hutchings, Joseph and Mary Evans, Charles Hammett, Richard Crang, Mary Fry, Frederick Beach, and Sydney Featherstone.

6 MARKET STREET:

This has been a newsagent's shop since at least 1906, when earlier owners were the Evans and Fishwick families. In 1830 it was probably the premises of Elizabeth Vernon, draper and tea-dealer.

THE FOUNTAIN HEAD INN:

A short-lived pub appeared in 1852, between Market Street and The Quay. Called the 'Fountain Head Inn', it contained a malt-house with its own kiln & cisterns, bar, parlour and tap-room. Also a small garden in which pigs were kept. It was bought from the late Joshua Williams by John Pentecost who ran it for just two years before emigrating to Australia.

CROSS OVER BUDE STREET AND CONTINUE ALONG MARKET STREET

We will just look at the buildings on the right as we go down this street.

7 MARKET STREET:

'London House', to the right of the Coach & Horses, was the draper's shop of Jerome Beara between 1880 and 1921. The shop extended around the corner into Bude Street and we will hear more of this later. The Post Office moved here in 1931 into Frederick Cork's drapers shop. Mr Cork later moved his shop and Post Office to the quay, and London House then became a haberdashery, then a shoe-shop, and then a greengrocers.

Opposite this shop was the entrance to Beara's Market, now rebuilt into apartment flats.

8 & 10 MARKET STREET:

Opposite the Royal Hotel was the grocery and ship's victualler's shop run by the Lawday family. Lewis Lawday started the family business around 1875, which continued until Fred Lawday died in 1938. Prior to that number 10 was Farleigh's Grocers, a sub-branch to their main shop at Barnstaple. They opened their shop here in Appledore in 1852, moving to these larger premises in 1857.

TEAS AT WHOLESALE PRICES.
THREE POUNDS of Superior BLACK TEA for 10s. 6d., or Three Pounds of FINE KAISOW FLAVOURED TEA, for 11s. 6d., at
FARLEIGH, BROTHERS,
Wholesale Grocery Warehouse, Cross-street, or 13, High-street, and Market-street, *Appledore*.
A Large Assortment of CHRISTMAS FRUITS, comprising MUSCATEL, VALENTIA, & SULTANA RAISINS, FINE CURRANTS, ST. MICHAEL ORANGES, &c., &c. [3319]

(North Devon Journal: 14th February 1861).

12 MARKET STREET:

· Scobling's, boot and shoes, 1901-1926.
· Lamey's, boots and shoes, 1930s.
· Thomas Ostler, hairdresser, 1930s.

14 MARKET STREET:

· Mary Buse, dairy and general grocer, 1891-1901.
· Sidney Woolland, hairdresser, 1914.

16 MARKET STREET:

· Charles Huxtable, bootmaker, 1891.

18 MARKET STREET:

· John Thomas Slader, china and household goods, 1880-1926.
· William and Bertha Down, 1926-1939.

One of the Bodley ovens sold by ironmonger and plumber John Thomas Slader.

20 MARKET STREET:

Formerly known as Bristol House.
· Samuel Fursey, boot and shoes, 1871-1893.
· John Tuplin, boot and shoes, 1901-1923.
· Catharine Tuplin, grocer, 1926.
· Mary Heddon, shopkeeper, 1935-1939.

After the 2nd World War this was Jack Wetherden's hardware and grocery shop, and is now the 'Sea Chest'.

In 1892 Miss Fursey offered these premises for sale, including the coal stores on the quay plus two cottages in the adjacent 'Fursey's Avenue'.

22 MARKET STREET:

Situated at the back of the Trinity Buoy Store, this house has the name 'Trinity Cottage'

Market Street in the 1890s (top), and again showing John Thomas Slader's china and glass shop circa 1900 (bottom).

and was the home of the buoy keeper in the 1870s to 1890s.

24-30 MARKET STREET:

These four properties have very attractive Victorian bay windows, but curiously there are no early records to show that these were ever shops and appear to have been largely domestic. The censuses describe mariners and sailmakers living here but not shopkeepers.

34 MARKET STREET:

- James and Eliza Chappell, dairyman and butcher, 1901-1910.
- Minnie Taylor, shopkeeper, dairy, 1914-1939.

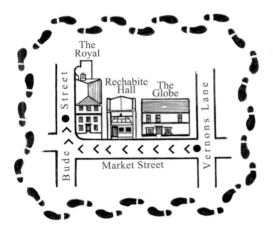

AT THE JUNCTION OF MARKET STREET AND VERNONS LANE - STOP!

Retrace your steps back to Bude Street. On the way, we will look at the buildings on the other side of the street.

31 MARKET STREET:

- **Martha Clemett, grocer, 1881.**

25 MARKET STREET:

Next to the former Globe Inn we currently find Schooners Delicatessen. However, for most older Appledore residents, this was Boyle's Grocery shop which ran from 1926 until the 1990s, although this building has probably been serving retail customers for centuries. It was Cox's grocery shop from about 1905 to 1926 and prior to that it was Elizabeth Hamlyn's shop for about fifty years. In 1856, seventeen year-old Betsy Ross was sentenced to six weeks imprisonment with hard labour for stealing a blue knitted guernsey frock from Elizabeth Hamlyn's shop. When Elizabeth's husband Thomas Hamlyn died in 1908 he owned quite a number of properties which were all sold off. These included three houses in One-End Street, seven properties in Market Street and two houses in Vernon's Lane - not bad for a grocer!

23 MARKET STREET – THE GLOBE HOTEL:

Next to the Swan Inn, was another of Appledore's old inns, The 'Globe', dating back to Elizabethan times when it would have originally had a river frontage and been well-placed to be a haven for thirsty sailors.

Old photographs of this building show a hanging glass globe outside acting as its sign (book 1, page 17). The globe was believed to be a sign of Portuguese wine merchants. The earliest mention of the Globe name is around the 1740s when Samuel Tetherley becomes proprietor of the 'Globe House'. However, the inn is probably far more ancient, and the lands upon which it stands were part of the 'Baples Estate' acquired sometime around 1500. The Baples were a noted local landowning family dating back to Sir Roger Beaupel, Lord of Landkey in the 13th century descended from one of William the Conqueror's knights. When Charles II was staying at Barnstaple in 1645, he stayed at Grace Baple's lodgings but left without paying his bill – I guess that's what you call Royal privilege.

John Powe, licensed victualler, owned Globe House from 1758 to 1783.

In 1888, William Tatem was summoned for being drunk on the premises and was fined £1. This seems a little harsh seeing as it was his pub at the time!

The rather striking eagle above the door has no particular significance. These eagles were fashionable items made in Bideford in the early 20th century and adorned various houses in the area. However, most were removed during the 2nd World War as the eagle was seen to be a symbol of Germany. The Globe ceased being a pub in 1968.

 The ghost of a young girl has often been seen here especially on Christmas Eve, and has been given the name 'Peggy'. She wears a blue skirt, white blouse, a straw hat with bright blue ribbon, and carries a skipping rope. Her long fair hair droops in curls over her shoulders and she gives a girlish giggle before vanishing into thin air. At other times the sounds of lewd sailor's songs have been heard downstairs and the smell of beer and tobacco can be smelt in the air. There is also a ghost of a man seen standing at a front upper window dressed in sackcloth-type clothes, thought to be a pimp standing guard on the girls upstairs.

The known landlords of this Inn from the 1740s until 1955 were: Samuel Tetherley, John Powe, Capt Brayley, Mr Tetherley, John Butt, Philip Lang, Thomas Lang, William Evans, James Moule, Mary Macallam, Mary Hooper, William Tatem, Thomas Stacey, and George and Isabel Moyse.

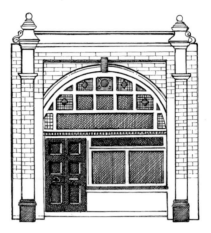

21 MARKET STREET:

The building here displays the sign 'Old Rechabite Hall', but who were the Rechabites and when was it a Hall?

The imposing arched façade was created in 1886 by John Gaydon a victualler from Barnstaple, who took on a traditional, but run-down old pub called the 'Swan Inn'. In fact the Swan had been closed for three years, but John Gaydon modernised the frontage with this sweeping arch and re-branded it as the 'Wine & Spirit Vaults'.

(Bideford Gazette: 18th Jan 1887).

In 1908, it was bought by the Order of Rechabites, a society dedicated to teetotalism who used it as their headquarters. The Rechabites probably thought that they had made a conquest by buying a pub and closing it down. Although they couldn't afford to change the vaulted front they did personalise the coloured glass with their emblem of the Raven & the Pitcher, which can be seen in the upper floor.

The Raven & the Pitcher comes from Aesop's fable where the raven was very thirsty but couldn't get into the pitcher to drink the water. So he worked all day dropping pebble after pebble into the pitcher until the water level finally rose enough for him to drink. This was adopted as an emblem by the Rechabites, who presumably thought that smart thinking and a clear head, gets you a drink.

Prior to 1886, the frontage probably looked much the same as all the other buildings along the street, with small sash windows and a dark interior. However, proof of its former past can be traced back in the deeds to at least 1747 when the inn was owned and run by mariner John Nicholls and his wife Jane. It was probably known then as the 'Swan Inn', although this name does not appear formally in the records until 1822 when Thomas Channon is the landlord.

The Rechabites moved out in 1930 and George Down turned it into a fish and chip shop. During the 2nd World War it was the Home Guard Drill Hall, and probably had a mini rifle-range in the garden as some live bullets were dug up here in the 1960s. Other historic finds from the garden were some old clay pipes and a musket ball.

Various owners then ran it as the 'Appledore Café & Ice Cream Parlour' and also as a general grocery shop. In the 1960s and 70s it was a trendy teenage café until it was converted into a private house in 1980.

The following landlords are known to have run the Swan Inn from 1822 until its closure in 1908: Thomas Channon, Philip Guy, William Stapleton, Thomas Harvey, Elizabeth Cann, Martha Scott, Richard Hocking, William White, Robert Barrow, Sarah Oatway, John Gaydon, Thomas Thatcher, and Ushers Ltd.

ANOTHER TUNNEL?:

Apparently during the War when the Quay was being re-built, a tunnel was discovered leading from the old Quay to underneath No 21. It had partially collapsed and was filled in shortly afterwards.

 A strange incident occurred in the early 1960s when the building was being renovated. Christine Patterson who lived there at the time, remembers her father finding a small celluloid doll with remnants of clothing concealed behind a lathe and plaster wall. He though it might be of interest and the doll was given to her mother in the kitchen. When Christine came in her mother showed her the doll, but only briefly. The doll flipped out of her hand into the air, and disappeared. They searched everywhere but the doll was nowhere to be seen. It still hasn't been found to this day. Is that spooky or what?

Street party celebrations in One-End Street for the Queen's Coronation in 1953.

The Down family outside their shop and fish and chip restaurant at 21 Market Street in the 1930s.

19 MARKET STREET:

• **William Sharrock, greengrocer, 1891.**

GIBBS LANE:

Gibbs Lane seems to be rather lacking in historical references. It is first mentioned by name in the 1851 census when there are seven properties listed, most of which contained just three rooms each.

Like most streets it had no formal naming-ceremony, its name evolving from common usage. In this case it was named after Theodosia Gibbs who kept a shop at the bottom of the lane (number 15 Market Street), which became known locally as 'that lane next to Mrs Gibbs', ie: 'Gibbs Lane'. She was born Theodosia Hartnoll, an Appledore girl, daughter of the village shoemaker, and was married and widowed twice by the age of 46. She kept a grocery and draper's shop here from the 1820s until her death in 1856, by which time the name 'Gibbs Lane' had stuck. It's only fitting that it should be named after one of Appledore's shopkeepers who served the village for more than thirty years.

15 MARKET STREET:

In 1871, ferryman Billy Johns and his family lived at 15 Market Street when he was involved in a police chase, which caused great excitement in the village. Johns had assaulted his wife during a quarrel and a warrant was issued for his arrest. Constable Stevens found him on the quay and tried to arrest him. A crowd gathered but weren't quite sure which side to be on. Johns then jumped into his boat and pushed off into the river, but the Police were unable to follow. The Customs Officer then took his launch out and eventually managed to catch up with Johns in the estuary. When they got close, Johns jumped overboard and tried to swim to freedom. He was pulled from the river, handcuffed, and brought back to Appledore where he was paraded dripping wet through the streets followed by a large crowd of people.

13 MARKET STREET:

• **Isabella Mara, grocer & tea-dealer, 1855-1866.**
• **Samuel Fursey junior, bootmakers, 1866-1869.**
• **William Bowden, grocer, 1869-1888.**
• **Gates 'Drapery Bazaar', 1882-1906.**
• **Payne's, draper and milliner, 1906-1934.**
• **Bert Ostler, hairdressers, from 1939.**

EARLY SMOKERS:

Clay pipes have been found in the back garden of 13 Market Street, now believed to be some of the earliest ever discovered in Devon, being traceable back to manufacturers in Barnstaple in the early 1630s. Tobacco shipments were first brought into Britain in about 1565 and Bideford is sometimes stated to have been the first place where this cargo

The remains of a clay pipe in the form of a bearded man, found in Appledore.

arrived, eventually proving to be very prosperous for the town. Between 1700 and 1740 Bideford imported more tobacco than any other port in England, except London. The tobacco import business created many wealthy local merchants and was of vital importance to its economy.

11 MARKET STREET:

- **John Beer, baker and confectioner,1875-1893.**
- **Lewis Beer, grocery shop, 1901-1910.**
- **Daisy Short, baker's shop, from 1934.**

Some poltergeist activity was recorded here in the late 1960s with objects flying across the room, books appearing mysteriously on window cills, apples spinning round the shop, etc. An exorcism was undertaken and all has been quiet since.

ROYAL HOTEL:

This long-standing commercial inn can be traced back by name to 1822 when Richard Berwick owned the licence, although the premises appear to have been a coaching inn for many years prior to that, so quite which 'Royal' the inn is named after is anyone's guess.

The structure you see today was built by the subsequent owners William and Honour Bolt sometime during their ownership between the 1830s and 1859. Overnight stabling was provided in the yard at the rear of the hotel.

Other commercial interests appear in buildings off this yard. In the 1860s Joseph Laird ran a dentistry business here. Offering himself as a 'mechanical and operating dentist, and supplier of artificial teeth', one can only imagine the standard that was employed at this time.

> ## ARTIFICIAL TEETH.
> ### MR. J. LAIRD,
> Mechanical & Operating Dentist & Chemist,
> BUDE STREET, APPLEDORE,
> Attends at Mr. RICHARDS' Saddler, High-st., Bideford,
> EVERY TUESDAY FORENOON.

(Bideford Gazette: 14th Jan 1868).

Just for the record, the following landlords are known to have run this establishment from 1822 up to the 2nd World War: Richard Berwick, William and Matilda Bolt, John Braund, Lawrence Heywood, Lewis Boundy, Ernest Main, Elizabeth Oatway, Frederick Raymont, Edward and Annie Randall, Alfred Vanstone, Albert Childs, Bertram Berry, Robert Chugg, and Bernard Bicknell.

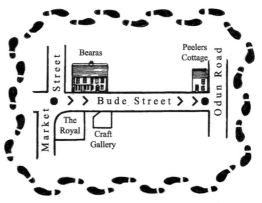

TURN RIGHT UP BUDE STREET

BUDE STREET:

Bude Street is one of Appledore's up-market streets. Faced on both sides with an assortment of master mariner's and merchant's houses all built and re-built at different times, it creates a veritable assortment of architectural styles. Grand facades built to impress sit next to older structures which hide cob walls dating back to the 1600s. It is not an ancient thoroughfare as it didn't actually lead anywhere useful, except to farmland on higher ground above the village. The oldest feature here is probably the line of the street itself which is first recorded by name in 1735 as 'Gaping (or Gapeing) Street', a name which was used into mid-Victorian times when for some reason it started to become known as 'Bude Street'. It probably took this name from 'Bude House' the grand house that looks down the street from Odun Road at the top, although why its name changed is unknown.

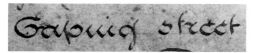

Bude Street was originally cobbled, which helped the horses grip on the steep slope, although in 1904 the surface was in a deplorable state, patched up by local masons and full of ugly and uncomfortable pits, some so large that you could lie down in them. Bude Street was one of the first streets to have underground sewer pipes when in the 1860s 'Annery pipes' were laid, which diverted the sewage away from the houses and deposited it on the beach below the Quay. There, combined with fish-offal and other abominable nuisances the smell accumulated, and if the wind was in the wrong direction an intolerable odour hung over the town – so it's just as well those old photos don't come with smells attached!

Bude Street was good enough for the young William Yeo who lived in one of these houses until 1856 when his grand Richmond House was completed at the top of the hill. Other master mariners lived here and names such as Thomas Gibson, Thomas Randall, John Gorvin, Thomas Bowden, Richard Screech, Josiah Evans, Charles Lesslie, and George Cawsey are very familiar to anyone tracing maritime history in Appledore. We shall encounter more of these people on our tour up the street.

SPEEDY DRIVERS:

Watch out for speedy traffic here, although this is not entirely a modern problem. In 1861 William Handford was summoned for riding furiously through the streets of Appledore. He was spotted by a Police Constable leaving the Royal Hotel about 9:30pm and riding at a reckless speed up the street. The Policeman could not say that he was drunk, but he did note that it took two men to get him up on his horse. He was fined 6d.

2 BUDE STREET – BEARA'S:

The first shop we pass in Bude Street was the tailor and drapery business of the Beara family. The business was established in 1809 by John Beara from Instow who was followed by his sons Alexander, John, and then his youngest son Jerome Beara. The drapers & gentlemans' outfitters business ran here until Jerome Beara died in 1921.

Following the departure of the Bearas this shop became a branch of Lloyd's Bank, and then the National Provincial Bank. The substantial wooden counter, which can still be seen here dates from the early 1920s and is an original bank fitment. This was just a sub-branch to Bideford and only opened on Tuesdays and Fridays between 10:30am and 12:30pm.

The extended frontage of number 2 includes a plasterwork roman-key string-course, and some decorated pilaster capitals, giving an indication of the status the Bearas gave to their business.

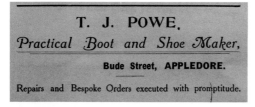

Advert for Thomas Powe, bootmaker at 4 Bude Street in 1906.

EARLY CHAPEL?:

In the back garden of number 2 is a curious stone building with niches recessed into the façade. These niches are now empty, but could originally have held statues which perhaps gives a clue to this building's former use. There are rumours of an early non-conformist movement in Appledore around 1650 when members held religious meetings at a 'barn' in a garden near Bude Street. This building fits the bill, and it is possible that this could be an early meeting-house. The ground floor comprises a single plain room about 15-feet square with a broken flagstone floor. There are no traces of furnishings or decoration and only the end wall has ever been plastered. It's difficult to put an age on a stone building, but this could be Appledore's first chapel. However, a congregation of twenty would have been a packed house.

High up on the outside is a circular recess containing another mystery. It is an incongruous carved symbol, consisting of a circular centre with the sign of a cross and an outer star-burst design. It is almost identical to the Coldstream Guards badge which is based on an order of chivalry and used in the Order of the Garter. But what's it doing displayed here?

5 BUDE STREET:

On the right hand side we have the Appledore Crafts Company. Look at the panel above the door though and you'll see the name of an earlier owner. In 1885 William John Land opened his grocery shop here which contained a wine-merchants and stationers. In 1887 he was appointed village postmaster, after the previous postmistress Mary Prance was tried for embezzlement of Post Office funds. Although she was found not guilty, she did lose her position.

 Born at Alwington, William Land had good business skills and two years later he was appointed chairman of the committee of local tradesmen. He negotiated an agreement from all the Appledore traders that they should close their premises at 8:00pm every evening (apart from Saturdays) in order to give the shopkeepers some time off. Late-night Saturday shopping is not new! This decision was passed around the village by printed bills and by the town crier. William Land ran the shop and Post Office for over thirty years until his death in 1916, after which his nephew William Stevens continued the business until 1931. The Post Office then moved to Market Street, but the grocery shop stayed here run by George and Florence Radford.

Land's Courtyard or Ackford's Court.

Behind Land's shop through some double-doors is 'Land's Courtyard', although originally this was known as 'Ackford's Court'. Several generations of the Ackford family lived there who had worked as sawyers in the village since the late 1700s. Robert Ackford moved to this court in the 1850s, and so it became known as the 'Court where the Akfords lived'. It was still known as Ackford's Court until 1931 after which the name is dropped. Inside the courtyard is a strange feature over one of the doors – a huge carving of a cockle-shell. No-one knows who put it there or what significance it might have had.

10 BUDE STREET:

Various businesses have traded from this building, built in 1851, and which has now been converted to domestic use. George Baker, who was also a teacher at Appledore School, ran a grocery shop here from 1851 until his death in 1886. It certainly kept him busy, as the rear of the building was used as a maltings, and George Baker also advertised himself as an auctioneer, accountant, tea-dealer, land surveyor, ship-broker, insurance agent, and vice-consul for Norway and Sweden. When the shop was sold in 1886 one of the rooms was stated to be a 'counting-house' – presumably so he could count all his money.

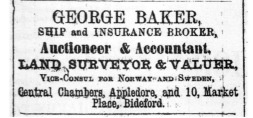

In 1891 a pawnbroker's auction was held here selling watches, chains, brooches, rings, clothes, linen, clocks, etc. In 1883, Edward Burnell-Jones from Wales took over part of the premises which then became his chemist's shop. This ran until 1910 after which William Neale Ellis bought this lock-up shop, although

(*North Devon Journal: 4th Nov 1890*).

Looking up Bude Street in about 1921. The chemist's shop of William Neale Ellis is on the left. Next on the left was the bakery of William Reed, so these are probably all his family standing outside the shop.

In 1890 transport to Bideford was provided three-times daily on the Three-Horse Break-Carriage 'Black Prince'. The carriage shown here in 1905 is Dymond's horse-drawn bus. His horses were stabled opposite the war memorial at Northam.

E. BURNELL - JONES,
DISPENSING & FAMILY CHEMIST,
APPLEDORE.

PHYSICIANS' PRESCRIPTIONS & FAMILY
RECIPES carefully prepared with the
Purest Drugs.

Horse & Cattle Medicines.

HORSE POWDERS, BALLS, DRENCHES,
BLISTERS, OILS, &c.

COW DRENCHES
Of every description from valuable and most
approved Recipes.

TEETH EXTRACTED.

(Bideford Gazette: 11th Dec 1883).

he chose to live in greater splendour in Bude House at the top of this street. Edward Burnell-Jones was a bit of an amateur radio enthusiast. In Feb 1923 the newspapers reported his success in having been able to tune in to an American radio station on his three-valve McMichael radio set. After 1931 Edward Short ran an outfitters shop here until the 2nd World War.

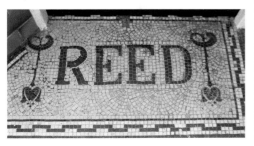

Toothache tincture bottle with Burnell-Jones label.

Through the tunnel at the side, in a house at the rear of this property (number 8), lived Madame Charlotte Jacquot, a teacher from Islington, who ran a language and music school here between 1874 and 1900 before retiring to Weymouth.

12 BUDE STREET:

The next shop up in the street still has the original shopfront and also the name of the former owner impressed into the mosaic floor tiles of the doorway. Alfred Reed ran a bakery business here from 1908 up to the 2nd World War. I have already mentioned the other side of his premises backing onto One-End Street, but there was a bakery business here before Mr Reed and another bakery here after he left, so a good many Appledore people have been fed from the ovens here.

A. REED,
Baker, Pastry Cook, and
Confectioner,
12, Bude Street, Appledore.

The building was reconstructed after a blaze that destroyed the previous house in 1847. Henry Williams was a maltster and tallow-chandler, but ironically one of his candles probably caused the destruction of his house and other adjoining buildings. Nearby residents smelled the fire and raised the alarm by ringing the chapel bells, but flames were soon raging in the malt-house in the back of his premises. Many of the neighbours were running about in their night-clothes, frantically clearing their houses of all valuables in the belief that the fire would soon spread up the street. Indeed it could have destroyed much of Bude Street, but luckily there was little wind at the time, plus heavy rain. Other neighbours tackled the blaze with whatever water was to hand, and after about two hours it was finally under control just as the new Bideford Fire Engine arrived on the scene.

14 BUDE STREET:

From its appearance this property is probably the most unassuming house in the street. The deeds of this house go back to 1805 when Thomas and Martha Prance of Glamorgan sold it to Henry Wilkinson of Appledore. However, the house's cob walls and proportions suggest that it is at least 200 years older again. Believed to be a former farmhouse it would have been one of the earliest buildings on this side of the street in the early 1600s.

16 BUDE STREET:

In 1921, this was the home of Thomas Riordean Randall who had a very lucky escape in December of that year. At that time he was Captain of the coasting steamship 'Stevenstone' newly built at Appledore. Randall was at Blythe in Northumberland with a cargo of coal to be taken to Denmark, but he was taken ill just before departure and left the ship. The First Mate then took charge. He was another experienced Appledore master mariner called Francis Prout, but an unknown disaster hit the ship on its voyage across the North Sea and it never arrived at its destination. The vessel was eventually assumed lost with all hands. These included the stand-in Captain Francis Prout and four other Appledore mariners: John McCullum, Nathaniel Cox, William Copp, and John Whitlock. The death of John Whitlock was especially tragic as he had married Eva Evans in Cardiff just 12 days earlier, she having made a special sea-voyage across from Appledore for the ceremony.

17 BUDE STREET:

On the opposite side of the road, number 17 Bude Street should have a well-documented history as it had deeds going back to about 1650. Unfortunately these were recently destroyed in a solicitor's warehouse fire, and all records were lost. (Anyone with old deeds, please copy them and keep them safe - it's our history too!).

19 BUDE STREET:

The deeds of this house go back to 1901 when the Parkhouse family was resident. From 1918 it was the home of harbour-master John

Hobbs, who was still in residence when the 2nd World War broke out in 1939. The house was then requisitioned by the Navy as offices and billeting for visiting sailors and officers.

21 BUDE STREET, BANK HOUSE:

This contained a sub-branch of Lloyds Bank from 1929 up till the early 1960s.

THE MELHUISH LANDS:

All of the land on the right-hand side of the street as far as Meeting Street was owned by the Melhuish family. They were Lords-of-the-Manor from 1692 until 1770, the title passing from Thomas Melhuish to his son Roger and then to his grandson William. Unfortunately, when William Melhuish died in 1770 a 200-year lease was put on all these lands, and in 1970 when the lease expired no-one could identify who the rightful heirs of the estate should be. No houses could be bought or sold until this was legally resolved. The matter was resolved the following year when full title was granted in Court to all house-owners on these lands.

Signature and seal of Thomas Melhuish.

22 BUDE STREET:

Deeds of this building go back to 1844 when William Yeo appears as one of the parties on the purchase documents. However, these documents refer back to an original lease taken out in 1723, so we can assume that this building probably dates back almost 300 years.

In 1925 the descendants of James Kellen Scott (who owned the Holt) conveyed the building to the Appledore Nursing Association set up by Lord Glanely (William Tatem), and it became known as the 'Glanely Home for District Nurses'.

24 BUDE STREET:

The home of William Beara from 1900 to 1959, bought from the Independent Minister at the time.

30 BUDE STREET:

In the 1881 census Richard Branch was living here. His occupation was described as a coachman, although the census doesn't say for whom. However, in a newspaper entry 55 years later his grandson described his grandfather as "coachman to Rev. Reynolds, vicar of Appledore for 53 years". The fact that the vicar had his own coachman does seem rather extravagant, but it is curious that the Branch family considered it such a prestigious job that they were still bragging about it half a century later!

"The street noises of my early youth were the romantic sounds of the clip clop of horses, the rumble of their wheels and the voices of the tradesmen bringing their regular wares - Mr Kivell, the baker; Mr Braund proclaiming the virtues of 'Clovelly herrings! Lovely Clovelly Herrings!' At the sound of 'Milko' from Mr Fred Steer you would take your jug out and he would turn the tap on the bottom of the churn to supply what you wanted. Appledore must have experienced noisy early mornings as three other milkmen - Ernie Cork, Albert Vaggers and Reg Griffey, also vied to provide our daily pints."
(Appledore Boyhood Memories, by E R Carter).

Mr. T. KELLY, A.C.O.,

PROFESSOR OF MUSIC,

35, BUDE ST., APPLEDORE.

—

THE NEXT TERM WILL COMMENCE ON
TUESDAY, JANUARY 20TH, 1891.

(Bideford Gazette: 13th Jan 1891).

LAW AND ORDER:

A few words at this point about Law and Order in Appledore...

During early Victorian times crime was prevalent in all parts of Appledore, even in up-market Bude Street. Originally some of the roof spaces in Bude Street were inter-linked so that someone being chased into a house could get into the roof space, climb along one or more houses, only to reappear from a completely different house. These 'smugglers hatchways' have now all been blocked up.

The Devon County Police Force was established in 1856, but prior to that there are reports of the town being frequently disturbed after midnight with brawls of drunken men and petty robberies constantly taking place. Prior to 1856 villages were expected to police themselves, and Appledore annually appointed a respected member of the community to keep control. However, this was not a job that anyone relished as it was a dangerous and thankless task, and eventually no-one wanted to do it. By 1852 lawlessness got so bad that the village decided to pay an outsider to do the job. 46-year-old James Baker from South Wales was offered the position, but he was not a great success and just two years after he was hired he was sacked. That left him in an awkward position, as he was no longer being able to support himself. He opened a small grocery shop but failed to pay his suppliers. He made arrangements to get back to South Wales, but on his day of departure found himself in Court convicted of fraud and was sentenced to forty days in jail. We assume he wasn't locked up in his own prison – that would have been ironic.

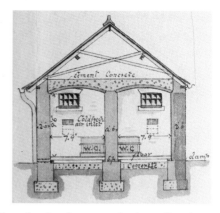

Plans showing the proposed prison cells to be constructed at the back of the Police Station. Note the concrete ceilings and small barred windows. (Devon Record Office).

42 BUDE STREET:

We are talking about Law and Order here because if you are now standing at the top of Bude Street, then you will be right outside Appledore's first Police Station. Number 42 Bude Street (currently named 'Peelers') was bought in 1856 to serve the new Devon County Police Force, and was converted from an old malthouse. The history of this house can be traced back to 1732 when widow Sarah Ellis leased the property for £8 per year from John Downe of Northam. From 1856 it generally housed two Policemen and their families, although these men were changed quite frequently. They certainly had an effect on reducing crime but lacked proper facilities to hold prisoners effectively. This was solved in 1888 when two self-contained cells were built at the back of this house, and they are still there today, each housing a more comfortable single-bed than originally intended. However, it is said that the ghost of one inmate, who was wrongly convicted for something he didn't do, still makes the occasional visit.

Before we finally leave Bude Street, watch out for runaway horses…

In 1909 Constable Perrin came out of the Police Station just in time to see a runaway horse and trap charging up the street towards him. It belonged to oil-seller William Taylor whose horse had taken fright in Market Street and took off at full speed. P.C. Perrin was able to climb onto the trap as it passed, work his way forward to the reins, and bring the cart to a halt before anyone could be hurt. He certainly deserved an 'Indiana Jones' medal for bravery.

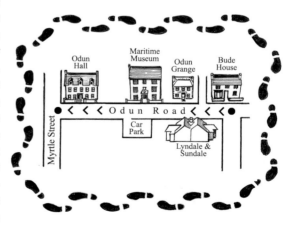

AT THE TOP OF BUDE STREET TURN LEFT ALONG ODUN ROAD

BUDE HOUSE:

Looking directly down Bude Street, stands 'Bude House', a handsome Georgian residence dating from the late 1700s although its early history is unknown as the house deeds were lost in a fire. It appears to have been the former home of a wealthy merchant or farmer, probably the Cock family, who originally owned all this farmland. However, we do know some of its later occupants:

DR PRATT:

In Victorian times Dr. Pratt served as Appledore's physician for sixty years. Actually that's not quite true, as there were *three* successive doctors called Dr. Pratt.

In 1832 Bude House was bought by 38-year-old Charles Edward Pratt from Lambeth, who came to Appledore to serve as its medical doctor. With him came his wife Mary Ann, and sons Charles and Frederick. The Exeter Flying Post in 1845 described how he coolly performed an emergency operation by candlelight on a 78-year-old Appledore woman who had a strangulated hernia. She recovered well and his skills were highly commended.

Charles Edward Pratt served as the village doctor until 1860 when his son Charles Pratt junior took over this vital role for a further twenty years. Then after Charles junior's untimely death his brother Frederick Pratt took over as Appledore's doctor, although he now lived in Marine Parade.

Frederick was destined to be a lifelong bachelor, that is until he reached the age of 57

ODUN ROAD

This street certainly seems to have had a number of colourful characters living here over the years, and we'll come to some of them in a moment. In the meanwhile - where does the strange name of this road come from?

'Odun' was said to be an ealderman or local leader in Devon at the time of the Viking invasions in the 9th century. Actually his name was 'Odda', not Odun, but he does get credited with a significant victory over the Vikings in 878. More of this battle later, but this element of British history was investigated by Thomas Hogg of Odun Hall who named his house and subsequently the street after this forgotten dark-age hero.

That at least is the official explanation, and it seems strange that Hogg got Odda's name wrong, but there is an alternative suggestion for where the name 'Odun' comes from. The Welsh word for kiln is 'odyn'. Production of lime was a major industry in the Torridge, with limestone and culm being imported from south Wales and burnt in lime kilns at many locations on the local river-banks. Ships unloaded their limestone in the Parlour at the bottom of the hill, but there is no known kiln near here. Maybe there was a former kiln somewhere nearby which is only remembered in the name of this road.

Aerial view of Bude House and farm taken in the 1930s.

when he married 18-year-old Ann Evans from South Wales. Quite what the attraction was here we don't know, but it certainly seemed to give the old doctor a new purpose marrying someone nearly forty years his junior. Frederick Pratt retired in 1892 at the age of 65, after which he really came into his own fathering four children by his young wife Ann before dying (presumably quite tired, but happy) at the age of 76.

BOXING AT THE MALTINGS:

Bude House used to be part of a complex of farm buildings with neighbour Ernest Cork farming the land leading up Staddon Hill. Amongst these outbuildings was a corrugated-iron maltings shed that brewed beer for the Seagate Hotel. This was pulled down in the 1970s and a small housing development created in its place, which retains the name of this trade - the Maltings. More secretive goings-on were happening in the 1930s though. At that time one of the chicken-sheds was used as make-shift boxing gym. Appledore grave-digger 'Big' John Williams used to earn his keep as a prize-fighter in fair-ground booths. He was then spotted by Bill Harkje, a German who now lived in Appledore, who took on the task of training him professionally. Secret boxing competitions were held here where Big John Williams would take on other local prize-fighters. There was talent here though, and John Williams went on to become boxing champion of Devon.

After the 2nd World War Bude House was sold by William Anderson of Wooda Farm to Owen Ommanney, a retired naval commander who had served in both World Wars.

COCKS ROW:

Heading along Odun Road we have a few interesting people to tell you about, but firstly a bit more on the history of this street itself which hasn't always been called Odun Road. Originally this was described as the 'Upper part of Gaping (ie: Bude) Street', and then later called 'Cocks Row' after the Cock family who owned the land on the upper side of this street. In 1830 Thomas Hogg came up with the name of 'Odun Place', which by 1900 had changed to 'Odun Road'. However, the 1851 census still calls the street 'Cocks Row', so I guess it depended on who you asked. Formal street signs did not appear until later in the 19th century.

CAPTAIN MEAD'S REVENGE:

On the left hand side are a pair of semi-detached brick-built houses called 'Lyndale' and 'Sundale', although when these were originally built in 1901 they were respectively named 'Endsleigh' and 'Heswell'. This pair of houses were built following a dispute by two neighbours on the other side of the road: Capt James Mead from Odun Villa and John Cock a farmer who lived in Odun Grange (then called 'Odun Farm'). Capt Mead wanted to render the back of his house but had to cross John Cock's land to do it. Permission was refused, the neighbourly dispute escalated and revenge was planned. When the land on the opposite side of the road came up for sale, Capt Mead bought it and erected these semi-detached houses here knowing full well that it would block the view

from his neighbour's house. Thereafter John Cock only lived in the back part of his house and didn't speak to his neighbour again. They were both obstinate men, but these houses still block the view a hundred years later reminding us all of their dispute.

LYNDALE AND SUNDALE:

Supposedly the first architect-designed houses in Appledore, Capt Mead built these two houses, one for each of his daughters. In 1939 'Lyndale' became Appledore's Police Station and Police House when 'Peelers' was vacated. This lasted until 1969, after which time we assume that Appledore was considered sufficiently law-abiding to manage without its own resident policeman.

ODUN GRANGE:

John Widgery Cock built this imposing house in 1878. The Cock family farmed the land leading up Staddon Hill, the name of the street here originally being 'Cocks Row'. Indeed this farmland was known as 'Cocks Field' as far back as the 1730s. In the 1870s, they also owned Bude House and the adjoining farm buildings, all of which became known as 'Appledore Farm'. This house was built as a modern residence for the Cock family which John Cock originally called 'Odun House'. However, in 1952 a subsequent owner changed the name to 'Odun Farm' and the name changed again in 1985 to 'Odun Grange' - the name that it still bears today.

In more recent memory, from 1925 Ernest and Alice Cork (no relation to Cock) ran a farm and dairy here. Some older residents still

remember Ernest Cork and his son Cyril delivering the milk in the 1940s from their horse-drawn float. Their horse having done the same round for many years was well trained, and soon learned to stop at exactly the right places each time without ever being told.

ODUN VILLA:

This was built in 1860 by John Darracott on land owned by the Hogg family, and was the home of master mariner Captain James Robins Mead from 1895.

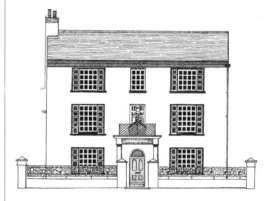

ODUN HOUSE – MARITIME MUSEUM:

The deeds of this house disappeared in 1855 when Independent Chapel minister Jerome Clapp left the village, allegedly taking quite a lot of Appledore's history with him - but more of him in a moment. The earlier history of this house ought therefore to remain unknown, but we are lucky because in order for the property to be sold, Elizabeth Fortune (a mariner's daughter born in Appledore in 1777) was asked to legally declare what she knew about previous owners. She stated that *"The house was built by Dr John Pyke (for whose family she had worked as a seamstress for 40 years), and in 1827 the house was sold to Major Thomas Hogg who let it to Sir George Burgeman, then to Sir Charles Chalmers, then to Jerome Clapp".* So thanks to Elizabeth Fortune we now know exactly who lived here. Elizabeth never married and died two years after making this statement.

> TO BE SOLD BY AUCTION, on Saturday, the 16th of August, at 5 o'clock in the Afternoon, at 'Parramore's Hotel,' in *Instow*, the large
> **FAMILY HOUSE,**
> At Odun-place, *Appledore*, lately occupied by the Rev. J. CLAPP, and previously by Sir C. CHALMERS;
> Containing 2 large Parlours, Drawing Room, 8 good Bed Rooms, Dressing Rooms, and all the numerous and various classes of Apartments and Offices that can be deemed requisite for the accommodation of an extensive Establishment; to which is attached a Stable, Coach House, and Walled Garden.

(North Devon Journal: 24th July 1856).

Dr John Pyke, surgeon, died in 1804 aged 43 so we can assume that he probably built this large house around the 1790s. It is certainly a grand house with huge reception rooms and the Tuscan-style porch with wrought iron balcony above which makes this a very imposing dwelling. John Pyke's widow continued to live here until the ownership changed in 1827. The Pyke family then moved to Staddon House further up the hill. After a couple of gentry tenants, the house was let to the new incoming minister of the Appledore Independent Chapel, the Rev Jerome Clapp.

JEROME CLAPP:

Jerome Clapp, father of the celebrated writer Jerome K Jerome, moved to Appledore in 1840 when he was appointed minister of the Meeting Street Independent Chapel. He was an architect by profession, but seemed to prefer the life of an Independent Minister and also trying his luck in dubious speculative ventures. He used his wife's inherited money for this, although none of these ventures ever turned out very well for him. His previous position as a Church Minister had been in Cirencester where he helped found a Chapel. His signature is still scratched on the window of a house in the town next to that of a Mrs Lawrence, with whom he was alleged to be having an affair. That could have been the reason for his hasty departure, but his time in Appledore wasn't much better.

Rev. Clapp rented Odun Hall for himself and his family, although he owned a number of other properties in Appledore plus a fifty-acre

farm that stretched from Bloody Corner to Hubbastone. It was on this land that his first failure occurred when he was duped into digging a silver mine - but more on this later. During his fifteen years at Appledore he appeared to have been well-liked as a minister, was actively involved in the temperance movement and various political causes. He even travelled to Brussels and Paris to attend peace conferences after the European revolutions in 1848.

Rev. Jerome Clapp.

Jerome Clapp seemed to enjoy giving his children unusual names. First there was 'Paulina Deodata' and 'Blandina Dominica', then came 'Milton Melancthon' and finally 'Jerome Klapka Jerome' (the famous author). Even his dog had delusions of grandeur being named 'Canino Fidel'.

In 1854 it all started going sour though. There were rumblings of discontent in Appledore and some financial disagreements which culminated in a physical fight on the church steps with local shipbuilder Thomas Cook and others. A subsequent Court appearance charged Clapp with assault, and after an alleged affair with Mary the church organist Clapp sold his farm in 1855 and left the village. There are still rumours in Appledore of an illegitimate son fathered by Clapp who was taken away in secret to be raised. This story still survives in a skipping rhyme chanted at the time by schoolchildren:

> *Miss Mary had a baby,*
> *She dressed him all in white,*
> *She took him out to Silford*,*
> *To keep him out of sight…*

There were about 15 verses in all, but this first one is all that has now survived.

Curiously also in 1855 Samuel and Susanna Fursey who lived in Market Street christened their new-born son 'Jerome Clapp Fursey'. It is odd that they decided to honour this disgraced minister at the height of his downfall. When Jerome Clapp left the village he took many of the church and other records with him, so we will probably never know the truth about this.

After leaving Appledore, Clapp moved to Walsall in the Midlands where he bought a failing iron-works and two colliery shafts, none of which actually got round to producing any coal. With all the money now gone he moved to East London, bought a failed wholesale ironmongery business, and finally died there in poverty in 1871. Ironically one of the coal mines which he owned in the Midlands (called the 'Jerome Pit') subsequently proved to be highly lucrative.

JEROME K JEROME:

Although the author Jerome K Jerome was born after his parents left Appledore, he did visit Appledore at the age of eight when his mother brought him here on holiday. She had dreams of regaining the farm and on their arrival Jerome junior recalls his mother being greeted by many old friends on Appledore Quay. This was after a frightening trip across the river from Instow on the ferry-boat in the early evening:

(* *Silford is about 2 miles away, south of Westward Ho!*)

"It was the first time I had been on a boat, and I was afraid, but tried to hide it".

This from the man that went on to write 'Three Men in a Boat' - one of the funniest books in the English language. How much did the short ferry journey across the river inspire him?

The ferryman also had his dog in the boat which Jerome recalls:

"I stumbled over something soft, and the dog rose up and up until it was almost as tall as myself and looked at me. I thought it was going to kill me and I shut my eyes tight; but it only gave me a lick all over my face that knocked off my cap. I also remember the walk up the steep hill. There were no lamps that I could see, but strange light was all about us, as if we were in fairyland. It was the first time that I had ever climbed a hill. It was just as if someone were trying to pull you backwards. It all seemed very queer."
(*My Life and Times, by Jerome K Jerome*).

JOHN DARRACOTT:

After Jerome Clapp left Odun House lay empty for some years until John Darracott came along in 1860. He was a mariner born in 1803, who first went to sea at the age of ten and got his own ship when he was nineteen. A devout Christian, he would often hold religious services on board his ship in whichever port he found himself in. He made a good living and retired from the sea at the age of forty but continued to manage the ownership of his own vessels which in 1850 included the 1,000-ton ship 'Ocean Queen'. The emblem of the North

Devon Maritime Museum that currently occupies this building is a harvest jug commemorating the 'Ocean Queen', so it is fitting that this was where the owner lived. In 1860 John Darracott moved from Meeting Street to this much grander residence which he called 'Odun House'. He was a great benefactor to the Baptist Church giving them the land on which the current Chapel is built. He was also deacon and treasurer there as well as running Bible classes. He died in 1882 aged 78.

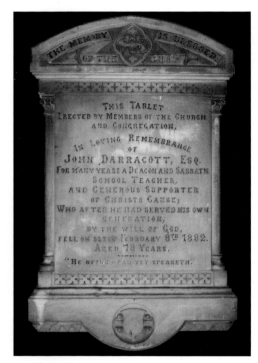

Memorial to John Darracott in Appledore Baptist Church.

MARITIME MUSEUM:

The award-winning Maritime Museum (belonging to the North Devon Museum Trust) opened here in 1977. A charitable organisation run entirely by volunteers, it preserves Appledore's Maritime Heritage in this wonderful location overlooking the river in which so much history was made. Don't miss the exhibits inside which include miscellaneous displays about the diverse elements of Appledore and its relationship with the sea.

The railings on the front wall were preserved from the short-lived pier at Westward Ho! Built around 1870 the pier was doomed never to survive the stormy conditions. It became fatally damaged in 1880 and was demolished shortly afterwards. The ship's figurehead on the balcony is not a historical one but a replacement for a previous head that rotted away. This head was carved in 2006 by Ron Slade and Barry Hughes.

THE VICTORIAN SCHOOLROOM:

Opposite the Maritime Museum is a recreation of a Victorian Schoolroom where parties of today's children are given a taste of what lessons and discipline were like over a hundred years ago. General notes were written on slates with chalk, but for handwriting practice nib-pens and inkwells were allowed to be used. A hand-bell called the children to lessons and there were also keep-fit regimented exercises in the yard. Another vital piece of equipment used regularly here, was the cane.

This recreated schoolroom opened on 21 May 1993 and was attended by year-six pupils from Appledore School dressed in Victorian costume. In this Schoolroom is a cupboard that used to grace the Appledore Wesleyan School. This cupboard was started in 1890 as a 'museum' to display items brought in by the children. Often these were articles that their fathers had brought back from sea voyages: exotic shells, a dead baby lizard, a swordfish's sword, etc. Also used in lessons at this time were items which today would be considered as Company sponsorship, eg: a box of Price's candles, four jars from Colman's containing different mustard plant leaves, a jar of dark treacly sugar from Abram Lyle & Co. However, in 1897 this object-lesson teaching was replaced by elementary science, and so these items were consigned to the back of the museum cupboard where they stayed until rediscovered nearly 100 years later.

SALMON BOAT:

Outside the Victorian Schoolroom is a salmon fishing boat, of which there used to be dozens in Appledore, all sadly now gone. This one has been restored by the North Devon Maritime Museum and is part of their historical displays.

Salmon fishing has long been a part of Appledore's business, whether legal or slightly-less-than-legal. It was said there was little chance of those who lived on the river ever going hungry. So many salmon were being taken from the rivers of England that in 1861 the Salmon Fishery Act set up boards of conservators to control fish stocks. Thereafter the salmon-fishing season started on 1st May and lasted until 25th September. The restrictions were disliked of course and consequently in 1948 a petition was signed by 124 Appledore fishermen complaining about these rules.

Of course the newspapers often recorded record-breaking fish caught in the river. In 1898 John Fowler from Appledore caught a 47lb salmon in the Torridge, which was quite large, but not quite as large as the 57lb monster

landed at Fremington in 1925.

Inevitably there are superstitions associated with almost any activity, but salmon-fishing seems to have more than most. Here are a few of them which Appledore fisherman had to slavishly follow:

• Once caught a salmon had to be laid facing the bow, never the stern.

• It was unlucky to say the word 'rabbit' in a salmon boat, or indeed mention anything else rabbit-related.

• Women were never allowed in a salmon boat - although they were of course allowed to skin and cook the fish for the men.

Failure to adhere to any of these would mean aborting the fishing trip and packing up for the day as there would be no further success in catching any salmon.

ODUN ROAD CAR PARK:

Immediately opposite the Museum is the Odun Road Car Park. There can't be much history here you would imagine. However this land was originally the front garden for Odun House (ie: the Museum) and was hidden behind a high stone wall, the cut-down remains of which can still be seen. Traditionally the land had been called 'Polly's Garden' since Victorian times, although no-one seems to know who Polly was. In 1860 when Major Thomas Hogg sold Odun House together with this front garden, he put a covenant on this land to say that 'no house or building of any kind is to be erected here by the new owner John Darracott or anyone after him'. Today therefore it still remains undeveloped, and used as a much-needed open space and car park for the village. Thomas Hogg erected the wall dividing the two halves of the car park to screen off the land that he sold, which was erected in 1860.

The last user of the garden was Ellen Galloway who lived in Odun House until her death in 1973. A reclusive lady, who took over her husband's profession after he died, and became the first woman tea-merchant in

Britain. She was devoted to her golden retrievers 'Sarah' and 'Ballerina' both of whom are buried here, and you can still see various dog's tombstones on the back wall of the car park. More curiously, no-one knows where Ellen Galloway herself was buried. She stipulated that her burial take place before any of her family were informed about her death. It is therefore rumoured that she was buried somewhere in this garden near to her beloved dogs.

4, 5 & 6 ODUN ROAD:

This pleasant row of cottages are the oldest surviving houses in the street. They were built in 1737 on land called 'Cocks Field' and were known for many years as 'New Buildings'. The man responsible for building these was John Benson of Knapp House, father of the notorious Thomas Benson. They were built to let to rich gentry, and in 1787 the houses were in the occupation of Joseph Halls, John Patten, widow Elizabeth Hogg, Samuel Tetherley, and surgeon William Wren. Ownership passed down a couple of generations of the Bensons before Thomas Hogg bought them in the early 1800s.

The house at the end of the row was the home of Appledore's physician, Dr William

Arthur Valentine, although his surgery was in Odun House (where the museum is now). Originally from Ireland, he served as village doctor from 1899 until his death in 1934.

Dr William Arthur Valentine (1870-1934).

THE KING OF NICOBAR:

Appledore has been home to some strange people over the years – which some might say continues to this day! However perhaps none stranger was a boy from the Nicobar Islands. William West, whose family lived at number 5 Odun Road, wrote some memoirs about his early life at sea. In 1875 when he was seventeen, his ship visited the Nicobar Islands in the Indian Ocean. There they befriended the natives, exchanged goods, and went on their way not knowing that they had a stowaway. A native youth was found hiding on board, who remained with them, learned to wear clothes, to speak English, and was eventually brought to Appledore where he acted as a servant for the family. They called him James Gladstone Nicobar, and he was certainly a curiosity at the Bethel Sunday School. Eventually the boy became homesick and a passage was found for him so that he could return home. He hoped that when he returned home he would be made King as the previous King had attained his position after famously making a sea voyage all the way to Calcutta.

A huge copper beech tree used to occupy the next space in the street from which the next house (Beechwood) takes its name. The tree was taken down in the 1980s, but schoolchildren always held their breath as they walked beneath it - although there was no apparent reason for this. Maybe it had something to do with the ghost though, as an elderly lady was often seen leaning against the wall under this tree. However, the lady always vanished into thin air when approached. Her identity is unknown.

ODUN HALL:

Thomas Hogg built this imposing house at 2 Odun Road around the late 1820s as a grand residence from which he had a panoramic view of the river. The house had a servants' wing on the left (now a separate house), a carriage house on the right, cellars underneath, and a semi-circular turning circle in front. All the land leading from the back of the house was part of the estate called the 'Parkland', and was often used for horse-riding.

Artist's impression of the proposed Odun Hall and stables.

Thomas Hogg commissioned some views of his estate looking from across the river at Instow. However, he either used an artist who never visited or he was sold an idea based on these 'artists impressions'. The scheme never quite turned out as grand as shown, presumably much to Thomas Hogg's regret.

In 1967 the house was bought by Appledore Shipbuilders Ltd who split the property into two self-contained dwellings. What they really wanted though was the space in front of the house which was converted into a car park for their workers in the Richmond Dock. The half-moon turning circle was demolished, the garden cleared, and the present car park constructed. It wasn't used for long though, because three years later the Richmond Dry-Dock closed and all the workers moved further up the river to a new site. The property here was then sold.

THE HOGG FAMILY:

The Hoggs appear in the parish records back to the early 1600s, but they only come to prominence in Appledore about 150 years later when William Hogg appears as the village apothecary and surgeon. The Hogg family can be a little confusing as all the interesting ones were called 'Thomas', but I will try and keep it as simple as I can…

1) Thomas Hogg is noted as being an attorney in Appledore in the 1760s from which he gained some social standing, although he did act for Thomas Stafford exiled in Oporto in 1761 with his uncle Thomas Benson. Hogg had property and land in Diddywell and died in 1786.

2) His son Major Thomas Hogg (whom I shall call Thomas Hogg II) was born in 1774 and climbed further up the social scale (he is the one credited with building Odun Hall in the 1820s).

Thomas Hogg II was interested in Appledore's history and investigated the legend of the Viking battle of 878. He elaborated on it and popularised the story, so that today we find it difficult to separate the truth from his elaborated myths. He was convinced that a Saxon leader called 'Odun' defeated 'Hubba the Dane' in a great battle, and Thomas Hogg proudly displayed a carved plaque in the entranceway of Odun Hall which gave a fanciful account of the episode. He named his house after the victorious Saxon leader Odun and consequently the road also came to take this name.

Odun Hall in the early 1900s. Note the semi-circular carriage turning-circle in front of the house. The land from where the photo was taken was the front garden of this grand house.

Odun Road in about 1900. Note the high garden wall on the left-hand side. In the distance there is a gateway into an orchard, this being the site where the houses of Myrtle Street now stand.

Although married, his only surviving children appear to have been illegitimate, the last of which (and apparently his favourite) was born just eight months before Hogg died in 1835 at the age of 62. His mistress on this occasion was Sarah Dimond, who obviously knew how to keep an old man happy! The child was named **'Thomas Howard Effingham Hogg Dimond'** – a mouthful of a name which perhaps needs some explaining:

  · **Thomas** – after his father.

  · **Howard & Effingham** – after Lord High-Admiral Howard of Effingham who commanded the fleet which defeated the Spanish Armada in 1588. Hogg seemed passionate about notable historical events and named his son after this saviour of England.

  · **Hogg** – after his own surname, an illegitimate child would often have the father's surname as a middle name.

  · **Dimond** – from Sarah Dimond who bore him the child.

However in his will Thomas Hogg II left his estate to his infant son Thomas (whom I shall call Thomas Hogg III) in trust until he became 21, but with one condition: he would only be allowed to inherit if his son took the surname of 'Hogg' rather than 'Dimond'. And so when the time came Thomas Howard Effingham Hogg Dimond applied for Royal assent to change his surname. Queen Victoria signed the licence and he then became **'Thomas Howard Effingham Hogg Dimond Hogg'** and inherited his father's lands at Fremington, Newton Tracey, West Horwood, Diddywell, and Odun Hall.

3) Thomas Howard Effingham Hogg Dimond Hogg III lived in Fremington, became a Major in the army and a local JP, and died in 1899.

4) His son – yes, that's right, he was called Thomas as well – 'Thomas Poltimore Dimond Hogg'. He inherited the Hogg estate and became vicar of Fremington. He died in 1941 (aged 82).

1 ODUN ROAD:

The house at the end of Odun Road used to be a wing of Odun Hall, but is now a separate dwelling. It was owned by the Kelly family, but Alice Kelly let the Independent Chapel use it as their manse for many years and left it to the church when she died in 1969.

 The house has a ghost who doesn't seem to like children. Nicknamed 'Harold' he is often only experienced as a grumpy presence walking through the house, although his dirty ragged wolfhound dog has been seen as a apparition, and Harold often moves all the lounge cushions into a pile on the floor overnight.

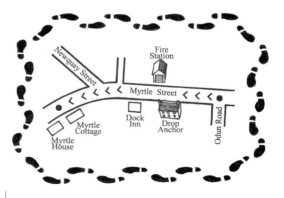

AT THE END OF ODUN ROAD TURN LEFT DOWN MYRTLE STREET

MYRTLE STREET

The road leading down into the village from this point was just a narrow track, but in 1870 at the bequest of William Yeo, it was widened to 20 feet in order to give better access to the Richmond Dry-Dock. We can therefore assume that the retaining wall on the left dates from around this time.

It's rather steep though, and after a heavy freeze in 1895 the newspapers reported that carts found it impossible to use, slipping helplessly down the hill, dragging the horses with them.

SLADE TERRACE:

The terrace of houses on the right-hand side was largely built by my great-grandfather William Kingdon Slade on the site of an orchard - part of the Tomouth estate. William Slade had spent all of his working life at sea as a mariner, but also bought vessels for use in the coasting trade giving him a comfortable income. In 1923 he decided to build a row of six houses (numbers 21 to 26), one for himself and one for each of his five children. These houses were therefore affectionately known as 'Slade Terrace'. His widow, Rosina Annie Slade, my great-grandmother, lived at number 24 and although she was born in 1865 I still remember her - a lively old lady who lived to be 99, just missing her century by six weeks.

The three houses at the lower end of this terrace (numbers 18 to 20) appear on a map of 1887, so are therefore much older.

OLD POST OFFICE HILL:

This part of Myrtle Street was originally known as 'Old Post Office Hill', indeed some older residents still

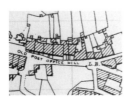

call it by this name. It still appears with this name on a map dated 1932. Today it is part of Myrtle Street.

APPLEDORE'S FIRST POST OFFICE:

At this point we need to stop and pay tribute to one of Appledore's unsung heroes. The first village Post Office was opened in 1820 operating a penny-post service. Located at number 17 Myrtle Street and currently known as 'Drop Anchor', it was run by Susan Sarah, wife of Thomas Sarah, a mariner from Falmouth. Susan ran the Post Office for forty years between 1820 and 1860 with the help of members of her family. We know that their eldest daughter Ann acted as a letter-carrier around the village. Her other daughters Catherine and Susan also helped their mother run a Dame School on the premises.

For one person to have run this Office for so long must be applauded as a great achievement. At the time of Susan's death the

Postmaster's position was paid £25 per year and the role was subsequently awarded to Samuel Fursey in Market Street.

Later on this was the home of John Beara, who ran his ships' brokerage business here.

 The ghost of a little girl has occasionally been seen here, just wanting it to be known that she is there. Her identity is unknown.

THE BROWN BEAR GARAGE:

On the site of Appledore's Fire Station used to stand the Brown Bear Garage. This housed the 'Brown Bear' bus run by Fred Hamlyn in the 1920s and 1930s. This was a local bus service which ran to Bideford every hour in competition with the National Omnibus Company and Dave Hocking's 'Pride of the West' bus service from West Appledore. Prior to 1914 a horse-drawn 'break' carriage ran every hour to Bideford.

"Mr Hamlyn's buses were brown, and Mr Hocking's were yellow and blue with the name 'Ensign'. In fact Dave Hocking started his service with a taxi in 1920, two years before progressing to buses. In 1936 Dave added to his business venture the sale of home-made ice cream which his family has continued ever since."
(Appledore Boyhood Memories, by E R Carter).

After the 2nd World War Frank and George Harris used the garage for their joinery workshop business. Next door at number 18, Edith Harris ran a grocery and sweet shop between the 1920s and the 1950s.

FIRE STATION:

Built in the early 1960s, this is not the first Fire Station in Appledore. Originally a fire engine was housed in a garage on the quay, and later it was housed in a purpose-built structure in Marine Parade near the bus stop. Back in Victorian times if a blaze broke out, a fire engine had to come from Bideford, and that was only after someone had ridden there to raise the alarm. The chances of a fire engine reaching Appledore before the fire had destroyed many houses was therefore remote.

Running around the back of the Fire Station is a small tarmac road known as 'Backfield'. More like a footpath than a road it is a lot older than it looks, and could well date back several hundred years. It ran between the rear of the houses in New Street to Mr Parkhouse's farm on the Tomouth Estate, and then down to the river near Benson's Quay. Now it is a route to garages serving the houses of Tomouth.

APPLEDORE PRISON:

Near to the Fire Station used to stand Appledore's jail. It was just a little village lock-up, but it could hold prisoners until they could be taken to the Magistrate at Bideford. Built in 1832, it was found that the previous arrangement of paying landlords to hold prisoners in their Public Houses was proving too expensive.

Crime in the early 1830s was getting to be a problem, but when caught the punishments

Empire Day celebrations at the bottom of Myrtle Street in the 1920s. Note the cobbled surface of Myrtle Street.

The Brown Bear garage formerly on the Fire Station site, seen here being demolished in the late 1950s.

could be draconian. In April 1832, Mr Williams and his son were both convicted of smuggling and fined £100 each. In the same month three Appledore men were convicted of burglary and sentenced at Exeter to be "transported to such parts beyond the seas for the term of seven years" (this would have been to Australia or Tasmania). They were William Cooper, Richard Gould aged 25, and Thomas Jewell aged 16. Their families were unlikely to have heard from them again because (even if they survived the journey and the seven years hard labour) there was no arrangement for them to return home after they had served their sentence.

Comments were made at the time in Appledore about crime being a lamentable state of society, attributed to a "destitution of religious instruction that contributed to the promotion of this evil". A meeting was held at the Tavern Inn to discuss what to do about all the 'nightly deprediations' which had recently occurred. The chairman Richard Vernon suggested that Special Constables be sworn in to patrol the village at night.

TOMOUTH ESTATE BUILDINGS:

The stone building next to the Fire Station is a surviving part of the Tomouth Estate farm-buildings, which in 1867 included: a lock-up house (ie: prison), large barn, shippen, stables, coach-house, slaughter-house, orchard, and three cottages. These 3 cottages faced onto Myrtle Street but were demolished around 1918, their condition having become too unsanitary. 12½ acres of land were also part of this estate but we will hear about this later. A well on this land was said to never run dry and capable of supplying 2,500 people, even in a dry season. These waters now drain into the sewers and today if you stand in the street on a quiet dry day, you will still hear the waters from this spring running underground.

The row of five terraced houses on the right were built around 1909.

THE DRUM AND MONKEY:

On the left-hand side next to the narrowest section of pavement possible, is 'Drum Cottage'. Formerly called 'Ark Cottage' it has a date of 1647 carved into its timbers. Although appearing to have sunk into the ground, the road level has been raised significantly here in the last fifty years.

The open space to the left of this house used to be occupied by a couple of old cottages, one of which was a pub serving the Richmond Dry-Dock workers called (not surprisingly) the 'Dockhouse Inn'. There is no record of a pub here before the Richmond Dock was built in 1856, and the name of the 'Dockhouse Inn' does not appear until the census of 1861 when the landlord is Thomas Harvey.

Although the name 'Dock Inn' was written over the door everyone knew it as the 'Drum and Monkey'. There is a story that a soldier returned to the village after having fought in the Napoleonic Wars bringing with him his drum and pet monkey, both of which he left in the pub. These became fixtures, and so the regulars there would pop in to see the drum and the monkey. Eventually the monkey died and was buried in the back garden. Quite what became of the drum no-one knows.

However, as this pub does not seem to appear until 1856 and the Napoleonic Wars ended around 1815, this does seem rather a long time for a monkey to survive. Or it could all just be a good old Appledore story!

The 'Dock Inn' shortly before its demolition in 1955. The 'tropical café' set up here was part of the Appledore carnival. (J. Gouldstone).

The same view today showing the space where the buildings used to stand.

Thomas Harvey stayed as landlord until 1893. Later landlords included: Edwin Waters, John Cobbledick, Charles Rummens, and Sidney Lamey. The pub closed in 1926, then became the fish and chip shop of James and Lilian Yeo until 1936. The building was eventually demolished in 1955, having become too dilapidated.

ALL CHANGE AT THE JUNCTION:

Standing at the junction of Myrtle Street and New Street a hundred years ago the view would have looked very different. The end of the Richmond Dock came much further up the street and a tall-masted ship would probably have been seen towering over the buildings, maybe even the bowsprit coming out over the wall. To the left of the dock was a three-story warehouse building, not actually on the dock site but where the road is now, creating a narrow roadway through to Marine Parade. This building was demolished in 1933 to enable the road to be widened.

MYRTLE COTTAGE:

This long-fronted house with dormer windows set back behind a high wall was originally two dwellings known as 'Myrtle Cottages' and dates back to at least the early 17th century. In 1808 these cottages were given by the charitable bequest of 79-year-old Elizabeth Wyott to the Independent Chapel for the 'benefit of the minister for his comfortable subsistence, maintenance and support'. This charity was wound up in 1908 and the properties were sold by auction. At that time they were let to fishmonger William Rook at a rent of £2 a year, and plumber Henry Channon at a rent of £7 a year.

WESLEYAN CHAPEL:

Appledore's first Wesleyan Methodist Chapel still stands here, hidden around the back of Myrtle Cottage (it's the building on the left up the drang, just behind the gateway, now called Hideaway Cottage). Built in 1825 it had a double-storey interior, 40 feet x 24 feet in size, with an upper gallery and seats.

Methodism started in Appledore in 1818 with meetings held at the house of Thomas Dennis in New Street, but the movement grew and soon needed a permanent home. A chapel was built in 1825 and used for about 25 years, but was eventually thought to be a little out-of-the-way. In 1850 Thomas Geen donated some land further up the hill where a new chapel could be built. The old chapel sat here unused for a number of years, was used as an apple loft, and was eventually sold in 1862 before being converted into 2-storey private accommodation.

> *APPLEDORE, DEVON.*
> TO BE POSITIVELY SOLD by PUBLIC AUCTION by Mr. F. LEE, Auctioneer, the residue of a very long absolute Term of Years, of and in all that BUILDING known as the **OLD WESLEYAN METHODIST CHAPEL**, with the SEATS, GALLERIES, & FIXTURES therein, situate on the Narrow Quay, opposite and near the Dry Dock in Appledore aforesaid, containing by admeasurement, 40 feet or thereabout in length, and 24 feet or thereabout in width.

(Bideford Gazette: 22nd July 1862).

Further up this private drang is an old cob-cottage, probably dating from the early 1600s. The foundations of other thick stone walls have been uncovered in the back garden here suggesting that the Docton House buildings were far more extensive in previous centuries.

Myrtle House in 1934 showing Hutchings 'Wireless & Electrical Depot'. Standing in the gateway is Betty Hutchings holding 3-year old son Michael.

Hutchings van outside Myrtle House in 1935, decorated to mark the Silver Jubilee of George V.

MYRTLE HOUSE:

Myrtle House was probably built just prior to 1700 as a development on the Docton House lands next door, and was known as 'Myrtle Cottage'. In the 1730s the Benson family were in ownership, and Thomas Benson built the extension on the left-hand side. A rear wing was added in 1845 and the house also contains a staircase and other period features from the same date. From 1903 it was the home of the Hutchings family. The room facing the road was the Hutchings' bakery and latterly used as an electrical supplies shop.

Opposite Myrtle House in the Richmond Dock wall you can still see two blocked-up openings which were part of the demolished warehouse building removed in 1933. The building was actually outside the dock site, so if you stand in the road then you would have been inside the building.

THE APPLEDORE MYRTLE:

In the front garden of Myrtle House is an old myrtle bush, possibly as old as the house in front of which it stands. Bought back from the Mediterranean by sailors several hundred years ago the Myrtle tree was supposed to bring good luck, and there are many associations with

Aphrodite the Greek the Goddess of love (also known as Myrtilla). It is therefore not surprising that this was a favourite gift for sailors to bring home to their wives and girlfriends.

Earlier in the 20th century there were myrtle bushes growing in almost every garden in Myrtle Street giving the street its name. Most of these bushes were killed off in the icy winter of 1947, but the one in front of Myrtle House survived and eventually recovered. The bush seems to have adapted to the local climate and is different from other myrtle bushes as it has much smaller leaves, and rarely produces berries. Known as the 'Appledore Myrtle' it is evergreen and flowers from August to Christmas.

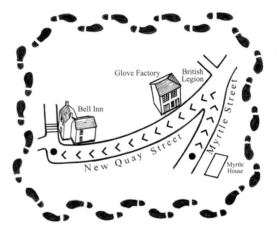

RETURN TO THE JUNCTION AND GO ALONG NEW QUAY STREET

TUPLIN'S SHOP:

If you stood at the junction of Myrtle Street and New Quay Street a hundred years ago you would have been inside Tuplin's grocery shop which stood at the apex of this corner. The Tuplins were a family that had been in the parish since the 1770s when the wonderfully named 'Digory Tuplin' appears.

The shop had to be demolished in 1933 as part of the road-widening scheme for Myrtle Street. My father recalls his experience of this shop when he was a child:

"Just down the street was a small sweet shop, which also sold tobacco and groceries (a sort of mini village store). Mother used to take me there shopping and I noticed some children came in and bought some items without money by saying that their mothers would pay. A few months later a most embarrassed shopkeeper, Kate Tuplin, had to very diplomatically tell mother she owed five shillings - a small fortune for those days. Mother was always very careful about never getting into debt and questioned this inference. The explanation was that I had been coming into the shop regularly asking for sweets and saving 'Mammy'll pay'."

(Appledore Boyhood Memories, by E R Carter).

BRITISH LEGION CLUB:

On a historical tour of Appledore's highlights the former British Legion Club probably wouldn't figure too highly. However the site on which it sits does have a considerable history, in fact this is probably close to one of the ancient centres of Appledore at the head of a sheltered creek. We'll start from what we can see now and work back...

The Appledore branch of the British Legion was formed in 1946, and held its first annual dinner in the Church Schoolroom on 8th April 1947. At this gathering, Rev. Muller expressed regret that they had no permanent Headquarters so a search was undertaken for a suitable site. The present buildings opened in 1950 including the adjacent Appledore Hall, and were held in trust on behalf of the people of Appledore. The Legion also acted as the social club for the adjacent shipyard, but recent financial circumstances forced the Legion Club to close at the end of Feb 2009.

When William Yeo developed the Richmond Dry-Dock in 1856 he needed workshops and

stores which could not be fitted onto the site itself. William Yeo acquired this site, and a blacksmith's shop was built on it to serve the needs of the yard. Later the buildings were used as a storage garage for Dave Hocking's buses; and during the 2nd World War as a vehicle maintenance workshop, part of H.M.S. Appledore - of which we will hear more later.

The wall-mounted Post Box round the corner is now becoming a rarity, this model having being produced in late Victorian times. It has Queen Victoria's crest on it and is first mentioned as being here in a directory of 1902.

THE APPLEDORE ALMSHOUSES:

In the 1850s a corner of the Legion site contained the Appledore Almshouses, now demolished. (Firstly an apology: it appears that Roger Melhuish did not build these in 1702 as I stated in my first book – this seems to in fact have been the Almshouses in Northam). I now believe the Appledore Almshouses were built around 1682 by Sir Thomas Berry, then Lord-of-the-Manor, as a private charitable venture. Later in 1702 two charitable bequests were made to the parish by James Cocke and Elizabeth Langdon providing £300 to be used for the poor of Appledore. Twelve acres of Tomouth land behind the almshouses was purchased to provide an income for the upkeep of these almshouses, which were used to accommodate any needy people of Appledore.

A fourth house was added later.

In 1851 James Peak lived in one of these Almshouses. He was a 25-year-old teacher of navigation to young boys for 1 shilling per week. He lived with his widowed mother after his father died at sea. He was considered one of the best teachers of navigation in the west of England, and many young Appledore sailors learnt their craft from him.

The almshouses survived William Yeo's 1856 redevelopment of this area, but not for long. In May 1859 (it was a Friday 13th), sparks from a nearby chimney fell onto the thatched roof of the almshouses and it soon caught light. The fire threatened to spread to neighbouring properties and the West of England Assurance Society's fire engine was summoned from Bideford which eventually managed to stop the fire spreading. No lives were lost but the old almshouses which had stood for about 175 years, were completely destroyed. John and Charlotte Sage and their family who were living there at the time had a lucky escape, as did most of their furniture

which was rescued by neighbours. The almshouses were not rebuilt and this disaster paved the way for the sale of the whole Tomouth Estate, as the land that supported them no longer had this financial purpose.

This street was so named after Thomas Benson's 'New Quay' built in 1745 to which this road led. The street later became known by Appledorians as the 'Underway'.

THE GLOVE FACTORY:

On the right the large 2-storey building with huge upper windows is known locally as 'The Glove Factory' because that's what it was in the latter part of the 20th Century. The building was probably built as part of William Yeo's 1850s Richmond Dock development, constructed as a sail-manufacturing loft with its huge windows giving as much light as possible to the sailmakers working inside. It appears to be the subject of this first-hand description in 1888:

"Across the road from the dock gates is a substantial run of lofts. Rock salt is stored below, rigging above, and sail-makers are at work with their needle and cotton, whose size and shape would drive a seamstress crazy were she called upon to use them. Half of this sailmakers loft is boarded off, Mr Cock having kindly placed a portion free of charge, at the disposal of the church ladies, who hold a women's sewing class here." (Strongs Industries of North Devon).

The Appledore ladies employed at the Sudbury Glove factory. Sixty women and one man are in this picture - guess which one was in charge!

A motley collection of Appledore's children seen here on the beach below the Bell Inn slipway in about 1900.

Glove Works Opened at Appledore

Later the building became Lamey's sail-loft, but after the declining need for sailmakers the building became derelict and it was not until after the 2nd World War that it was used again. Sudbury Gloves (originally a Nottingham company who had recently opened factories in Bideford and Torrington) opened a manufacturing workshop here on 26th February 1947, in which it was hoped that fifty ladies could be employed. The latest system of gas heating was installed on the walls and fluorescent electric lights were provided above the working benches. Over half of the gloves went for export. The factory closed in the early 1990s and has now been given a new lease of life as an Art Studio and exhibition display space.

DOCK HOUSE:

The large house to the left of the glove factory - 2 New Quay Street - was known as 'Dock House', and stood immediately opposite the work entrance gate to Richmond Dock. This three-storey building (plus a 4th storey loft-conversion in 2008) contained Ernest and Mary Blackmore's fish and chip shop run between 1949 and 1954.

OBSCURE SAINTS:

The house at 6 New Quay Street might appear to be the home of a Rock and Roll fan being adorned with the name 'St Elvis', however the house first appears with this name in 1933 before the King of Rock was even born. St Elvis is actually an obscure Celtic Saint called Ailbhis (anglicised to Elvis), who was believed to have baptised St David in Dyfed. The neighbouring house 'St Valerie' is no less obscure, this being the name of a 2nd century Roman martyr. But what are these saint's names doing here?

GNAWED BY RATS:

Conditions in New Quay Street have certainly improved over the years. Elsewhere I have described the standard of 19th century housing, but a report in 1827 describes how the three-week-old son of Richard Brooks of New Quay Street had his fingers badly bitten and flesh gnawed by rats whilst sleeping in bed. Rats were a major problem in the past, impossible to control, and when flooding of low-lying areas occurred hundreds of them used to be seen swarming away from the waters. No wonder the rats took refuge on the ships.

THE BELL INN:

Another of Appledore's ancient inns traded here until 2004. The building still stands on the corner but is no longer used as a pub. The 'Bell Inn' name can be traced back to 1822, but it is quite likely that this inn, opposite a well-used slipway access to the beach has been here for many centuries. In the 1820s the landlord was Samuel Cann, a surname well known in the village today.

After the 2nd World War, Eddie Chapman was a frequent resident at the Bell when visiting his brother Wyn who was a director at Appledore Shipbuilders. Eddie Chapman was a double-agent in the War, known as 'Agent Zig-Zag', regarded by the Nazis as a super-spy whom they awarded an Iron Cross for his heroics. However, he deceived the Germans with false information, managed to divert many flying bombs, and even volunteered to assassinate Hitler. Various books have been written about his wartime exploits. After his death his ashes were scattered from the Bell Inn slipway.

There have been quite a few ghostly sightings in the Bell Inn. One of these was of a man dressed in Victorian clothes who has been seen to walk through an upstairs brick-wall. There used to be an opening at this point leading to a neighbouring cottage, now demolished.

More flamboyant is the phantom sailor seen wearing a three-cornered hat often seen walking into the bar area from the street outside. In 2004 a visiting American lady saw him enter the pub, assumed he was in fancy dress, and tried to greet him. However she soon realised otherwise when the sailor walked straight through her outstretched arm and vanished into thin air. No doubt her screams will resonate here for a while too!

LYING IN A POOL OF BLOOD…:

In 1864 at 'Sea View Place' near the Bell Inn, lived 23-year-old Elizabeth Fisher, daughter of Joshua and Elizabeth Fisher. Her mother woke up one morning and found their daughter lying in a pool of blood on the bedroom floor. Her throat had been cut and murder was suspected. No-one else was in the house and yet the mother had no reason to murder her own daughter. Dr Pratt was summoned and

examined the body whereby he found the murder weapon still sticking into her throat – a shard from a 'bedroom utensil'.

At the subsequent inquest it was eventually determined that the young lady, who suffered from epileptic fits, must have fallen over in the night, smashing the chamber pot resulting in part of it penetrating her throat. No charges were brought against the mother, but it did keep the newspaper reporters busy for a few weeks.

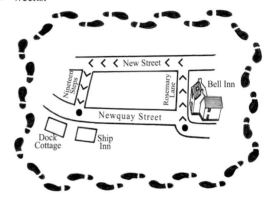

TAKE THE NARROW DRANG UP TO NEW STREET AND TURN LEFT

ROSEMARY LANE:

This lane up the side of the old Bell Inn used to be known as 'Rosemary Lane' supposedly after one of the publicans, although I can find no trace of an owner with this name. However, the ghost of a lady in a long dark dress has often been seen here before vanishing.

Quite when New Street was 'new', is difficult to say. There are houses here of all different dates, but the majority date from the late-19th and early-20th centuries. These would be replacements for earlier houses on the same site whose standards probably didn't meet even those of the Victorian working classes. Occasionally you will see an older house amongst the others (eg: numbers 17, 19, and especially 28) which suggest an origin in the early 1700s, and may be an indication of the street pattern laid out around this time. That would make sense, as it was a boom time for trade with the Colonies 300 years ago, and the need for sailors (and housing for them) was at a premium.

Although quiet today, New Street would have been vibrant in the past. It had its own shops - Powe's groceries at top of Rosemary Lane, also Hooper's, Chappell's, Hardings, and White's fish and chips.

DISGUSTING HABITS:

In 1866 the North Devon Journal reported the findings of a Public Health Report after an outbreak of cholera in the village. This painted a picture of the wretched conditions which stated that "it was almost impossible to give an adequate idea of the disgusting habits to which the lower classes are compelled to resort". Wells were found to be impregnated with decayed vegetable and animal matter, and could only be used for cooking; the water for drinking purposes having to be fetched from a considerable distance. At the bottom of New Street an open well was examined and found to have sewage from nearby drains oozing into it through the pebbles. Its contents were said to be regularly used for drinking purposes – it's no wonder that beer was more popular than water.

ASSAULT, MURDER AND SUICIDE:

The newspapers of the time recorded other traumatic events in New Street:

In 1824 blacksmith William Wood received a visit from a bailiff who was coming to take goods in lieu of un-paid rent. Mr Wood had felt justified in withholding his rent due to the house being in such a dilapidated state, and saw the bailiff off by hitting him on the head with an iron bar. Unfortunately this fractured the poor man's skull and Wood was taken away to be sentenced at the Assizes.

In 1878 26-year-old Annie Sydney, wife of mariner Thomas Sydney, committed an even worse offence. Obviously suffering from mental problems which were described as a "nervous despondent state", she was spotted hauling herself out on the anchor chain of a schooner moored off the Bell Inn slip carrying her six-month-old daughter, and trying to drown herself in the river. She was rescued and taken back to her house where they found the gruesome reason for her attempted suicide. The baby she was carrying was already dead, its throat cut with a bread knife, the murder weapon being found still blood-stained and hidden under a pillow. Mrs Sydney was taken to the Assizes where the jury found that wilful murder had been committed and she was committed to the Asylum.

NINETEEN STEPS:

Our tour leaves New Street and heads back down to New Quay Street which was widened to its current width in 1870. The narrow steps at the far end were originally known as 'Nineteen Steps', a name which is no longer used today – probably because there are now twenty-three of them!

THE SHIP INN:

Opposite the bottom of these steps, at 19 New Quay Street was the final pub at this end of the village. The 'Ship Inn' can be traced back to the 1820s when Thomas Bowden was landlord. However, there are references in 1807 to a 'Ship & Tow Boat Inn' at Appledore which could well be this public house. In 1867 the pub was sold with 'rights to beach' for repairing vessels. The Inn closed in 1927 and then became the 'Ship Dairy' run by Albert Vaggers.

Next to the Ship is 'Dock Cottage', home of the Harris shipbuilding family in the early 20th century. It was built in the early 1800s and was the home of the last male Benson to live in Appledore. Thomas Brown Benson who died in 1876, was the great-grandson of the notorious Thomas Benson: merchant, landowner, Sheriff of Devon, disgraced MP, smuggler, fraudster, privateer, and downright villain, who lived at Knapp House further up the river. It is of him that we shall hear next.

Letting notice for Benson's New Quay (North Devon Journal: 2nd Dec 1830).

BENSON'S NEW QUAY:

Looking though the large gates into the gravel yard at the top of New Quay Street, you will see the remains of Appledore's maritime and economic past. Here in 1745 Benson's New Quay was constructed after which New Quay Street was named. Thomas Benson was a shipping entrepreneur who owned dozens of ships trading to Spain, Portugal, the American Colonies and also fishing vessels to Newfoundland. There were only limited unloading wharves available to him and he wanted to quicken the turn-around time of his ships in order to increase his profits. He built a 300-foot-long stone quay here complete with warehouses, unloading areas, and easy access to the cheap labour of Appledore. But most of all it was away from the prying eyes of Customs Officials in Bideford.

The stone quay still survives and can best be seen from the river. One of the original three-storey warehouse buildings can also still be seen here, although it's now in a badly dilapidated state. However, it can still give us an impression of the activity that went on here over 250 years ago: the bustle of unloading, the shouts of the sailors, and the smell of the fish and other cargoes. It was a vibrant and prosperous time but it was all just about to turn sour for Thomas Benson.

THE BENSON FAMILY:

What can you say about Thomas Benson, one of Appledore's most notorious characters? Certainly his activities should not be allowed to tar all the Benson family with the same brush. They were a noble family who brought prosperity not only to themselves but to Appledore as a whole. The Benson family in Appledore can be traced back for eight generations to a Thomas Benson born about 1560.

John Benson (the notorious Thomas's father) was the only son amongst seven children as was his father before him, so all the family wealth was concentrated down the male line. John Benson married Grace Melhuish (daughter of the Lord-of-the-Manor) and, again ignoring the unimportant female children, had three sons of which Thomas was the youngest. Fate was with Thomas though as the eldest son died before his father and the family wealth was left to 2nd son Peter, but he also died a few years later and Thomas Benson inherited the whole of his estate: ships, land, property, money, and status. It was an Estate worth about £10 million in today's terms.

THOMAS BENSON:

Thomas was not one to sit around enjoying his wealth. He had to be wheeling and dealing. He was contracted to transport convicts to America, but instead took them as far as Lundy Island, of which he was the lessee, where he set them to work building walls and cultivating the land. Benson also used Lundy Island as a depot for goods brought from abroad, storing his contraband in a cave on the island.

Two of the contracts which Thomas Benson signed to transport prisoners to America. Supposedly he signed both of these himself, but these signatures don't look very similar to me. More fraud going on here I think!

Benson was also heavily involved at a peak time for the tobacco trade when Bideford was 2nd only to London in the quantity of tobacco it imported from America - at its height importing nearly 3,500 tons every year. However Benson did things his way. He landed his tobacco at the New Quay where he paid the import duty. He then 'exported' the tobacco to Lundy and legally claimed back the tax paid. The tobacco was then processed there and smuggled back to the mainland. The Customs officers were at a loss to know how to deal with this as Lundy did not come under the control of any mainland port. However, Thomas's downfall came when he hatched a far more audacious plot…

THE NIGHTINGALE:

In 1752 Benson had an old brigantine called the 'Nightingale'. She was barely seaworthy but he loaded her with lace, silk, cutlery, pewter, woollen goods, and fifteen convicts, all of which he insured heavily. She sailed from Appledore on the 28th July but only got as far as Lundy Island where the cargo was removed. Her crew were then paid to take

the ship out again and set fire to her making sure that this was witnessed by a passing ship. The vessel sunk and the crew managed to get ashore with the convicts who were then locked up in a barn at Knapp House. Benson then claimed for the loss of the ship and its cargo.

However, people were curious to hear a first-hand account of the disaster so the mate James Bather was plied with drink in a Barnstaple pub and the truth came out, which didn't take long to reach Benson's enemies. Benson's fall-guy Captain Lancey was hunted down and arrested at the Swan Inn at Northam (which Benson also owned). Lancey was taken to Newgate Prison in London. Benson went to London to try and get bail for the imprisoned crew who he would then smuggle out of the Country. He failed. The trial went ahead, the truth came out and Lancey was executed at Wapping.

Thomas Benson was fined over £7000 for smuggling offences and his estate was seized as security, but he fled to Oporto where he had merchant friends. He continued his business dealings from Portugal, and there are even rumours that he once returned to Knapp House during his self-imposed exile. Benson died at Oporto in 1771 at the age of 64.

THE STATION THAT NEVER WAS:

A railway to Appledore had been planned for many years. Since the successful opening of the line connecting Bideford to Barnstaple in 1855, the next logical step was to extend this to Appledore and Westward Ho! A two-mile route was planned down the riverbank which was to terminate in Appledore at Benson's New Quay.

The scheme was approved by Parliament in 1866 as the 'Bideford, Appledore and Westward Ho! Act'. However, no sooner had this been approved than there was a financial crisis and banking collapse so the raising of the £60,000 needed for its construction came to nothing.

The promoters struggled on for a few years trying to raise the necessary support, but the scheme was eventually abandoned. It was to be another forty-two years before the dream of a railway coming to Appledore was realised.

Before we turn up Tomouth Road to continue the tour, we will wander a little further up the riverbank as there are some interesting stories to uncover here. There have been a number of quays facing onto the river between here and Boathyde, and we will hear about the New Quay Dock in a moment. First we have a silver mine to locate…

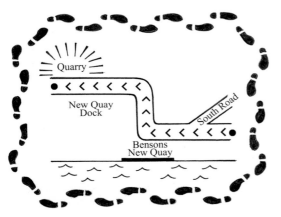

GO ALONG NEW QUAY STREET TOWARDS THE HUBBASTONE QUARRY

THE APPLEDORE SILVER MINE:

Don't get too excited about un-tapped riches here - it was all actually a con. In 1851 Jerome Clapp owned the farmland here and was excited when told that there was lead and silver to be found on his land. He employed some miners and they started tunnelling in from the beach near to Hubbastone Quarry. Jerome's father Benjamin was a silversmith in

Bath, so presumably he was looking to make a family business out of this. A shaft was also sunk from the field above and indeed the mine captain did emerge with some silver nuggets. Clapp was congratulated on his good fortune and continued to pay the miners. However, a year later no more nuggets were found and it was realised that the silver had probably been planted there, and he had been duped. The mine was closed and the entrance sealed, although the tunnel and shaft are still believed to be there.

NEW QUAY DOCK:

We've heard previously about the Richmond Dry-Dock but there was another dry-dock in Appledore, also built by William Yeo, when he realised how successful these facilities could make him. This one was known as the 'New Quay Dock' and was 270 feet long and 44 feet wide with its adjoining yard covering four acres. For some reason this dock wasn't exactly straight and the bend in the middle gave it the nickname of the 'Banana Dock'.

After Yeo died the dock fell into decline and was in turn rented by shipbuilders Thomas Cook and William Pickard, but eventually leased in 1881 to John Westacott, a shipbuilder from Barnstaple. Westacott advertised for work but after four months none had been forthcoming and the depression was hitting everyone hard. That changed in November of that year when a barque that had been booked

A Thames 'dumb' barge being constructed in the 'Middle Yard' of Robert Cock and Sons in 1902.

The ketch 'Emily Barrett' undergoing works in the New Quay Dry-Dock.

in for a refit sailed into the river. Indeed, it was so important to many livelihoods that Westacott's man ran breathlessly into Church disrupting the service to loudly announce the news of the ship's arrival.

> WANTED, 25 SHIP CARPENTERS; four months constant work guaranteed.—J. WESTACOTT, New Quay Graving Dock, Appledore

(Bideford Gazette: 3rd October 1882).

In 1888 the writer Hugh Strong visited Appledore, and wrote a lively account of the New Quay Dock, which then employed between 100 and 150 men:

"The yard is entered by the blacksmiths' shop; there are three forges in the smithy. The bellows and anvils are silent now, for the smiths are at their mid-day meal, which they take in a snug corner of the forge. Stretching away from the blacksmiths' shops are the lofty spacious stores. Here oakum, paints, nails, and iron, are one after another presented to our eyes. Out among the timber, in the dockyard, we hit upon splendid spars, 75 feet long. On our right are the carpenters' and joiners' shops, with the tool chests of the workmen in the rear. Sail, moulding and rigging lofts extend over the saw-pit. Then the lumber stores extend along the yard end, and the rock salt, which preserves the timber and prevents dry-rot, is stored there."
(Strongs Industries of North Devon).

Philip Kelly Harris (1852-1938).

John Westacott was declared bankrupt in 1891, and the era of wooden shipbuilding came to an end in 1912 when the Harris family launched the last wooden merchant ship built at Appledore. She was the 'P.T.Harris', and was tragically lost at sea four years later on a voyage from Greenock to France. She had five Appledore sailors on board, none of whom was ever seen again.

DISASTROUS APPLEDORE BLAZE
SERIOUS DAMAGE TO SHIPYARD

In 1947, fire destroyed a three-story building on the site used for rigging and sail-making, and a carpentry and joinery workshop. The glow of the fire was noticed at 4:20am by Mrs Blackmore of 47 New Street and it caused thousands of pounds worth of damage. In 1973 the Dock was filled in, although the structure still survives underneath the concrete of the New Quay yard. Maybe one-day it will be dug out and restored?

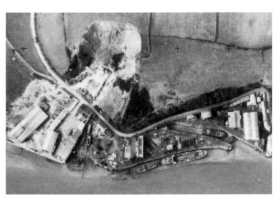

Aerial view of Hubbastone Quarry and New Quay Dock in 1959.

HUBBASTONE QUARRY:

A large chunk of hillside has been taken from this quarry over the years and used for road and building stone. We don't know when quarrying started, but the Bensons were paying land tax for a quarry here in 1777 and almost certainly used its stone to build Benson's New Quay in 1745. In the early 1900s many tons

Various vessels undergoing repairs in the New Quay Dock around 1900.
The ship in the lower picture was obviously quite leaky,
as she had a windmill-powered pump to keep her dry.

Going, going, gone! The destruction of Chanter's Folly in 1952, it having become too unsafe to let it stand any longer. The demolition was carried out using cables. (North Devon Athenaeum).

In 1937 the Shell Petrol Company devised an advertising campaign to decorate their first fleet of lorries built to deliver petrol to garages. They commissioned 29 original posters of various follies throughout England and Wales, to show the different places that Shell petrol could take you. This one showing Chanter's Folly and the New Quay Dry-Dock was painted by Clifford and Rosemary Ellis. (Shell Art Collection).

were being taken each week, some by horse and cart, others in barges from a small landing stage. During road works some time ago buried rail-tracks were discovered which were originally used for the transportation of stone to the quayside in wagons. Quarrying stopped about 1930 and the yard was taken over by haulage contractors W. Lamey & Sons. In the 1950s the Barnstaple Brick and Tile Company set up a manufacturing factory on land in Hubbastone Yard before relocating to Poole around 1960.

CHANTER'S FOLLY:

A folly-tower teetering on the edge of the Hubbastone Quarry was a familiar sight up until 1952. It can be seen in many old photographs, built in 1841 by Thomas Burnard Chanter who was at that time leasing the rights of the Manor of Northam. The tower was fifty feet high and built on the highest part of the estate so that Chanter could see his ships coming over the Bar and then have sufficient time to arrange for stevedores to unload the cargo at Bideford. A good view could be had from the very top, but in later years this was restricted by the growth of trees thus giving the tower its more recognised name of 'Chanter's Folly'. There is an unverified story that when Chanter kept the first watch after the tower was completed he saw his son's ship wrecked on Bideford Bar. The entire crew was drowned and Chanter never set foot in the tower again.

Thomas Chanter was personally contracted to supply all the timber for the building of Brunel's Great Western Railway between Gloucester and Exeter, a distance of some 107 miles. The timber was imported from Canada (in today's terms a contract that was worth several million pounds). The works were completed in 1844 and made Chanter one of the wealthiest merchants in the south-west of England. It is therefore likely that Chanter funded the 1845 construction of Appledore Quay out of the profits from this contract. In a roundabout way we can therefore claim that Brunel paid for Appledore Quay to be built.

"When I was a boy the floors and stairs were very rotten and rickety. In the summer holidays I enjoyed the company of two of my male cousins, Ted and Sid Lamey. Other members of our gang included their cousin, Jackie Lamey, and friends such as John Thomas, Walter Tuplin, Dennis Cox, Frank Curtis, Donald Moyse, Desmond Leslie, Jack Evans and Owen Reveley. Every year we used to climb the steep quarry face to scratch our names on the crumbling plaster inside Chanter's Folly. Of course we could have gone the long way round, up the lane, and across the fields, but that provided no challenge or excitement."
(*Appledore Boyhood Memories*, by E R Carter).

Although the tower was sufficiently strong to survive a lightning strike in 1927, the interior was gutted in 1945 by some excited Naval Ratings celebrating V.J. night. The damage done to the stonework made it unsafe, and in November 1952 the tower eventually had to be demolished, despite having been listed as having special historical interest.

On his visit to Appledore as a child in 1867 Jerome K Jerome was taken around the old farmland which the family owned and he explored Chanter's Folly: *"There were picnics on the topmost platform of the old, grey, ruined tower, that still looks down upon the sea. One spread first: apple jelly and then Devonshire cream upon one's bread, and lived upon squab pies and junkets, and quaffed sweet cider out of goblets, just like gods."*
(*My Life and Times*, by Jerome K Jerome).

DELAWARE COTTAGE:

In the yard below the quarry used to stand a curious pagoda-like house belonging to shipbuilder Richard Taylor Blackmore (see book 1, page 112). In 1881 he bought an old barque at a boat auction in Bideford. She was called the 'Delaware', and he floated her down to Hubbastone where he broke her up and used her superstructure as the main part of his house which came to be known as Delaware Cottage. The two lower stories were the deckhouses of the old barque; on top of which he put the ship's galley used as a bedroom for his sons which could only be reached by a ladder. In the decking were thick glass deadlights from the ship and carved on the beam could still be read 'Accommodation for five seamen'. In the living room were the original ship's lockers, opening with lids acting as seals with brass rings. Some of these held coal, others were the old bosun's stores containing thimbles, deadeyes, tools and screws. Outside the house stood two ships figureheads, all painted white. The house survived until 1923 when it was demolished and replaced by the suburban terraced houses seen here today.

HUBBA THE DANE:

This place is called 'Hubbastone', supposedly named after the Viking leader 'Hubba' who was slain near here after a decisive battle against the Saxon men of Devon. He was buried on the riverbank under a large stone, or cairn of stones. This story is based in dark-age legend and has been embellished by well-meaning antiquaries of the past so that today it is difficult to separate legend from fact.

What we do know is that in the year 878 twelve-hundred Vikings came over from South Wales intent on making their presence known and probably landed their ships somewhere around the river Torridge. A battle took place and the Vikings were driven back, largely defeated, but the survivors had time to bury their leader (actually called 'Ubba') under a large stone before sailing off in their ships to lick their wounds. The facts of this are sparse and were popularised by Thomas Hogg and later by local historian Charles Chappell. Charles Kingsley also wrote this romantic prose about it in his 1855 novel 'Westward Ho!':

> *"Within that charmed rock,*
> *so Torridge boatman tell,*
> *sleeps now the old Norse Viking,*
> *in his leaden coffin,*
> *with all his fairy treasure,*
> *and his crown of gold".*

Recent research has suggested that the Viking battle took place inland at Castle Hill near Beaford, but we still have the legend about Ubba being buried at Appledore. The Hubbastone itself seems to have vanished in late Victorian times, probably underneath one of the dock developments, and its very existence is therefore now doubted. However, the Devonshire Association confirmed the existence of this stone in 1879 when the Barrow Committee investigated it, but the same organisation in 1902 found that many people testified to its existence but no-one knew what had happened to it. In 1904 an old inhabitant recounted a story that Jerome Clapp had found the Hubbastone in the 1840s and lifted it to see what was underneath. There he found a bottle containing parchment supposed to tell the history of this battle, although this parchment had been obliterated by water. Perhaps the best evidence linking this site with Ubba is in the Hubbastone name itself, handed down through the centuries giving us a tribal memory of what happened here over a thousand years ago.

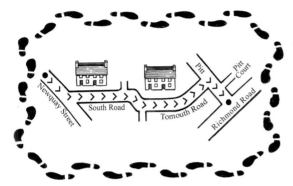

GO UP SOUTH ROAD INTO THE TOMOUTH ESTATE TOWARDS PITT HILL

If you walk further up the river you will come to what was (when opened in April 1970) the largest covered shipyard in Europe, Appledore Shipbuilders Ltd, the surviving modern face of the Torridge Shipbuilding Industry.

Further up-river are Boathyde, Knapp House, and eventually Bideford. Gracefully spanning the river there is the new Torridge Bridge whose caissons were built in the Richmond Dock and floated up river before being sunk into place. During construction of this bridge a greenstone Neolithic axe was found in the river indicating that prehistoric people also found these waters a good place for hunting and fishing.

Our historic route through Appledore re-traces its steps now and passes through the housing estate of Tomouth. On the surface this might look like a moderately well-designed post-war Council Estate, but there is still history to be uncovered here. Go back along the New Quay Street to South Road.

TOMOUTH ROAD

'Tomouth' is probably the oldest name in the village dating back at least a thousand years. It described the original settlement around Parlour Creek where the Richmond Dock now stands. However, given that the name 'Appledore' doesn't appear until the early 1300s, then 'Tawmouth' could actually be the original name of this early settlement. In 1068 it was called Tawmuda (pronounced 'Towemutha'). Later we find it spelt as Tavemuth, Towemouth, and latterly Toumouth.

Map showing the Tomouth Estate fields in 1840.

Three-hundred years ago the Tomouth Estate lands consisted of a farm and twelve acres of fields. These were purchased in 1702 to support the charitably-funded almshouses and known as 'Cocke's and Langdon's Charity'. In 1813 the lands were let to Thomas Hogg who created a rope-manufacturing facility known as a 'rope-walk' on the site. This rope-walk was roughly along the line where Tomouth Road adjoins Pitt Hill, and in 1871 was giving work to nine men and six boys. By 1881 the yard had

Aerial view of the Tomouth lands in October 1945 - Myrtle Street is at the top, and New Quay Street is on the right. Note that South Road was constructed before the 2nd World War, ending in a turning-circle at the top of the hill. House building re-commenced on the Tomouth estate after the war. (National Monuments Record Centre).

1938: One of the first Council-house tenants receiving the key for their new property in South Road. Minnie Bale and her husband Harry (with cap, left of centre) were re-housed from the condemned buildings in Canns Court.

been closed down and the rope-making materials sold.

The land was turned into a housing estate in the 1940s, but there were calls for the land to be used for houses back as far as 1863 when accommodation of every kind was badly needed. The vicar of Northam commended the Tomouth site and wrote saying that:

"There is a great need of fresh houses to accommodate the increasing population, owing to the new Dry Dock, and new ship-building yards. There is little room for the erection of new houses; and I regret to observe a tendency to build upon the very lungs of the place, the small

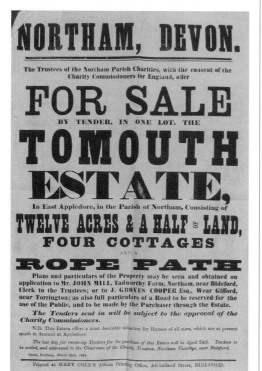

gardens at the back of some of the houses." (And who says that infilling development is new?).

In 1866 the land was offered for development and three tenders were submitted. William Yeo submitted a bid as he wanted to get involved in other ventures. Yeo's bid of £2,500 was accepted, although coincidentally this just happened to be the exact reserve price for the land, and

subsequent rumours of collusion were voiced. However, Yeo did nothing with the land and in 1872 he died, and the promise of cheap housing for the people vanished along with him. The development saga of this land was to rumble on for another seventy years.

A valuable well of water existed at Tomouth, which in the hot summer of 1866 supplied all the inhabitants of Appledore even when all the other wells had dried up. The Vincent and Duncan collar factory on Appledore quay found that this was the closest place from which a reliable supply of water could be obtained. In 1887 they laid nearly 600 yards of pipes to this source, only applying for permission from the landowner after they had carried out the work.

In 1884 Robert Cock was renting the lands and there were again calls to make this available for housing. The fields were let in various lots but no development was forthcoming.

In 1906 it was proposed that a Council School should be built on part of the land adjoining Pitt Hill, but this was subsequently rejected for a site further up the hill.

Early in 1914 the Northam Council pressed for working-class houses to be built here, but then the 1st World War started and the plan was shelved.

In was not until 1938 that a Council-funded development finally started, only to stop again when the 2nd World War broke out. South Road had been constructed leading up to a turning circle at the top (this can be seen from photos taken during the War). After the War building work proceeded with great speed and the first new houses were ready in February 1947. These houses were highly prized as they came complete with upstairs bathrooms.

As Council housing goes this was actually a very well-planned estate which should have been an example to other Councils. Its commanding position overlooking the village and the river still makes it a desirable place to live.

'Pitt' is a strange name for a road, which might even be unique, if there wasn't another street with the same name in Bideford.

Old photographs of this street show houses on the upper side of Pitt Hill and open fields on the lower side. That was because the lower side was controlled by the Tomouth Charity Trustees leaving just the upper side available for building. The original name of the road was 'Stoope Hill' and is recorded as such in documents from the 1670s which mention 'Tomouth and Stoopehill'.

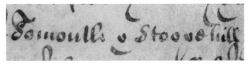

The slightly later name of 'Pitt' (first seen in 1735) probably came from a clay-pit somewhere on the upper side of the road which served an adjacent brickworks. The deeds of number 8, date back to 1735, when the lands here were owned by the Docton family who granted John Hall permission to build a house adjacent to this 'brickfield'.

There is evidence of earlier houses in this street, the house adjacent to number 11 appearing particularly ancient. Numbers 3 and 6 have dates of 1745 on them which suggest significant development of this street took place here around the time that the Bensons were bringing prosperity to Appledore in the first half of the 1700s.

Half-way up Pitt Hill 'Wintor House' with the Edwardian balconies was built in 1910 as the Manse for the Baptist Church, a role which lasted until 1979.

MUSICAL MICE:

If you stand very quietly in Pitt Hill you might just be able to hear the singing mice. Admittedly they haven't been heard for a while now, but in 1904 a resident heard two of them singing merrily (as mice do) despite all his attempts to scare them away. It must have been true – it was in the papers! You might also be lucky enough to hear them - especially after a few drinks. Even greater newspaper headlines for a Pitt Hill resident in 1913 when Samuel Short was awarded a prize for growing a 24lb cabbage. Ah – the true stuff of history!

PITT COURT:

Hidden away at the bottom of Pitt Hill lies Pitt Court, a surviving terrace of houses from the 1700s. These are strangely separated from similar houses in Appledore at this time by a few hundred yards, almost forming a separate hamlet. Their former out-houses can still be seen on the opposite side of the Court and it is good to see the original cobbled surface still surviving unscathed by ubiquitous tarmac. A single courtyard well served all the houses here, although it was stated in 1894 that the water from it had been unfit for drinking for the past twenty years.

The first house in Pitt Court was a sweet shop in the 1930s run by Mary Ellen Channon and adjacent 'Algoa House' was home to the Kelly family who from late Victorian times ran a nearby grocery shop.

NUMBER 1 PITT HILL:

Actually number 1 no longer exists! Richmond Road was widened in 1932 and the house at the bottom of Pitt had to be demolished to enable the extra width to be created. You can see the modern brick gable-end of number 2 constructed at this time. For much of Queen Victoria's reign this now-vanished house was the home of Harriet Williams who died in 1897. She was the wife of mariner Richard Williams, but spent most of her life as a widow. Richard Williams was employed by William Yeo and served him well as Captain on his brig the 'British Lady' on the Atlantic route to Canada. However, tragedy struck Richard Williams in 1851 when he died whilst on a voyage and left his widow Harriet and their five children at their house here in Pitt. Whilst his death was not unique in the hazardous world of seafaring, what is amazing is that we have a photograph of Richard Williams.

This remarkably early picture was taken in a photographer's studio in Quebec in February 1851, not long before Richard's death. Richard Williams is on the left and 37-year-old William Yeo is on the right. (Basil Greenhill Collection in North Devon Record Office).

THE UNICORN INN:

Opposite the bottom of Pitt Hill stands 'Prospect House', adorned with a date-plaque of 1878. Both the name and date are misleading as the house has a much earlier history than that. It used to be a coaching inn called the 'Unicorn Inn' dating back in licensing records to at least 1822, at which time Thomas Halls was the landlord. The pattern of pebbles in the pavement outside is believed to be a sign to tell illiterate coachmen that they were able to get good lodgings here for their horses.

The pattern of pebbles in the pavement outside is believed to be a sign to tell illiterate coachmen that they were able to get good lodgings here for their horses.

In 1857 John Carter (my great great great grandfather) took over as landlord from Thomas Halls. John and Caroline Carter had ten children, the ninth of which was Matthew Henry Carter born at the Unicorn Inn in 1858. Sadly Matthew died aged eleven when thrown from a pony he has been warned not to ride. The inquest into his death was held at the Unicorn Inn (many inquests were held at inns), but it is poignant that this was also his birthplace.

From 1901 the Kelly family ran a Grocery Shop here until 1938.

> **FREEHOLD DWELLING-HOUSE, GARDEN AND PREMISES,**
> formerly the "Unicorn Inn," but now known as "Prospect House," situate near Pitt, Appledore, in the occupation of Miss Moore as tenant thereof. The house contains two Sittingrooms (one of which was formerly used as a shop), Kitchen, large Store Room, w.c., &c., 5 Bedrooms and large Attic. There is a side entrance which also leads to the garden.

(Bideford Gazette: 19th November 1901).

DRIVING OFFENCES:

Motoring fines are not new, even in the days before cars. In 1870 Joseph Spear received a 'parking ticket' for leaving his pony and trap outside the Unicorn Inn for longer than was necessary to unload. He was fined 7s 6d.

Drink-driving is also not new: in 1883 John Baker was summoned on a charge of being drunk in charge of a horse and trap in the streets of Appledore. He was fined £1.

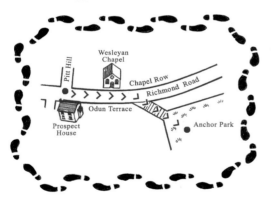

FROM PITT HILL TURN LEFT UP RICHMOND ROAD AND THEN INTO ANCHOR PARK

MR KIDDLES COTTAGES:

On the right are a row of houses which appear in the 1891 census as 'Kiddle's Cottages'. These are now known as Odun Terrace, but who was Mr Kiddle, and how is his name linked to these houses? Was he the builder, landowner, or what?

Actually Richard Neller Kiddle was a dentist in Bideford, but in 1888 he bought Odun Hall (just round the corner in Odun Road) which included a large back garden. On this garden he built this terrace of seven houses as an investment and the following year sold Odun Hall on again, followed by each of these seven houses. They were known as Odun Terrace because they were in the back garden of Odun Hall. Mr Kiddle made a tidy profit, sufficient to set up a new dentist's practice for himself in Lewisham. It seems that developers who appear, build what they want, make some money and move on, are not new in Appledore.

GOOSANDER SCHOOL:

Behind Kiddles Cottages stands a house called 'Goosander'. A boarding and day school for young ladies and gentlemen was run here in the 1850s and 1860s by Misses Sarah Baker and Jane Baker. They were daughters of George Baker who was the boys' teacher at the Appledore National School, later acting as village Postmaster, etc. (see 10 Bude Street).

THE CIRCUS COMES TO TOWN:

In the early 1930s a travelling circus came to the area. Keen to promote their show they arranged for a tight-rope to be strung across the road from Odun Terrace to the houses on the opposite side. Their tight-rope walker made several trips across this wire, creating considerable interest, mostly from people who wanted to see him fall. They were disappointed!

Dark Lane:

From here on the road up the hill is known as Richmond Road, but this has not always been the case. Appledore people knew it as Dark Lane - indeed some still do. It was so named because of the overhanging American Oak trees planted on the edge of the Richmond House estate, which virtually touched the houses on the other side of the road causing the lane to be dark, even in summer.

In 1898 Northam Council agreed to rename it 'Richmond Road' instead of the rather gloomy Dark Lane. Whilst this new name was formally accepted at the meeting, the chairman did comment that it would "always go by the name of Dark Lane". He was proved to be right, the old name still appearing on street maps until the 1930s. However, the trees were cut down in 1938 and the road widened to allow Western National buses access to the Quay. Thereafter there was no reason to call it 'dark', but their stumps can still be seen in the grounds of Anchor Park.

Memorial to Thomas Geen in the Wesleyan Chapel.

Wesleyan Chapel:

The date on the front of this former Wesleyan Methodist Chapel tells us when it was built (1851). It was opened on 1st May of that year, the congregation having out-grown their former premises at the bottom of Myrtle Street. Shipbuilder Thomas Geen gave some of his land upon which to site this Chapel, which was built by Appledore mason Thomas Dennis at a cost of £402.

The Chapel was lit by flickering candles for the first eight years of its use, but in 1859 these were replaced with a much better light source known as moderator lamps. These were hung from the ceiling and ran on pressed olive oil. They also had the wonderful facility of being able to moderate the flow of oil to the wick - hence their name. Modern paraffin oil-lamps would not arrive in the village until a bit later, and gas lamps not be installed until 1877.

The Chapel's congregation thrived for many years, but in the last couple of decades membership dropped to a handful and the high maintenance cost of the building finally forced its closure. The final service was held on 12th October 2008.

WESLEYAN SCHOOL:

The Wesleyans were very successful in running their own school though. In the 1850s the National School was in operation next to St Mary's Church, but a need was felt for another school to cater for the children who belonged to the non-conformist chapels, rather than the church. The Wesleyans went ahead with this scheme costing £300, and began by raising sufficient money to start construction by selling 800 tickets for a public tea at 1 shilling each. Their benefactor Thomas Geen laid the foundation stone in 1861 over a time capsule containing a message, newspapers and coins. Sadly he didn't live to see the completion of the school the following year, dying shortly before the opening celebrations in 1862.

In 1903 there were five classes being taught in the main room and an inspector reported that the children were well-behaved and well-taught, although under somewhat difficult circumstances. Infants were still being taught here until 1951, but with educational changes they were finally moved to the Council School further up the hill.

The Beare family outside their house in Chapel Row, now Richmond Terrace. They lived in the first house in the row from the time of its construction for the next eighty years.

CHAPEL ROW:

Next up the hill the houses are called Richmond Terrace, but when built in the 1860s these nine cottages were known as 'Chapel Row'.

Further up the hill the next terrace of houses was built in 1909 in front of the Council School which opened in the same year. This Council School became the main school for Appledore. During the 2nd World War Appledore school children were supplemented by 74 evacuees from London, plus some of their teachers. This made for some interesting communication problems with the cockney accent contrasting with rich Devon dialect in what was called the 'Battle of the Accents'. When they left many of the London children had acquired Devon accents, so I think we won that battle.

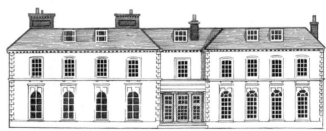

RICHMOND HOUSE:

From Anchor Park we get our best view of Richmond House, a grand dwelling built in 1856 by William Yeo at the same time Richmond Dry-Dock was under construction. With his father James he had built up a sizeable shipbuilding business using Canadian timber, and by 1858 he claimed to have crossed the Atlantic 45 times. He made himself into the village 'squire' and often had the final say on who was employed in the village. If you crossed him you would find yourself sacked with no possibility of work in his shipyards.

Dr Mark Horton (in his guided tour during the 2007 Book Festival) described Richmond House as the 'most vulgar house in Appledore' – William Yeo: lording it over the village with the ostentatious show of wealth and power. I personally think this was a little mis-founded.

A Wesleyan Sunday School parade in the 1930s in Marine Parade.

The Wesleyan School class of 1907.
Back row: [unknown], Lizzie Fisher, Olive Cornish, Laura Hocking, Ida Mitchell, Katy Ransome, Susan Westlake,
Elsie Cawsey, Rita Oatway.   Middle row: Daisy Short, Paul Parkhouse, George Sanders, Frederick Huxtable,
Dave Hocking, Tom Cooksley, Ada Kelly, Thomas Stacey, Dolly Slade, John Marshall, Doris Gorvin.
Front row: Beatty Hocking, Harold Blackmore, Mary Gregory, Frank Ford, Thomas Screech, [unknown],
Florence Fisher, Lily May, Edmund Peake, [unknown], Nellie Powe.

Firstly the house could not be seen by the villagers, as it was completely hidden by trees, and secondly the house was much smaller when William Yeo built it. A later owner doubled the width of the façade in the early 20th century, so it wasn't originally the huge structure that we see today.

The grand staircase in The Holt.

SCHOOL TREATS:

It was certainly a grand house and William Yeo did like to show it off. School treats were held annually in the grounds. In 1863 a joint schools celebration was held with an estimated 2,000 people attending. Given that the population of Appledore was not much more than this at the time, it seems the whole village must have turned out.

"The town was decorated with flags of all nations, which floated gracefully in the breeze,

and banners were thrown across the streets. At 2:00pm the children and friends, with the minister, Rev. E Reynolds, met at the School Rooms, where they were joined by the Bideford Rifle Corps Band. A procession was formed, which perambulated the streets, the teachers and children carrying some beautiful banners and flags. They proceeded to Richmond House, where they met with a hearty welcome from the liberal and respected owner and his fair daughters, who kindly led the way to the grounds which were tastefully adorned with a profusion of flags." (North Devon Journal: 16th July 1863).

White Lodge, the former gatehouse lodge of Richmond House, sadly demolished in 2005.

William Yeo was also a benefactor to Appledore – I guess it came with the job. In the cold winter of 1871 he arranged for fifty tons of coal to be distributed to the poor of the village. However, the following year he was dead at the age of 59 – followed six months later by his wife Elizabeth. They are buried together in an imposing marble tomb at the top of Appledore churchyard, originally surrounded by iron railings. He was not a likeable man and probably deserved his nick-name of the 'black ram' a corruption of his surname 'Yeo' (which pronounced with a Devon accent sounded like 'ewe'). William Yeo had six daughters but only one son. Sadly this son died at the age of eight and no-one was left to carry on the business. Subsequently depression hit the Appledore shipbuilding trade. The remaining family moved away in 1875 and William Yeo's furniture and effects were sold off at auction. However, the house does still contain many original features, including library cupboards hand-built from exotic hardwoods.

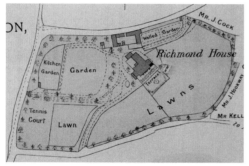

Sale particulars of Richmond House in 1903.
(Devon Record Office)

THE HOLT:

In 1903 the house was purchased at auction for £2,500 by Major-General Boyes from Abbotsham, who declared that the house would now be known as 'The Holt', a name which it bears to this day. Later the house was bought by the 3rd Earl of Eldon as a wedding present for his son the Honourable Denys Scott, who married Lillie Amy Stuart in 1907, a descendant of the family of the Marquis of Bute. They had five children and two cats called 'Winston' and 'Algernon'. Denys Scott doubled the size of the façade by adding the nursery wing on the right-hand side and by 1938 when the trees were cut down to widen 'Dark Lane' the house boasted seven gardeners, seven indoor staff, and a chauffeur.

"Denys Scott originally came from a family of coal owners in the north of England. He was a sidesman at St. Mary's Church, which he attended regularly, but otherwise was not particularly active in the life of the village. He was a keen member of the Royal North Devon Golf Club, not a particularly outstanding player, unlike his brother Michael who at one time became British Amateur Champion. Michael also won several Australian Championships, the French Open Championship and captained the British team competing against America at St. Andrews for the Walker Cup in May 1834."
(Appledore Boyhood Memories, by E R Carter).

Denys Scott was in command of the Local Defence Volunteers during the 2nd World War. He died in 1962 and Scott Avenue, built on part of the Holt lands, was named after him.

 For a house that isn't that old, it seems to have more than its fair share of ghosts. The last two owners have both seen a lady in a long red dress and matching bonnet coming down the stairs and going out the front door. She is often accompanied by a strong smell of perfume, which other independent observers have also smelt. She matches the description of Madeleine Scott (sister-in-law of Denys Scott), who was French, had auburn hair, was beautifully dressed, and always wore expensive perfume.

There is also a ghost who has identified himself as Fred Scott. This would be Frederick Scott, son of Denys Scott, who was quiet and kind, but eccentric. He has appeared as a jittery man looking out of the window of the nursery in which he was often locked as a child.

A small girl and her dog have also been seen running up and down the hallway, but they have now been exorcised. Their identity is unknown, but she could be Sibyl Scott, the five year old daughter of Denys Scott who died in 1919.

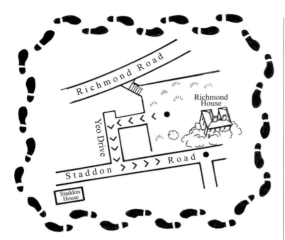

FROM ANCHOR PARK GO THROUGH THE ALLEYWAY TO YEO DRIVE AND UP TO STADDON ROAD

In 1970, the Staddon Estate lands were part of Odun Farm and were sold for development. A Daily Telegraph travel-writer wrote in that year: *"There are two Appledores: the one on the hill is modern, and therefore not worth looking at; the one by the water is ancient and therefore handsome."*

As our journey around Appledore passes through both parts, I'm afraid we have to look at both.

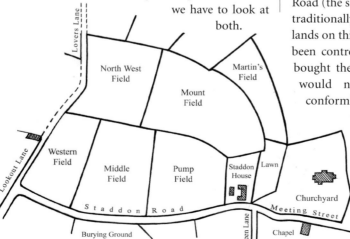

Map showing the Staddon Estate fields in 1840.

A modern housing estate shouldn't contain much of historical significance, but historically Staddon Road is the original route down to the river at Appledore sea-front. A further ancient track branches off and goes over Lookout to the river at West Appledore. However, don't be deceived by this modern straight tarmac estate, this trackway has been here for over a thousand years.

THE BURYING GROUND:

The 1840 tithe map shows that the lower side of Staddon Road consisted of four fields: 'South Field', 'Three Corner Close', Lookout Field', and the 'Burying Ground'. The last of these with the curious name of the Burying Ground, appears roughly in the area between the top of Yeo Drive and the back of The Holt. Traditionally 'burying grounds' (as opposed to a burial ground or cemetery) suggested a place where non-conformists buried their dead, using the ground in rotation as the bodies decayed - but is there any evidence for this here?

A) We have an old non-conformist Chapel at the top of Meeting Street, dating back towards the mid-1600s (more on this later), and they would have needed somewhere nearby to bury their dead.

B) The land on the upper side of Staddon Road (the side where St Mary's Church now is) traditionally housed a Catholic Chapel. The lands on this other side of the road would have been controlled by the Catholics or whoever bought their lands afterwards, and therefore would not have been used by non-conformists.

C) The land closer to Appledore was probably already in use as farmland so the closest usable space for burials would have been this plot here, a little away from the village on the sheltered side of the hill, next to the road and with peaceful views looking up the river.

Any bodies would by now have dissolved, so the only evidence we have for this cemetery is circumstantial, and the field name of the 'Burying Ground'.

Engraving of Staddon House c.1830.

STADDON HOUSE:

Before we head towards Lookout and down to West Appledore, we will first hear about the history of Staddon House which stands in its own grounds a little further down the hill near the top of Meeting Street.

The origins of the 'Staddon' name are unknown, although it is possibly taken from the Saxon words 'Stod' and 'Dun' meaning horse-farm. The house and former estate that bears its name was probably built in the early 1700s, but it is equally possible that a Mr Staddon bought the land and built himself a grand house here. The Staddon surname appears in Braunton, Fremington and Barnstaple around this time. Indeed there were Staddons still living in Appledore until the 1880s.

The original Staddon lands included the upper side of Staddon Road as far as Lookout Lane, so this would certainly have been a grand estate in the 1700s. The estate changed hands in the 1740s, and the house is marked on Donn's map of 1765 when Mr Ford was in residence. The inscribed plaque currently on the gateway to Staddon House reading "circa 1780" is therefore wrong – ignore it!

Aerial view of Staddon House and grounds c.1930.

In 1780 Samuel Pyke was paying Land Tax and Window Tax for Staddon, but the Pyke family left the house in the 1790s and it was let to various tenants in succession – firstly to local shipbuilder Richard Chapman, then in 1810 to Moses Chanter, merchant and former mayor of Bideford, including his son Thomas Burnard Chanter who grew up here watching the ships coming and going in the river below. Captain Charles Gribble was a later tenant in the 1820s, but the Pykes were still in ownership of the house and all the estate lands until the 1840s.

When Appledore's first vicar was appointed in 1845, Staddon House was used as the vicarage and Rev. Edward Reynolds and his family moved in for their term of service at Appledore – a term that would actually last until his death over fifty years later.

At that time the property was described as having: 3 sitting rooms, 2 kitchens, a large hall, larder, dairy, shoe-hole, pantry, coal cellar, wine cellar, store room, 2 meeting rooms, 3 large bedrooms, 3 small bedrooms, 2 servants bedrooms and 2 water closets. Outside was a barn, cow house, granary, potato house, stable for 3 horses, coach-house, ash pit, servants WC, walled kitchen garden and 2 acres of land. A grand house by any standards, which even William Yeo couldn't match with Richmond House.

COUNT TOLSTOY:

After the 1st World War the house was bought

by Howard Wicksteed who became a local squire. He was a Lieutenant in the Devon Territorials, and during the 2nd World War he was second in command of the Home Guard.

In 1934 there was great rejoicing when Wicksteed's daughter Frieda Mary got married. She was just 18 but had met a Russian Count by the name of Dimitry Mihailovich Tolstoy, a survivor of the Russian Revolution and descendant of the celebrated family of the author Leo Tolstoy. Dimitry had escaped Russia with a death sentence pronounced on all members of the aristocracy and arrived at Southampton as a refugee. How he met Frieda is unclear, but the village celebrated in style and the streets were adorned with flags.

Frieda Mary was the first North Devon bride to fly to her honeymoon. The couple set off from an airstrip on the Northam Burrows in a Desoutter cabin monoplane, known among aviators as the 'honeymoon express'. Denys Scott's son Jack piloted the plane, and the bride's travelling outfit was a two-piece ensemble in chequers, with hat of the same material. Aeroplanes flying around the Taw and Torridge were becoming more familiar after 1934, when a flying club was established near Braunton Burrows and many people were taught to fly there. In 1940 the site was taken over by the R.A.F. and it became the Chivenor Air Base. Thereafter Wellington bombers carrying out raids were a more familiar sight.

Frieda Mary's marriage to Count Tolstoy ended in divorce and in 1945 she married novelist Patrick O'Brian, who was the author of the 'Master and Commander' series about life in the Navy in Napoleonic times. They lived in Staddon House until 1949. Her son Nicholai Tolstoy wrote about his childhood growing up there:

"Though Staddon was spacious and elegant, and enjoyed a setting of rare natural splendour, it could not be described as a grand house. However, the interior appeared particularly fine on account of my grandfather's magnificent collection of 18th century satinwood furniture, porcelain and china, paintings, and other beautiful works of art. So far as I was concerned, the most valuable objects were a carved paddle; and an executioner's club whose round head was shaped like that of a bird with a skull-penetrating beak. The King of Fiji also presented my grandfather with a canoe, which he profanely converted into a chicken hutch."

('Patrick O'Brian: The Making of the Novelist', by Nikolai Tolstoy).

THE KING OF SIAM:

In 1940 Staddon House was briefly let to another refugee. The deposed King of Siam (now known as Thailand) came to the throne in 1925. Educated at Eton, Prince Prachadhipok Sakdidej had not expected to ascend to the throne. He abdicated in 1935 and lived in exile in south-east England for a number of years. When the German bombing started, like many others evacuating the populated areas he moved to a safer area. He rented Staddon House with his family, having previously stayed there in 1931. He stayed for about ten

months and later arranged for a picture of himself to be sent to every house in which he had lived.

APPLEDORE IN THE CIVIL WAR:

Like everywhere else in the Country Appledore couldn't help getting involved in the English Civil War. This raged from 1642 to about 1649, with North Devon mainly being on the side of Cromwell and Parliament. In the parish of Northam there was said to be a ratio of 617 Parliamentary supporters for every 1 Royalist Petitioner. Nevertheless, control of the land at Appledore changed hands twice during the War and was, as you might expect, strategic because of its position overlooking the estuary. The best position to control this estuary was from the highest point on the hill above the village - so that is where a fort was built.

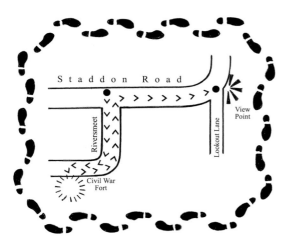

TURN RIGHT UP RIVERSMEET AND THEN RETURN ALONG TO THE END OF STADDON ROAD

To see the site of the fort, although there's not much left to see now, turn right from Staddon Road and go up Riversmeet to the top. The remains of the fort are in the private field in front of you.

CIVIL WAR FORT:

The fort here was quadrangular with bastions at the angles, and was probably built by Major General Chudleigh who also built the fort at East-the-Water, Bideford. Heavy cannon were positioned in the fort with sufficient range to reach vessels in the estuary. In fact they were so heavy that it took a team of sixteen horses to move each one. A deep well also exists near the fort, now capped off, but still believed to be unfilled. Who knows what Civil War items might be found at the bottom of this.

The fort at the top of Staddon Hill was manned by local troops on the side of Parliament, but a push by the Royalists under Colonel George Digby in August 1643 forced the fort to surrender along with Bideford, Barnstaple and Torrington. It was such an easy victory that Appledore was very demoralised. However, before the end of the War the tables were to be turned again.

THE BATTLE OF STADDON HILL:

Obviously local soldiers could not be trusted to secure a Royalist fort in Parliamentary territory, so a garrison of forty Royalist ex-Cornish miners was brought in. However, by June 1644 the Parliamentarians had retaken Barnstaple, who then tried to re-take the fort at Appledore under the command of Colonel John Luttrell from Saunton. Their soldiers sailed down the Taw, moored their boats in Skern Bay, and climbed up the hill to the fort. There was no element of surprise though, and the attack dwindled into an ill-conceived siege. The attacking Parliamentarians found they were now being shot at from within the fort,

and were stranded in enemy territory cut off from any support. All attempts to take the fort were rebuffed. The Cornish miners eventually killed about 120 of the battle-weary troops and routed the remaining ones, driving them back to their boats. It was a fiasco for the Parliamentarians and a victory for the Royalists. Prince Charles visited Appledore the following year, no doubt inspecting his victorious troops here.

It was short-lived though and the fort again changed hands on 20th April 1646, when the Parliamentarians efforts gave them the upper hand and they were able to regain all the strategic points in Devon. The battle was effectively over here and shipping could now come and go more freely, but the conflict took much longer to resolve nationally. Perhaps the greatest thing for which Appledore should be thankful was that disease, which often accompanies warfare, never took hold here.

THE NAPOLEONIC WAR:

During the Napoleonic War with France (1803-1814), the coasts of England were threatened with invasion. Martello Towers were built along the south coast and the old Civil War fort at Appledore was re-fortified. A naval battery consisting of six 18-pound guns was installed here to protect the estuary from enemy ships. The guns had an accurate range of up to a mile but were still felt to be a little

remote from the river, so they were re-sited onto Greysands Hill near to the estuary mouth, a location still known today as 'The Cannons'.

QUEEN BOUDICCA AND THE DANCING GIRLS:

Many village celebrations, fetes and sports days were held in the fields on Staddon Hill. In 1912 Rev. Alfred Green and a committee of other village organisers arranged to hold a Historic Pageant here. The programme of events included a dramatised play 'Britons v. Romans' with George Vaggers as the Roman General, defeating Queen Boudicca, who then poisons herself (after having made a stirring speech). Afterwards there was a second pageant 'Alfred v. Hubba', complete with an epic battle, jesters, and dancing Viking girls. The event ended with polkas and waltzes accompanied by the Appledore Town Band under bandmaster William Parkhouse. All jolly good fun on a summer's afternoon.

AFTER THE PAGEANT there will be

DANCING.

MUSIC SUPPLIED BY THE . .

Appledore Town Band
(Under Bandmaster W. PARKHOUSE).

Programme of Dance Music.

1—POLKA	... ...	" Pretty Polly "
2—WALTZ	... ...	" Evening Echoes "
3—SCHOTTISCHE	... ...	" Merry Molly "
4—TWO STEP ...	... ...	" Red Star "
5—QUADRILLE	... ...	" Piccadilly "
6—WALTZ	... ...	" Beauty's Bower "
7—BARN DANCE	... ...	" Princess "
8—TWO STEP ...	... ...	" Number Two "
9—LANCERS ...	... ...	" Coronation Gems "
10—SCHOTTISCHE	... ...	" Topsy "
11—WALTZ ...	... ...	" Dainty Dolly "
12—QUADRILLE	... ...	" Belgravia "
13—POLKA	... ...	" Rosebud "

"God save the King."

WESTWARD HO!:

From the viewpoint at the end of Staddon Road, we can look across towards the developing resort of Westward Ho! - and that's probably as close as we want to get. If you like Appledore then you're probably not going to like Westward Ho! This town was so named in 1863 by property developers keen to build a fashionable new resort, which extolled the benefits of the healthy wide expanses of the Northam Burrows and the new 'Scotch game of golf'.

However in 1889, a contributor to 'Punch' magazine remarked that the village was:

"...in a poor way, but trying to live up to its reputation. Its houses seemed to have been planned by different architects, each one trying to outdo the other in building something uglier and drearier than the last. When Shakespeare wrote the line "Dreary, flat, stale, and unprofitable" he must have had Westward Ho! in his prophetic eye."

Whether the place has improved in the intervening 120 years I will leave you to judge!

THE BURROWS:

The Northam Burrows are far more interesting, although 650-acres of grazing sheep, salt marsh, and golfers might not immediately seem fascinating. However, this is part of the North Devon UNESCO Biosphere Reserve and a site of Special Scientific Interest. It also contains some significant 2nd World War heritage remains. A two-mile long ridge of pebbles protects the Burrows from the sea, but there are concerns about the long-term ability of this ridge to protect the land behind it. On the Burrows is a visitors' centre with displays and information on the eco-structure of the surrounding area. It can be a deceptively dangerous place though – in 1910 sixteen-year-old Robert Hocking, a bargeman from 40 Market Street, received a cut on his foot from a bulrush and died a few days later from blood poisoning.

The Burrows are first mentioned by name in 1632 by Torrington-born antiquary Tristram Risdon, who describes them *"lying full upon the sea, defended from the rage thereof by a ridge of chesell, where sea-holly groweth plentifully, whose roots are used as a sweetmeat and aphrodisiac."* Obviously he had his priorities right!

The Burrows have always been common land available for the use of the parishioners, mostly because the land was unusable for commercial farming so the Lord-of-the-Manor graciously allowed local people to use the pasture for free. In 1642 these rights were confirmed in a document signed by twelve inhabitants, including Etheldred Darracott and John Beaple. More detailed rights were confirmed by Roger Melhuish in 1716 who listed these in detail, including:

• Anchorage for local vessels was free, although 'foreigners' had to pay for this.

• Running a ferryboat across the Taw and Torridge could be done by anybody, although an annual fee of 2s 6d was payable to the Lord-of-the-Manor.

The Manorial rights have now devolved to the Town Council, but our rights today are enshrined in these historical documents.

Potwalloping on the Burrows in 1910.

Potwallopers:

These rights were known as 'Potwalloper's Rights', the term being taken from an archaic reference to voters in certain Boroughs of England where anyone who could boil (or wallop) a pot (ie, have a hearth, and thereby a fixed home) was entitled to vote. In Northam the term has now evolved to refer to the act of parishioners reinstating the pebble-ridge to protect the common land.

"Many years ago there was a custom instituted called 'Potwalloping', when the householders of Appledore, Northam and Westward Ho! met annually, usually on Whit Monday, to throw back the pebbles that winter storms had displaced. I think the ceremony was held in connection with Northam Revels, and an ox was roasted with everyone receiving a generous share. In 1932 there was a big turn-out of horse-drawn carts, boy scouts, girl guides and unemployed workers. Children filled their model trains and tenders with the scattered pebbles, and tugged them back to the ridge. A selection of refreshments included ham, beef, bread, cheese, cider, beer, tea and biscuits."

(Appledore Boyhood Memories, by E R Carter).

A National curiosity:

In Victorian times the Burrows was recognised as one of England's natural wonders and people came from far and wide, to take in its bracing air. In 1856 five hundred people came by excursion train from Exeter to see its marvels, 'being conveyed from the Station by all possible means of transit'.

In 1850 two thousand people attended an entertainment on the Burrows - a large party dined there in a booth provided by William Bolt from the Royal Hotel in Market Street. There were public games including: donkey racing, jumping in sacks, running for a ram and climbing the greasy pole for a leg of mutton. In the 1880s horse races and polo matches were also held on the Burrows.

Protecting the Burrows:

Traditionally the Burrows often flooded, as salt marshes are supposed to do, however it was felt that if a causeway was constructed across Skern Bay then the Burrows land could be better controlled and used by the villagers. Today we have this causeway - generally known as the 'tip-road' as it led to the Council rubbish tip on Greysands Hill. This embankment was started before the 2nd World War, being built up lorry-load by lorry-load as the waste was deposited here. However, it took until 1977 for the embankment to be completed sufficient to prevent the sea from flooding the area behind. An embankment was proposed as early as 1858, suggesting that a line should be drawn from Badstep to Greysands for this defence. Apart from anything else this would 'create a delightful sea and river-view walk from Appledore', which often seemed to be the Victorians' prime concern.

The Moving Pebble-ridge:

The pebble-ridge is a fascinating natural feature formed from sea-rounded pebbles washed up the coast from Hartland. They provide a barrier to protect the land of the Burrows, but there are always threats that the sea will break through. In 1896 the Burrows was reported to be completely under water as the sea rolled in a great mass of foam over the top of the pebble-ridge, and cattle could be seen walking up to their necks in water.

Nothing can withstand the power of the sea, not even a ridge formed from a million tons of pebbles. It is constantly being pushed backwards, calculated to be at the average rate of three feet per year. This can effectively be demonstrated at low tide, as if you walk directly out from the ridge from Westward Ho!, you will come to the remains of a couple of shipwrecks buried in the sand about 240 yards out. One of these is the 'Sally', dashed against the ridge in 1769, her hulk left embedded in the sand. The sand has held her firmly in place, but today the ridge has moved 240 yards further inland.

Remains of the ketch 'Sally' wrecked on Westward Ho! sands in 1769.

GOLF:

The Burrows is home to the Royal North Devon Golf Club, said by some to be the oldest golf club in England (however, there was a club formed at Blackheath in 1608, and another at Manchester in 1818, but I will let the golfers argue the point on this one!). The Club on the Burrows was formed in 1864 thanks to the vicar of Northam, whose sister married a Major General from St Andrews who introduced him to this 'fine Scotch game'. However, it can claim to be the oldest Links course in England. The first match was played on 10th November 1864, when Lieut. Colonel Hutchinson holed the round in 119 strokes and won the first silver medal. There was also a club for lady members who in 1870 numbered over one hundred, although they had a separate course so as not to mix with the men.

The remains of the Lifeboat house on the Burrows in 1910, next to the 7th green of the golf course.

In 1876 much of the pebble-ridge was reported as being washed away and hundreds of golfers turned up, fearing that it would be the last time they could ever play there because of the certain destruction of the links during the coming winter.

"J. H. Taylor, a local lad, learned his trade here, winning the Open Championship five times and becoming one of the greatest golfers of all time. The sand-hills were a favourite area for rambling and exploring. One evening I was playing there with a cousin. We mislaid an old golf club we had borrowed, and while looking for it, forgot the time, and did not realise it was getting dark. Without warning a thick sea-fog joined the darkness, and we were totally dis-orientated trying to find our way through the bulrushes, ditches and other hazards. We became separated, and I fell into the very muddy drainage stream. At least by following it closely we eventually found the exit gate, where we were met by my super-anxious, distraught mother, accompanied by neighbours and friends armed with torches. One had a megaphone, and I wouldn't have been surprised to see a St. Bernard dog!"

(Appledore Boyhood Memories, by E R Carter).

WATERTOWN, ASSELLS AND DIDDYWELL:

There are three small settlements visible from this viewpoint which occur within the parish of Appledore, so we will give them a mention here…

Watertown is possibly first mentioned in 1334 as being the home of Ralph atte Water, an affectation which may have given the place its name. Later on it was the home of the Melhuish family, before they bought the Lordship-of-the-Manor of Northam in 1692 and moved up the social scale. Thomas and Grace Melhuish owned land here in 1664. In the 1851 census

Watertown consisted of just two basic dwellings.

Assells, at the bottom of Broad Lane, does not appear to have any ancient recorded history, although in 1750 there were two tenements here – Upper Assells and Lower Assells. John Wood bequeathed money from the income of Lower Assells to the school at Northam. In 1851 there were about five dwellings here. The place-name also appears in documents as 'Tasells' or 'Tosells Fields'.

Diddywell is mentioned as far back as 1330, appearing as 'Dodewille' deriving from Dudda's spring or well. The remains of a Manor House are indicated on maps, although this never appears to have been the home of any Lord-of-the-Manor. The Hogg family owned the house in the late 18th century. They were looking to raise their social standing so this could have been their way of appearing as gentry. Much of the Diddywell land and part of Tossels Ground was owned by Thomas Howard Effingham Hogg Dimond, as part of the lands inherited from the Hogg family.

THE GREAT EASTERN:

Brunel's largest and supposedly greatest ship was the Great Eastern, launched in 1859 after five years in construction. She had the capacity to carry 4,000 passengers right around the world without refuelling. She was blighted from the outset by the accidental drowning of her appointed Captain whilst he was trying to reach the great ship in a small boat. Further

deaths occurred on board due to an explosion during sea-trials, and the ship was believed to be cursed. Indeed she was probably responsible for sending Brunel to an early grave at the age of 53.

I mention this ship here because the Captain subsequently appointed to take care of the ship on her maiden voyage was James Bowen, who lived at Diddywell. He was a former captain and marine surveyor who had retired to part of Diddywell Farm. He was obviously still highly thought of, but was forced to decline the position on health grounds and so the honour went to someone else. On the Great Eastern's maiden voyage she carried just thirty-five passengers, was never a success, and was converted for cable-laying just four years later. When she was sold for scrap in 1888 it took eighteen months to take her apart.

CHURCHILL WAY:

If we take an imaginary walk towards Northam, there are a couple of items worthy of mention in that direction:

At the end of Staddon Road we join Churchill Way, re-named from 'Appledore Road' when the road was upgraded here in the 1960s. Its name was changed after the death of Sir Winston Churchill, who incidentally was once rumoured to have stayed at Knapp House. The houses on Richmond Green were built in 1964.

Down Churchill Way on the left at Marshford, lies the hallowed turf of Appledore Football Club. There has been a Football Club in Appledore since at least 1892, but the land here was given for the use of the club in 1946. In 1977 it was the arrival point for Appledore's first Royal visitor since the Civil War. Prince Charles landed here in his helicopter, when he came for a ship-naming ceremony at Appledore Shipbuilders. He was launching the 'Scillonian III' - the ferry that currently serves the Scilly Isles.

Richmond House in the original design built by William Yeo. The façade is twice as wide now – it was extended by Denys Scott in the early 1900s.

Appledore has only had two Royal visitors, and both have been Prince Charles and heirs to the throne. The first was in 1645 during the Civil War and the second was in May 1977 when under happier circumstances the Prince of Wales arrived for a naming ceremony at Appledore Shipbuilders. Here he is meeting Joe Need, the Mayor of Northam. Local M.P. Jeremy Thorpe is on the right. (Western Morning News).

THE POOR HOUSE:

Further down the road at the 'Marshford Crossroads' lies a large building that was formerly used as the parish Poor House. It was sited mid-way between Appledore and Northam, indeed this cross-roads now marks the boundary between the two parishes. The building is shown on Donn's map of 1765, and was run by the Northam Parish Overseers for the old and infirm of the village. The parish burials record eighty deaths of inmates in the Poor House between 1813 and 1837, almost all of them elderly.

THE WINDMILL:

Just past the crossroads, on the top of the hill stood a large brick windmill (see Book 1, page 133), now vanished apart from its stone base. It was built in 1803 including an adjoining house for the miller, but replaced an earlier mill on the same site – land tax was being paid on this in 1777. A description of the mill in 1805 said that it was well built, and with a brisk wind its two-pairs of mill-stones could grind twelve bushels of corn an hour. However, the wind proved too much for this prominent tower, and in the early 1900s parts were unsafe and taken down, and a storm in 1920 finished the process. We will see what happened to the bricks from this structure a little later.

LOOKOUT COTTAGE:

At the top of Lookout Lane stands Lookout Cottage, originally built as two small cottages. They were constructed around 1847, and were first occupied by ship's carpenter John Ashton and his wife Jane who lived here for the next thirty years. It has probably the best view in Appledore, but also the most exposed. Indeed

when built, it would also have been rather remote standing on its own, a quarter of a mile from any other dwelling.

Go through the stile at the top of the lane and stop to admire the view from the field, although it's such a stunning view, it would be difficult to ignore it.

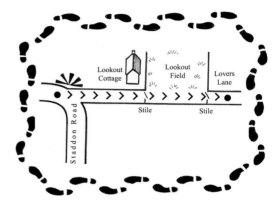

TURN RIGHT UP LOOKOUT LANE AND GO ACROSS THE FIELD

LOOKOUT FIELD:

Between 1947 and 1970 this field was used for the annual Appledore School Sports Day, after which the school got its own playing fields. The running and other races were keenly contested, so participants probably didn't get much time to admire the view.

Earlier celebrations were held in this field as illustrated in the following description of a harvest festival thanksgiving, when the whole village congregated here:

"There are few views to equal the one from Look-Out Field. It would be hard to find a more blustery one, no trees, just a thicket hedge grew

along its sides, and even this had bent to the prevailing south-west gales, only its thinness saving it from disintegrating altogether. On such a day as this the womenfolk sat and chatted of this and that, while the men in a separate group did the same. The young folk sported the field. The boys seemed to delight in chasing the maidens downhill, and laughed as they puffed their way back.

(Queen of the Estuary, by Harry C Finn).

APPLEDORE.

A

FETE & SPORTS

Under distinguished patronage will be held on

BANK - HOLIDAY, AUG. 3rd,

In STADDON CORONATION FIELD

(By kind permission of J. L. Round, Esq.), from 2-30 to 9 p m. Proceeds in aid of the Lads' Naval Brigade.

(Bideford Gazette: 30th June 1914).

As we wander across the field, we can take in a bit more history of the estuary itself. From here we can clearly see the river mouth and the Braunton Burrows on the other side of the river.

BIDEFORD BAR:

Across the mouth of the estuary lies a submerged sand bar. Like the pebble-ridge it consists of material washed up from further down the coast. In the 16th and 17th centuries Appledore was probably much easier for a ship to get into. Admiralty charts have shown that the Bar has shallowed by about 2 metres since 1855, and each year about 750,000 tons of new material is deposited here. In the 1540s the antiquary John Leland travelled down the Taw landing at Appledore on his journey down into Cornwall. He wrote that *"The haven entery is barrid with sande, and the enterie into it is dangerous".*

Imagine the view from here in 1588 though, when five ships from the Torridge sailed to join Francis Drake at Plymouth in the famous battle with the Spanish Armada.

"The view from my window is never the same. I look out on to Baggy Point, and find it different yet again, red-brown today, and sombre. Sometimes I wake up and feel there is something unusual; then I realise what it is – the silence. Most of the time, the sea maintains an uproar that I take for granted until there is a sudden calm. Today there is the stillness after the storm, and I am conscious of the lack of noise."

(A Window on the Sea, by Daniel Farson).

THE WIDOWMAKER:

It was said that Appledore had more widows per head of inhabitants than any other town in England. This coast has always been a danger for shipping. Even in good visibility there are few harbours in North Devon to shelter when the weather catches you unaware. Shipwrecks here can be counted in their hundreds and the loss of life in its thousands - it would take a huge book just to mention all the ones that are known about. A brief tribute can only be paid here to some of the unfortunate sailors whose lives have been lost within a couple of miles of this point.

The Parish burial registers record many untimely entries, such as these:

- *6th February 1838 - A drowned man, name unknown; and a further six drowned men.*
- *2nd November 1807 - Five French men who were drowned near Braunton Burrows, names unknown; and one English man drowned with the above, name unknown.*

SHIPWRECKS:

The earliest recorded wreck in the vicinity dates back to the time of Harold Godwinson - potential King of England in 1066. His mother Gytha founded the church of Stoke St Nectan at Hartland, because she believed this saint was responsible for saving her husband Godwin when his ship was wrecked on the coast here. The first recorded vessel to be wrecked approaching the river was driven ashore at Appledore in 1627. The ship was of English origin, but both it and the crew had been captured by the Spanish six months previously before they had made their escape and were able to get back to England. Whether they survived the wreck is unknown.

In 1669 a ship was wrecked on the bar loaded with muskets and ammunition destined for Charles II's army in Ireland. There was considerable trade with Ireland at this time – a 1682 Irish halfpenny was recently found near the path at the bottom of the hill here.

In 1770 the ship 'Juba' was wrecked on the Bar. It broke up and all the crew were drowned. All that was rescued was a cask of palm oil and a few elephant's tusks. In fact elephant's tusks turned up among the sand dunes after heavy storms for many years afterwards.

Wrecks in the 1800s are more frequently mentioned, made even more poignant with newspaper reports of bereaved families and bodies being recovered.

1682 Irish halfpenny found at the bottom of Lovers Lane.

North Devon Journal 1827: *"The town has recently been visited by the afflictive hand of Divine Providence, by shipwreck and other accidents on the water, several families have been reduced to great distress. Not less than seven widows and upwards of forty children have within a very few weeks been deprived of their husbands and fathers."*

North Devon Gazette 1859: *"During a terrible storm, five or six vessels foundered with great loss between Morte Point and Baggy Point, including vessels driven ashore at Appledore. Northam Burrows was strewn with wreckage, and nine bodies were washed up and buried in Northam Churchyard."*

To reduce the risk of shipwreck, in 1820 two lighthouses were built on the other side of the estuary at Braunton Burrows. There was a lower light near to the water, and a higher light some seventy feet above this. If the lights were aligned vertically you knew that you were in a safe channel to enter the estuary. These lights were removed in 1957 and the lighthouse demolished. Also installed in the estuary in 1820 were two navigation buoys which served the same purpose as the lighthouse during daylight hours.

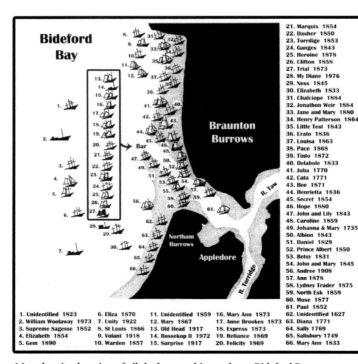

Bideford Bay

21. Marquis 1854
22. Dasher 1850
23. Torrdige 1853
24. Ganges 1843
25. Heroine 1878
26. Clifton 1858
27. Trial 1873
28. My Diane 1976
29. Ness 1845
30. Elizabeth 1833
31. Chalciope 1884
32. Jonathon Weir 1884
33. Jane and Mary 1880
34. Henry Patterson 1864
35. Little Test 1843
36. Erato 1836
37. Louisa 1863
38. Pace 1868
39. Tinto 1872
40. Delabole 1833
41. Juba 1770
42. Cata 1771
43. Bee 1871
44. Henrietta 1836
45. Secret 1854
46. Hope 1880
47. John and Lily 1843
48. Caroline 1859
49. Johanna & Mary 1735
50. Albion 1843
51. Daniel 1829
52. Prince Albert 1850
53. Betsy 1831
54. John and Mary 1845
55. Andree 1908
56. Ann 1878
58. Lydney Trader 1875
59. North Esk 1859
60. Muse 1877
61. Paul 1852
62. Unidentified 1627
63. Diana 1771
64. Sally 1769
65. Salisbury 1749
66. Mary Ann 1833

Braunton Burrows

Northam Burrows

Appledore

R. Taw

R. Torridge

1. Unidentified 1823
2. William Woolaway 1973
3. Supreme Sagesse 1852
4. Elizabeth 1854
5. Gem 1890
6. Eliza 1870
7. Unity 1922
8. St Louis 1866
9. Volant 1918
10. Warden 1857
11. Unidentified 1859
12. Mary 1867
13. Old Head 1917
14. Rossekop II 1972
15. Surprise 1917
16. Mary Ann 1873
17. Anne Brookes 1873
18. Express 1873
19. Reliance 1869
20. Felicity 1869

Map showing location of all the known shipwrecks on Bideford Bar.

"With a 12-foot diameter lantern, this was reputed to be the last timber-built lighthouse in the British Isles. Illumination was supplied by an acetylene mantle burner, giving a five-second light and a five second eclipse. Near the lighthouse was another unusual timber object - a large ball (about ten feet in diameter) made of wooden slats painted red. It was raised and lowered regularly on a pole about 30 feet tall by means of a winch, manned by the lighthouse keeper. The object of this exercise was to indicate the state of the tides to ships in the bay; being raised to the top when the river was at half flood; then lowered when it was half ebb. After dark a white light indicated the former state and a red light the latter."
(Appledore Boyhood Memories, by E R Carter).

Sea Chart from 1855, indicating the meaning of the lights and tide-indicators on Braunton Burrows. (UK Hydrographic Office).

THE MAID OF SKER:

The Braunton Burrows feature in R.D. Blackmore's novel 'The Maid of Sker' written in 1872. More famed for his novel 'Lorna Doone', the 'Maid of Sker' is set in 1782 and concerns the missing daughter of a Devon family, who was found washed up on the Welsh coast in a small boat belonging to the ship 'Wild Duck' of Appledore. There are tales of dead bodies being buried on the Burrows, an evil local Parson and a cult of naked savages. All total fiction of course!

In 1945 Alexander Korda used Saunton Sands for the desert scenes in his classic film of 'Caesar and Cleopatra'. The film starred Vivian Leigh, Claude Rains, Stewart Grainger and Flora Robson. The spectacular Technicolor epic was, at the time, the most expensive film ever produced and the sight of an army of Egyptian horsemen galloping along the sands must have been quite stunning.

The Braunton high light, built 1820 and demolished in 1957. The lighthouse-keeper's accommodation was built around the base of the tower.

Although only a few hundred yards from Appledore, Crow Point and the Braunton Burrows are just about as remote as you can get if you are travelling over land. It was for this reason that an isolation hospital was proposed here after cases of smallpox were reported in Appledore in 1871. Outbreaks of Typhoid fever, Scarlet fever and Diphtheria were also reported in 1897. Eventually a 'fever hulk' was moored off Crow Point, the nursing staff being transported there by the Appledore-Braunton ferry.

A silent film of Kingsley's 'Westward Ho!' was filmed on location here in 1919. Sadly all that now appears to have survived of this 6-reel spectacular is this still-picture from the movie (Bioscope Magazine 1919).

FISH TRAPS:

You might think that the only way for our ancestors to catch fish was to go out in a boat with a line or net and hope for good luck. No, they were much smarter people than that, they let the fish come to them. It demanded considerable constructional effort, but from prehistoric times, the building of fish traps were a sure way of getting a regular supply of fish and with no risk.

They consisted of wattle or timber V-shaped structures, behind which the fish would be trapped when the tide went out – they were crude but efficient. There were many of these in the Taw and Torridge including about four on the beach near Crow Point. They were not small structures – Bellamy's Weir was stated to be almost a mile long and twelve feet high at the apex, so it must have been quite a landmark from Appledore.

Evidence suggests that such traps were in use as far back as 867 when Aethelbald King of Wessex, gave ten hides of land at Braunton (that's about 300 acres) to be used to supply fresh fish for his estate.

However, these structures were obviously dangerous to shipping and mariners argued that they had a difficult enough job navigating large ships through the estuary, without huge timber uprights projecting into the river. Some Appledore sailors even took to cutting down some of the timbers. The matter was eventually resolved in 1851 when the production of a detailed chart showed the offending weirs, and sailors then had no excuse for not knowing

their location. It is from these charts that we have been able to identify the location of these lost weirs.

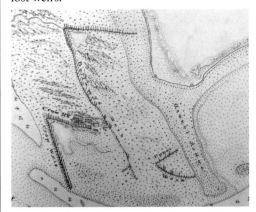

1851 chart showing location of the Torridge Fish weirs. (UK Hydrographic Office).

A DISASTER OF EPIC PROPORTIONS:

If you had been standing on this hill on 20th January 1607 you would have been witness to a catastrophe, the effects of which were remembered in Appledore for generations afterwards but which have only recently been rediscovered through historical detective work.

It was 8:50am on a Tuesday morning. The village was just waking up on a winter's morning, the two separate settlements of Irsha and Appledore clustering along the shoreline and yet also trying to shield themselves from the elements. Many of these poor houses were home to sailors who thought themselves lucky to have somewhere dry to sleep. The houses were strong enough to stand up to winter storms, but many were not strong enough to survive what was coming, and in ten minutes time they would be swamped by an onslaught from the sea. Unknown to the village a relentless tidal wave was already advancing up the Bristol Channel. Thought to have been created by an underwater earthquake somewhere between Cornwall and Ireland, an up-thrust of the seabed caused the displacement of a huge body of water. This large chunk of sea gathered inertia, turned into an unstoppable wall of water, and rolled up the coast of Cornwall and Devon gaining height as the land forced it back on itself. The tall North Devon cliffs hardly noticed as the extra-large wave rolled along them, but the wave was now approaching the low-lying land in Bideford Bay and the settlements along the river banks. A tsunami was coming, and there was nothing that anyone could do about it.

The wave entered the estuary with a height of about four metres, but further up the Bristol Channel the narrowing effect of the coastline pushed the wave to at least twice this height. It crashed over the pebble-ridge completely covering the Burrows - any livestock here would not have stood a chance. The Irsha Street houses were hit face-on, swamping and demolishing many of these properties. All fences and walls facing the water were washed away, and any timbers and other materials lying in shipbuilding yards were taken away by the water. A sixty-ton fully laden ship was picked up and deposited on dry land, beyond hope of retrieval. Around the corner the buildings in the area of Appledore quay probably survived better as the wave swept side-on up the river, but the destruction of property must still have been catastrophic for anyone living in the lower part of the village.

By the time the wave reached Barnstaple much of its power has

dissipated along the soft banks, but the wave still brought immense chaos to the town. The waters came half-way up the houses in the main street and went right over the top of Pilton Bridge. We have reports from credible witnesses in the town:

Adam Wyot, the Town Clerk, wrote that this was a flood the like of which was never seen before in the Town. The waters came into all the houses and cellars near the quay, burst open locked doors, demolished the walls of houses, and destroyed many thousands of pounds worth of salt, sugar, oats, fish, spices, wines and other commodities stored there.

Robert Langdon, the Parish Clerk, reported the death of James Frost and his two daughters Sabine and Catherine, who were lying in bed when the walls and roof of their house collapsed in on them. Other nearby houses close to the castle were also destroyed.

Another gentleman wrote an account the following day: "*All the houses standing upon the Key and neere to the Waterside, are quite covered over with the flood. Barges like water-coaches, are brought up into the streetes, and to mens doores, yea great barques sayle up and down amongst the houses. The lamentable shriekes of women, the cryes of poore children, the astonishment and wild lookes of all men, at the suddaine allarum given by this deluge, no man can truly expresse.*"

Contemporary wood-cut showing the flooded villages, and the desperate men and cattle.

Further afield it was reported that Burnham-on-Sea was destroyed, as was part of Lynmouth, where the deluge caused the river to change its course. Many settlements on the Somerset Levels were also consumed with the loss of an unknown number of lives.

RECONSTRUCTION:

There are no accounts concerning the aftermath in Appledore, although the Instow Manor Records report that a new stone quay was being built there in 1609 so this can hardly be a coincidence, and it probably replaced an earlier quay damaged or destroyed by the 1607 wave. In 1630 the Devon antiquarian Thomas Westcote crossed the river from Instow and reported that Appledore had within a generation turned from a backwater into a growing, thriving port. Could this refer to the reconstruction over the previous twenty years? For a long time afterwards there must have been strong reluctance to rebuild on land where houses had been destroyed, which explains why there are few properties in Irsha Street dating back more than 300 years. Truly it must have been a momentous disaster which stayed in the folk-memory of the people here for many generations.

LOVERS LANE:

The footpath leading from this field down to West Appledore is known as 'Lovers Lane'. This route is an ancient trackway dating back to prehistoric times when the first trading routes were being established across England. A saltern way (ie: a trade route for that precious commodity - salt) ran across the Braunton Burrows and ended near a small stone Chapel hidden in the sand dunes where travellers could stop and pray for a safe river crossing. On the Appledore side of the river the path led up and over the hill in a straight line towards Northam and onwards down into Cornwall. River crossings could safely be made by ferry at high tide when the currents were weak, but there was also believed to be a rough stone causeway leading out towards the sprat ridge in the centre of the river which could have assisted crossings at low-tide.

In 1911 farmer Oliver Heywood who owned this land suggested that Lovers Lane should be widened into a roadway to provide a proper route into West Appledore. He offered some of his land for this purpose but thankfully this didn't happen and we still have part of the original lane, a remnant of this ancient track.

"I was playing in the street with my cousin when we heard the lifeboat rocket, and he suggested a short cut up the hill and down Lovers Lane. After a wet period this lane was very muddy and very rough with odd stones and exposed tree roots. Of course I tripped over one of the hazards and by the time I had extricated myself from the mud, the lifeboat was down the slip-way and heading for the Bar. Being a Sunday I was wearing my best 'go-to-Chapel' clothes, so you can imagine the reception my mud-plastered outfit received at home. About ten years ago the local paper reported that on several nights a peculiar apparition which looked like a white object had been seen floating down Lovers Lane. I did not have the courage to write to the editor suggesting it was the ghost of my white shirt, before it had kissed the mud."

(*Appledore Boyhood Memories, by E R Carter*).

THE MOUNT:

We pass by 'The Mount', a drab Council housing estate from the late 1960s – not a good period for classic architecture! It was named after Mount Field upon which it was supposedly built, although actually it was built on 'Higher Style Field' and 'Barn Close'. Mount Field is where the Civil War Fort remains are and survives undeveloped. At the bottom of Lovers Lane is the much better Western Avenue development built around 1955.

TIN TOWN:

Western Avenue was built on the site of H.M.S. Appledore - a 2nd World War camp consisting of about twenty Nissan huts set up in 1943 which came to be known locally as 'Tin Town'. H.M.S. Appledore was the name for the whole of the training and operations area in the Taw and Torridge estuaries, including the land-based camps and administration centres. It held a significant role during the War; not only was H.M.S. Appledore tasked to patrol the estuary against possible enemy invasion, but also to provide training for secret missions and the development of potential weaponry that could be used on these missions.

APPLEDORE AT WAR:

The threat of German invasion brought the Royal Navy to Appledore in June 1940 and the place became a base for the operation of coastal craft. The flotillas operating in the Bristol Channel had many Motor-Torpedo-Boats and Motor-Launches needing to be serviced, repaired, and replenished. The sheltered area of the river Torridge and its shipyards were found to be ideal for this, and the river was literally buzzing with activity.

The old Naval Battery just past the Lifeboat House – which we will visit shortly – was taken over as the head-quarters of the military base in Appledore under the supervision of Harold Franklin. He was a retired Rear Admiral from Northam who returned to active duty with the rank of Captain, although everyone still called him 'Admiral'. Tin Town was set up to house special troops. Elsewhere in Appledore the Quay was requisitioned from the slipway to the steps and a wire enclosure put up to restrict public access. Many buildings were also requisitioned: the Seagate Hotel was filled with Landing-Craft crews, the present Library became the Harbour Office, and the Co-op (then Bearas) had a Mess room and Galley on the upper floors for Navy Officers. The vicarage was vacated and filled with serving Wrens. Private houses were filled with other visiting personnel, as well as refugees from London. Appledore was full to the brim and it had a job to do...

Frogmen training at Badstep in 1944.

FROGMEN:

Over a three-year period H.M.S. Appledore was a training area and experimental ground for all types of amphibious warfare, and many new techniques were developed here. The 'Landing Craft and Obstruction Clearing Units' trained men in underwater techniques needed to prepare the route for a sea-borne invasion force landing on a mined enemy beach. Wearing shiny wetsuits with large fins they looked very strange and became known as 'frogmen' - a name that was possibly even invented in Appledore. Their job would be to blow up any enemy mines placed to prevent allied craft

Ships weren't the only things wrecked here. This whale was washed up on the pebble ridge in 1921. The man sitting on it is Clarence Smale, rumoured to be the last paid hangman in England - although this just appears to be a story told to frighten the children. The whale's jaw-bone was later erected as an archway over a path at Kipling Tours.

Aerial view of the huts at 'Tin Town' erected at West Appledore during the 2nd World War. The houses of Greysand Crescent (built 1935) are on the other side of the road. Further down on Western Hill, two gun emplacements can be seen. (National Monuments Record Centre).

from getting too close in to the shore, so underwater explosions were often heard in the vicinity. The chief frogman was Harold Hargreaves, although there were about ten others, including Rene Le-Roy who formed a life-long bond with Appledore that continued until his death in 2001. They trained from the slipway at Badstep and also in Ilfracombe Baths.

Many weird and ingenious inventions were tried out on the sands at low water, some of which were more lethal to the users than the enemy: flailing rotating chains to set off mines in advance of a vehicle, amphibious flame-throwers, but worst of all was the 'Great Panjandrum'.

THE GREAT PANJANDRUM:

This was basically a huge rocket-powered Catherine Wheel, about ten feet in diameter. It was supposed to be set going from within a landing craft, make its unstoppable way up the beach scattering the enemy in disbelief, and with its 4,000 lbs of high explosives blow a tank-sized hole in the concrete sea-wall. It sounded credible, provided that it would work.

It looked promising but when tested it hit some bumps in the sand, a steering cable snapped, and it lurched towards the dignitaries who were eagerly watching the test. Finally it fell on its side and some of the rockets came off, flying wildly in all directions. Later in London the boffins who came up with this idea quietly filed it away in a filing cabinet, and it was never tried again.

The remains of some of the old wartime structures can still be seen on the Burrows. Air-raid shelters, radar bunkers, huge radio masts, and concrete 'dragons teeth' intended to slow the progress of any invading enemy were all constructed here. In 1943 and 1944 the Americans transformed the Burrows into a centre for Assault Training in preparation for D-Day.

The radio masts erected on the Burrows by the Americans during the 2nd World War.

Appledore was largely spared the friendly invasion of Americans during the war, even though three United States Divisions undertook assault course training in the river and on the Burrows, plus 3,500 United States boatmen and 500 demolition experts. They were here from October 1943 and were based on the other side of the river. Then suddenly in June 1944 they all disappeared – their crucial secret training was over and they all left on their mission to retake France with an invasion on the beaches of Normandy – D-Day.

H.M.S. Appledore still exists as part of the present military facility at Fremington Camp, but its mission in Appledore was terminated on 18th September 1947 when at sunset the White Ensign was lowered from the flagpole for the last time. It was saluted by the guard of Marines and the Last Post was played on the bugle. Prayers were said and the colours were presented to St Mary's Church where they still hang to this day, reminding us of Appledore's role in the war and the sacrifice made by so many of its families.

The lethal flailing chains of a prototype mine-clearing vehicle being tested on Westward Ho! sands as part of the lead-up to D-Day. (North Devon Museum Trust Collection).

The even-more lethal explosive 'panjandrum' awaiting unloading and testing. Its trial at Appledore caused more panic amongst the testers than any potential enemy, and the idea was quickly dropped.
(North Devon Museum Trust Collection)

The Appledore Home Guard formed in 1940.
Back row: Billy Hare, John Bowden, John Smale, Philip Labbett, Cyril Cork, Edwin Cawsey, Billy Short,
Edwin Harding, Billy Richards, Mervyn Harris, Stanley Jewell.
Middle row: Len Ford, John Cole, Richard Taylor, Bobby Richards, John Long, Fred Bennett, [unknown],
Arthur Brennan, Albert Cawsey, [unknown], [unknown], William Labbett, Frank Curtis, Jack White,
Jimmy Screech, Fred Beer, Ronald Evans.
Front row: Walter Hocking, Len Taylor, [unknown], Mr Penny, Bert Bennett, Arthur ~?~, Dennis Scott,
Mac Austin, Redvers Labbett, ~?~ Labbett, Tom Parsons, Daniel Fowler.
Seated in front: Bert Cooksley, Leslie Harris, Billy Harris. Robert Richards, Ronald Lamey, Stanley Shute.

"Today, officers and men of the Royal Navy and Royal Marines unite to give Appledore flags not only in
remembrance of the toil, but also in honour of those from Appledore who gave their lives in the 2nd World War.
We hand them to you with our goodwill for perpetual remembrance sake and for the ennoblement and
prosperity of our Country." (Framed text in St Mary's Church).

After the war the huts at Tin Town were used as temporary Council housing for about six years, before being replaced by the 1950s houses which exist today. Some Appledore residents still remember being housed in these huts but were not sorry to see them go, along with the cockroaches and mice with which they shared their accommodation.

The Littlejohn family standing outside their new home at Tin Town in 1945.

THE LINES:

At the bottom of Lovers Lane we cross over Torridge Road. Older Appledore residents still refer to this as 'The Lines' because the road follows the route of the single-track railway line that ran from Appledore to Westward Ho! There was a small station halt at the junction here - the only facility being a platform raised about one-foot above the track level. The next station halt was just 500 yards away at Watertown – this was not a train that got up much speed in between. Prior to the railway there was just a rough footpath between the fields and the cliff, but any wheeled carts had to use a rough track along the beach. The railway track was removed after the 1st World War and the route formed into a road in 1935.

On our left is the modern housing development of Pollywell. This field contained a reliable well of water that had served West Appledore and Watertown since at least the 1700s. The well was thirty to forty feet deep,

but was capped off in 1918 and a pipe taken from it to serve a nearby water-trough. The well is now covered by number 12, although the house is called 'Well House' and has a dummy well built in the front garden.

On the opposite side of the road stand the houses of Greysand Crescent built in 1935 from the distinctive cream-coloured bricks from Petersmarland near Torrington.

JUBILEE ROAD:

Jubilee Road was built at the same time as Torridge Road on the line of a former cart-track, and was named in honour of the Silver Jubilee of George V. The land on the seaward side was known as 'Soldier's Field' - recalling the military use of this land for estuary defences here. After the 2nd World War it became a football pitch and playing fields, and in the mid-1950s a putting green created by Sammy Guard and Reg Gale.

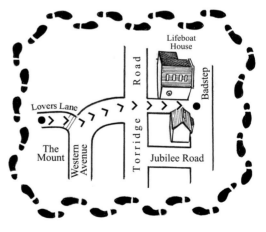

FROM LOVERS LANE CROSS TORRIDGE ROAD AND GO DOWN THE FOOTPATH OPPOSITE

BADSTEP:

The road here originally led down to the beach, and the ancient river crossing point to Braunton. A rough track also led round the foreshore towards Westward Ho! Known as 'Badstep', the name is probably just a contraction of 'Appledore Steps'. This does however suggest a time when there were steps leading down to a ferry. It has been used as a launching area for Customs boats and Lifeboats since the 1820s, the present slipway being built across the rocky shore in 1889 and extended in 1909.

Next to the slipway is a small pool of water which never dries up. This is not unusual in a place where the tide comes in twice a day, but this is fresh water fed from an underground spring.

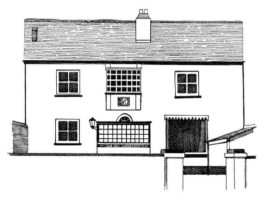

CUSTOMS HOUSE:

Facing out to sea is the Old Customs House. Built in the 1820s, it was then known as the King's Watch House and was a base from which Custom's Officers could keep an eye on vessels coming in and out of the estuary. The main business of Customs took place at Bideford - this was just a conveniently-placed outpost which functioned here until about 1900.

The battlemented walls represent the only defence that the estuary had in 1860, when the early Royal Naval reserves were stationed here, even though the men only had hand-held guns for protection.

The large window on the right-hand side of the frontage was originally a boathouse, into which the Custom's boat was taken when not in use. It was launched down a steep slipway (now vanished) immediately opposite this window. In 1829 the first Appledore lifeboat was stored here, it being found that she could launch much quicker from this location than the barn further up the road in which she was usually kept. The cockerel plaque on the front was probably brought back from someone's travels to Portugal where this is a sign of welcome.

Opposite the Customs House is a small rocky promontory with battlemented stone walls, suggesting that defensive cannon were once sited here. Within this a boathouse built during the 2nd World War housed a large searchlight and generator designed to sweep the estuary for enemy boats. There was another searchlight-post further along the road at the back of number 59 Irsha Street.

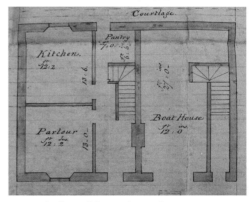

Originals plans of the King's Watch Customs House (North Devon Record Office).

CHOLERA:

The duties of a Customs Officer are often dangerous, but in August 1866, 30-year-old officer Anthony Oatway probably didn't see this one coming…

It was a hot Sunday morning and he was on duty checking a vessel recently arrived from across the Bristol Channel. He boarded the ship and was offered a drink of water by the crew. What he didn't know was that there had been an outbreak of cholera in Wales and the water was infected. He later experienced vomiting and diarrhoea – ten hours later he was dead. Others were infected too, and there was concern that in the densely-populated and badly-drained houses of Irsha Street this could turn into an epidemic. Oatway's death was closely followed by two neighbours, and also Oatway's adopted daughter who first felt the symptoms coming back from his funeral - she too was dead within two days.

Over the next two weeks there were nine deaths from cholera, including 17-year-old Elizabeth Curtis from Irsha Street and Sarah Bynon from Meeting Street. The worst tragedy fell on Thomas and Ann Richards from Vernons Lane who lost four of their children (Ann 14, William 8, Philip 7 and Evan 3). Thomas Richards returned home from sea to find his house empty and his wife and two remaining children moved to a temporary structure in a remote field overlooking Watertown.

Tar barrels were burnt in the streets, disinfectants were used liberally all over the village and prayers were said in the Chapels. Many more people caught the disease but survived, and after a month it was all over. The last man to succumb was Humphrey England from One-End Street who took it with him on board ship to Marseilles where he died, the news of his death reaching Appledore two weeks later.

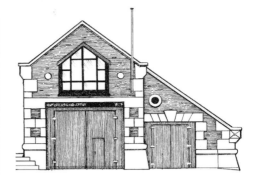

LIFEBOAT HOUSE:

At the top of the Badstep slip stands Appledore's well-designed Lifeboat house which opened in 2000 on the site of a previous boathouse built in 1889. Inside you will find displays listing rescues carried out since a formal rescue service was established here in 1825. Today it houses the inshore lifeboat and Appledore crew headquarters – the main lifeboat being permanently moored in the estuary channel.

There have been a number of lifeboat-houses around the estuary:

After the 1st lifeboat was temporarily housed in the Customs Watch-house, a permanent home was sought. In 1831 it was agreed to build a stone boathouse at Watertown with the boat being kept on a four-wheeled carriage, enabling it to be quickly taken to the water by a team of horses.

A 2nd lifeboat house was built on the Northam Burrows in 1852 to permit a lifeboat to reach vessels beyond the Bar more quickly. This closed in 1897 and the building was demolished in 1913. A pole with a cross on top was erected in its place to act as a mark for sailors. The horses which were used to launch these boats were kept in a field on the Burrows, and when they heard the lifeboat rockets they

The lifeboat house and Badstep slipway. The rough track led from here across the beach to Watertown and Westward Ho! The house in the distance was formerly used by the RNLI as a boathouse and stables.

would jump the fences and get to the boathouse before the crew. When not on the Burrows the horses were stabled in the house at the bottom of Jubilee Road, now called the 'Old Coastguards House'.

A 3rd lifeboat house was operated from the Braunton Burrows between 1857 and 1919.

After the 1st World War, all the lifeboat houses were forced to close due to a lack of both able-bodied men and horses.

The Badstep Lifeboat-house was built in 1889 on land given by local historian and landowner Charles Chappell.
"The lifeboat 'Jane Hannah McDonald' was pulled into Appledore to her new home, placed on a carriage, and a team of horses, men and boys hauled her up to her new locality amid cheers for the life-boat, the Institution, and the local Committee. Seeing Mr Charles Chappell, the donor of the freehold upon which the new lifeboat-house is built, coming along the beach, the men ran to him, shouldered him, and with rounds of cheers carried him to the boat."
(Bideford Gazette: 21st Dec 1889).

A lifelong bachelor, when Mr Chappell died three years later his coffin was carried by members of the lifeboat crew.

R.N.L.I.:

The history of saving lives at sea goes back many centuries. The first organisation formed for this purpose was established by the Bishop of Durham in 1721, when men on horseback were employed to survey the coast of Northumberland in bad weather and raise the alarm if any boat was seen to be in distress.

Before lifeboats rescue work was done by pilot-gigs. Appledore had two well-known six-oared gigs, the 'Siren' owned by the Evans family, and the 'Volunteer' owned by the Hockings. John Sanders had an eight-oared gig called 'Preserver', however an Act of Parliament in 1812 made it illegal for any private boat to have more than six oars (to limit the speed of

boats in order to clamp down on smuggling). From 1815 Appledore had a portable 'Manby Mortar Apparatus' which enabled a line to be fired at a ship in distress, but there was no national organisation for undertaking rescue at sea.

Owners of pilot gigs undertook rescues when necessary, and in 1824 Appledore pilots were awarded £20 (about £1,500 today) by the Magistrates for bringing a Brig safely into port. It was also dangerous - for which there was no compensation. Earlier the same year a pilot-gig overturned and Michael Johns was drowned along with two others. His body was not recovered until six-months later, and sadly left a wife with six children.

A launch of the Appledore lifeboat in the 1870s.

By 1824 various boats were stationed around the coast of Britain but not controlled by any overall body. The Lifeboat Institution was formed in this year which later became the Royal National Lifeboat Institution. It is still totally funded by charitable giving, no grants or funds are received from government, so please give it your support and of course your money. It is an Institution of which we should all be proud. In early Victorian times a French vessel was wrecked on the south coast. Upon being asked how he knew that this was England, the Captain allegedly replied *"Sacred Pig of Heaven (or the French equivalent), I knew it was England by the way the lifeboats came out for us"*.

Anyway, appeal over - on with the history…

The horse-drawn procession taking the new lifeboat 'Jane Hannah McDonald'
from Bideford Station to Appledore in 1910.
The arrival of a new lifeboat was always a cause for great celebration.

A self-righting test carried out on the 'Robert and Catherine III' in the New Quay Dry-Dock in 1911. She was the
last oar-driven lifeboat used at Appledore before motors were fitted. Miss Leicester of Bayswater presented three
lifeboats to Appledore, all called the Robert and Catherine.

LIFEBOATS:

Appledore's first lifeboat arrived on 28th Feb 1825. Called the 'Volunteer' she was eighteen-feet long, weighed about one ton, and was pulled by four oarsmen. She was transported on a wheeled carriage by a team of horses, and could be launched from various points on the Northam Burrows. She could hold up to twelve people and had an air-tube on each side for buoyancy. Built for safety not speed, she was lined with cork. She saved a total of 85 lives during her thirty years of service.

Since the 'Volunteer' Appledore has had many boats, given and named by various benefactors. The 'Hope' given in 1862 by Mrs Ellen Hope had a service-record second only to that of 'Volunteer', saving 59 people between 1866 and 1882. The arrival of each boat was the cause of pride and a grand celebration in the neighbourhood. In 1870 the 'Mary Ann' arrived by train at Bideford Station, where she was conveyed to Appledore by a team of six fine horses. Flying Union Jacks and manned by the lifeboat crew wearing cork jackets, red caps, and medals, she took two hours to make the journey watched by thousands of people. William Yeo who contributed £100 towards the new boat was present at the launch. In 1922 the first motor-lifeboat arrived, however since 1938 the lifeboats became too large to fit in a boathouse and have since been moored in the river.

RESCUES:

Much has been written about Appledore's lifeboats and rescues and I cannot compete with previous histories on this subject. Grahame Farr's book 'Wreck & Rescue in the Bristol Channel' tells you about more rescues from this station than you can imagine. Between 1825 when formal rescues took place at Appledore and 2008, it is calculated that 786 lives have been saved from this station.

The first real rescue was in 1829 when the 'Volunteer' made two trips across the Bar in a terrible storm and rescued twelve men from the sloop 'Daniel'. Owen Nile Reordean-Smith was the helmsman and earned a silver medal for this daring rescue, as did the other two crew-members William Brinksmead and Philip Guy. William Hurry and Isaac Matthews were given cash rewards. Owen was the son of a Naval Officer and was supposedly born on board a ship at the battle of the Nile in 1798 – hence his unusual middle name.

The most famous rescue undertaken by an Appledore crew was just after Christmas 1868. A tremendous storm was blowing on-shore and there was boiling surf as far as the eye could see. The Austrian barque 'Pace' was being blown onto the shore by the pebble-ridge, and at 2:00pm she went aground and started to break up. The lifeboat 'Hope' was launched and so began a heroic rescue, which took three journeys to the stricken barque. Despite her rudder being torn off, the boat overturning, and the coxswain being badly injured, at least nine men were saved from the 'Pace' for which the RNLI awarded silver medals to Joseph Cox (coxswain), his son Joseph Cox junior and John Kelly in recognition of their outstanding service.

The Appledore lifeboat 'Jane Hannah McDonald' drawing huge crowds to witness her launch at Bideford in 1910.

The 100th anniversary of the Appledore lifeboat. This photo taken in 1925.
Back row: Sidney Cann, [unknown], Stephen Craner, John Craner, George Cann, John Cann, John Allen,
Stephen Bignell, George Craner (coxswain). Front row: [unknown], John Bowden, John Rees, Alfred Evans,
Fred Butler, George Craner junr, Arthur Hammond.

A presentation and group photograph of the RNLI committee and crew in March 1931, on the retirement of
Harri Clough Whitehead, Hon.Sec. for 30 years.
Back row: Col. Eardley Wilmot, George Carter, Capt Incledon Webber, Evans, A Bowden, Stephen Bignell, Capt
Charles Sumner, George Craner (coxswain), F N Hulton, Tom Hornabrook, W A Cryer, Sidney Cann, John
'Webber' Craner, George Cole, Harold Miles, Stephen Craner.
Front row: Col. O'Donovan, Denys Scott, Rev Muller, G F Shee, Harri Whitehead, Capt E Drury, Dr William
Valentine, Maj-Gen Sir Robert Stuart, Lt-Com H W Wheeler.

Tombstone in Northam Churchyard for sailors from the 'Pace'.

Henry 'Bosun' Carter (a cousin of my father) served as coxswain from 1964 to 1969. On New Year's Day 1966 he was in charge of the lifeboat 'Louisa Anne Hawker' in the rescue of a pregnant woman from Lundy in hurricane force winds. Due to the terrible conditions the boat was unable to get back into Appledore until two days later, the crew having spent forty hours at sea.

AWARDS AND MEDALS:

No lifeboatman (or woman) does such service for praise or reward, but receiving such an honour is indeed gratifying and records their selfless acts for posterity. In addition to the RNLI medals awarded to Joseph Cox and some of his crew in the rescue from the Austrian barque 'Pace' in 1868, the Emperor of Austria also honoured both Joseph Coxes and John Kelly with silver crosses of merit. Awards were also made to William Yeo for his active involvement on shore during the rescue, and to customs officer William Nichols.

One of the RNLI medals awarded to Joseph Cox. (North Devon Museum Trust Collection).

The rescues continue to this day, and mention of all the serving coxswains and life-saving rescues is not possible in this brief history. Today the boats are much safer and well-designed for all conditions, but men are no less willing to put their lives at risk to save others. Twenty-nine medals have been awarded to Appledore crew members for gallant rescues since the station began in 1825.

Not all awards were for active crew-members though. In 1851 Appledore boat-builder Henry Hinks entered a competition to design a lifeboat. From his small boat-yard at the back of the Irsha Street houses he had been building boats since the 1830s, and he faced stiff competition from 280 other entries around the world. His design was awarded 2nd place at the Great Exhibition of 1851, and the Duke of Northumberland (then President of the RNLI) presented him with the prize of 100 guineas. The following year he was awarded a contract to build two lifeboats and his features were incorporated into all lifeboats for the next sixty years.

In 1965 Sydney Cann retired after 53 years service to the RNLI, 32 of these as coxswain. He had received the RNLI Silver medal and the British Empire Medal for his services.

MEMORIAL:

It is sad that there is no memorial here, not only for the thousands of sailors who have lost their lives within sight of this point, but also for the lifeboatmen who have died whilst trying to rescue them. Thankfully the Appledore RNLI has had no deaths amongst its serving crew for over 140 years, but the ones that were lost should still be commemorated.

In 1833 the Appledore lifeboat was launched to try and rescue the crew of the 'Mary Ann' which was being driven onto the shore near Westward Ho!, but their mission was doomed as the conditions were just too bad to help. All the crew belonging to the vessel in distress drowned. The Appledore lifeboat overturned and was washed up on the shore half an hour later with some of the crew still clinging to it, but three of its crew were lost.

Benjamin Pile left a widow and nine children, Samuel Blackmore left a widow and two children, and John Peake (whose body wasn't recovered until a week later) left a widow and three children. The coast was covered with fragments from the wreck including a writing desk from the ship containing the ship's papers.

The parish registers record their burials, along with two of the recovered men from the 'Mary Ann':

28th November 1833 – Samuel Blackmore, aged 33.
28th November 1833 – Benjamin Pile, aged 49.
28th November 1833 – An unknown drowned man.
29th November 1833 – An unknown drowned man.
9th December 1833 – John Peake, aged 46.

The only other loss of a lifeboatman happened at the same time as the rescue of the 'Pace' in 1868. Another barque wrecked in the same gale was the 'Leopard', from which three lives were saved but 36-year-old David Johns was drowned attempting to get a line onto the ship. The Board of Trade awarded £50 to his widow.

Well-worn trackway across the beach.

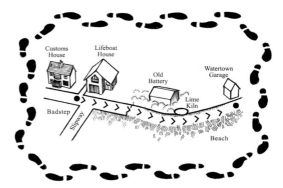

FROM BADSTEP TAKE THE PATH ALONG THE BEACH TOWARDS WESTWARD HO!

(Make sure the tide is out – otherwise the lifeboat will have to come and rescue you!).

Here you will find obvious signs of a trackway, with ruts showing where the wheels of carts have cut grooves into the rock over hundreds of years. This was the main road out of West Appledore leading towards Westward Ho! In 1884 there were calls for a proper road to be built here as the only alternative was to go back to East Appledore, up Bude Street and over the hill. The cliff-top footpath here was no better, constantly being eroded, and people using it were forced to cross the fields instead. This road was suggested at a Council meeting, although committee-member Mr Pickard said he thought that this was the wildest scheme he had ever heard proposed.

THE BATTERY:

If you look up from the beach you will see a couple of timber bungalows close to the cliff edge. They don't look much, but they were actually built to be Appledore's first line of defence.

The main Appledore lifeboat on the slipway around 1900.

Crowds still gather for the launch of a new lifeboat. This is one of the RNLI's Inshore Boats being blessed at Badstep by Rev. Peyton-Jones in August 1975

The Royal Naval Reserve was formed in 1860 to provide a reserve of trained men which the Navy could call on in times of need. Appledore men soon joined up and attended 28 days of training each year, but this was all undertaken in Bristol and meant disruption to their service on commercial vessels.

In 1894 the Navy realised that more recruits would join if they were able to train locally, so it was agreed that a Battery should be built at Appledore. The field beyond the lifeboat station was purchased from the West Farm estate. Within a few months a defence facility was constructed, but in good-old Dad's Army style the Navy failed to supply any actual guns until about nine months later.

The facilities comprised a 50-foot by 25-foot gun-shed constructed from 12" thick English oak walls lined with zinc, a timber-framed drill shed, a brick-built magazine, a spacious parade ground and a concrete sea-wall. The largest gun here was a 64-pounder, there was also a 6" breech-loader and some early machine-guns.

About a hundred Appledore men joined up, and at the opening ceremony in 1895 Mr Martin drilled the men through the streets of Appledore led by the town band with crowds cheering. Cutlasses were waved, flags were flown, and the procession was followed by nearly 2,000 schoolchildren and spectators. 'God Save the Queen' was sung on the Quay, at Richmond House and again at the Battery. Tea was provided for the volunteers and 850 schoolchildren in the Church Field.

The Reserve Force only ran for about eleven years and closed in 1906 due to Navy cuts. In 1910 the site was sold and the buildings were converted into two bungalows.

The site was brought back to use during the 1st World War for gunnery practice. Two twelve-pound guns were sited in the bay windows and used for training. The shells were fired at targets sited at Greysands after which

Mr Cox was sent to retrieve the cricket-ball sized missiles, but occasionally some shot is still found at Greysands.

During the 2nd World War the Battery became one of the bases for H.M.S. Appledore.

Vernon's lime-kiln and Badstep, painted by Ayres Simmons in 1896.

THE LIME KILN:

Just beyond the Battery bungalows can seen the site of an old lime-kiln, although this kiln has now almost completely vanished due to erosion. Originally there were seven such kilns along the Torridge between Appledore and Bideford, the best preserved of which can be seen just up-stream from Instow which was restored as part of the Tarka Project.

In 1630 Tristram Risdon reported that *"a new invention has sprung up and been practised in Devon, by burning lime and then spread upon the arable land, this hath produced a plentiful increase of all sorts of grain amongst us".*

Limestone and coal from South Wales was brought over in small one-masted smacks, carrying about 10-15 tons at a time. It was burnt in these kilns and the resulting mixture spread on the fields to counteract acidic soil conditions and to improve drainage. Lime was also used as a coating for buildings and for mixing with gravel to make floors. Some limestone ship owners also took to bringing in brandy, wine and tobacco, transferred from French ships in the Bristol Channel. Customs Officers were appointed specifically to keep an eye on these limestone ships.

*64 boys and 5 officers posed for this photograph in 1911 when the Brigade was under the command of
Lieut. J. Hinks. Rev Scholey sits at the centre of the officer group.
Their headquarters were in the old Battery buildings beyond the lifeboat-house.*

*Naval personnel pictured outside the Battery during the 2nd World War.
Back row: Bill Badcock, Alfie Bennett, John Bowden, Arthur Badcock, Leonard Braund, Percy Shackson,
Walter Ford.
Front row: Billy Lamey, Lt Jimmy Mead (Secretary to the Admiral), Admiral Harold Franklin, Patricia Smith
(Wren Petty Officer), and Freddie Cane.*

This photo was not taken in Appledore - it was actually taken in India. It shows members of the 6th Devonshire
Regiment in 1914 but these are all Appledore boys.
Back row: E Burnham, John Farthing, John May, James Parkhouse, William Parkhouse, Edwin Lamey.
Middle row: J Saunders, Archibald Peake, Gordon Vaggers, John Scilly, George Cooke, John Lang.
Front row: Oswald Bennett, Arthur Ash, J Prouse, Leslie Gray, Charles Cole, Thomas Berry, Richard Powe.
Standing at each end: William Berry (left), William Scilly (right).

Piles of limestone seen here on the riverbank opposite Hubbastone waiting to be carried to the lime kilns.
(Colin Green Collection at North Devon Museum Trust).

The kiln here was known as 'Vernon's lime-kiln' after the Vernon family who owned the land here from the early 1700s. Richard Vernon is listed as being a lime-burner here in 1830 and the kiln was still producing lime until the 1860s. The depth of the cart-wheels in the rocky path along the beach bear testimony to its centuries of use.

The now-demolished 'Gillhouse', and Vernon's lime kiln.

In 1845, 90,000 tons of stone was brought into the Taw and Torridge rivers to serve the kilns along the riverbanks, the stone being deposited on limestone grounds at Appledore and transferred to smaller barges. As most able-bodied men were away at sea, the women were forced to work in any way they could. If stone needed shifting then it was the women who did it. In 1851 there were over thirty people in Appledore working as limestone porters. Most of these lived in Irsha Street, and all were women. From 19-year-old Sarah Jenkins to 65-year-old Sally Passmore, they all toiled at this back-breaking manual work.

In 1843 five local merchants who were controlling the limestone trade tried to reduce costs and cut the wages of the porters. For women who were on such low wages and who worked in such harsh conditions this was the last straw – they went on strike. No vessels were unloaded for a week, the ships couldn't trade, and eventually the merchants had to give in and reinstate the wages to their former level. Power to the women of Appledore!

THE GILLHOUSE:

What was the Gillhouse? No-one seems to know, but just behind the lime-kiln used to stand a substantial dwelling called 'Gillhouse' or 'Gillhouse and Folly'. Presumably the 'folly'

name comes from being perched precariously on the edge of a disintegrating cliff.

In 1713 mariner Richard Vernon was living in the Gillhouse which had an outhouse, barn, stable and garden. Five years later the land was leased to John Benson, and by 1842 Thomas Chappell from West Farm had acquired the lands from the Vernon family, including the lime-kiln. By 1888 the property was described as the Gillhouse Garden behind the former warehouse or cellar called Gillhouse. We can therefore assume that part of the property may have fallen into the sea by this time and the rest was demolished.

1855 map showing Vernons lime kiln and the adjacent Gillhouse and garden plot.
(North Devon Record Office).

THE BREAKER'S YARD:

Numerous ships have been constructed here over the centuries, but Appledore is also where ships were brought to die. Not all ships sank or were abandoned, those that reached the end of their useful lives were broken up and

The ships' graveyard in Skern Bay. Henry Hinks ran a breaker's yard here ending the life of numerous working vessels.

The Old Coastguard's House, formerly 'West India Hill Boathouse' used by the RNLI as a store and committee room. In the 19th century it housed the lifeboat and was then used as stables for the lifeboat horses. Note the gas-lamp still in use on the corner, and the unprotected cliff-edge.

any scrap materials salvaged. Many people around Appledore say they have 'old ship's timbers' in their houses - on the basis that the timbers look old and therefore must have come from a ship. Whilst many of these timbers may have been acquired from working shipbuilder's yards, that's not quite the same. However amongst all these claims there are in fact a number of house timbers with an undoubted maritime background.

Many vessels were brought here into Skern Bay to be broken up by Henry Hinks who ran a breaker's yard here. Most vessels have now vanished, although there are still some remains recognisable as lengths of old timbers sticking up from the mud. These are the remains of the schooner 'Goldseeker' built in 1873 and the Thames barge 'Shamrock' built in 1899.

The most famous vessel brought here was the 'Empress', previously known as the 'Revenge'. Her name was changed in 1890 when she became a training ship (see book 1, page 141). She was a former battleship with 91 guns, weighing 5,500 tons, and was the flagship of the Channel fleet.

In 1924 William Jenkins was an ex-pilot living on the Quay and was brought out of retirement to bring the ship safely into Skern. Children were let out of school early to see it. Henry Hinks allowed people on board for 6d and the money went towards the building of the new Bideford Hospital. The Captain's writing desk, wash basin and part of her keel are now in the North Devon Maritime Museum. Some of her timbers were used as the roof beams for All Saints Chapel at Instow, and some of her timbers were used to make doors for Kingsley Hall in Westward Ho!

"Beyond the sea was lapping the lower timbers of the dismasted wooden battleship 'Revenge', which with portholes and brown poop and projecting bowsprit, lay like the body of a gigantic cockchafer on the flat Skern mud. Noises of knocking came from the high hull."
(The Pathway, by Henry Williamson).

Who builds a wall like this?

Further round Skern Bay, can be seen the remains of this brick sea-wall. It was constructed from bricks taken from the demolished windmill near to Marshford crossroads, hence the rather unusual bond-pattern of previously used bricks and their slightly curved profile.

Here can also be seen the remains of the boat-building shed used by Alan Hinks to build the replica ships 'Nonsuch' in 1968 and the 'Golden Hinde' in 1973.

Watertown Garage in the 1960s.

THE GAS WORKS:

A Gas Company was formed in 1875 to supply gas for street lighting and private households in Appledore. A site at Watertown was felt to be the best place for this, which today is the Watertown Garage. A limited company was formed and a £3,500 scheme started. Street lighting was felt to be long overdue. Barnstaple had had public gas lamps since 1833 and it had long been said that Appledore, with its narrow and tortuous streets, was positively dangerous after dark. Many serious and fatal accidents had happened to people falling off the quays into the river or on the beach below. In 1866 William Yeo chaired a meeting to see how a company could be formed and to search for a suitable site, but it would be another nine years before this came to fruition.

In June 1875 the scheme was celebrated in a marquee near the site, with a grand dinner, toasts to the 'success of the Appledore Gas Company', and an evening display of fireworks.

Two gasometers were built here, six retorts and four miles of piping around Appledore. The gas was produced from coal brought direct to the site from South Wales.

The remains of the ovens in which the coal was burned to produce the gas. These still exist in a chamber under the floor of the Watertown Garage.

The secretary of the Gas Company, George Baker, lit the first lamp on 15th January 1876 and in all a total of sixty-five public lamps were installed around the village. The remains of a couple of these can still be seen on some houses, such as this one on the wall of 48 Market Street.

"Jimmy Day was a very conspicuous character, not only because he was well above average height, but because he was the local 'town crier' and the official gas lamp lighter. Before the novelty wore off, we used to follow him around, intrigued how he made the lights come on with his long pole. It's funny, but I can't remember anyone even climbing up the lamp-posts to switch them on and off."
(Appledore Boyhood Memories, by E R Carter).

The Gasworks closed in 1930.

The Gasworks Manager's house was sited between the gasworks and the gasometers.

FROM WATERTOWN RE-TRACE YOUR ROUTE BACK TO BADSTEP

Badstep   Watertown

OLD COASTGUARD'S HOUSE:

At the bottom of Jubilee Road we have a house teetering on the very edge of the cliff, a more exposed position would be difficult to imagine. This is currently called the 'Old Coastguard's House', although that is actually one thing the building has never been.

The building appears on the 1840 tithe map, and the outcrop of rock and the green in front of Hillcliff Terrace (known locally as 'Western Hill') appear in earlier documents as 'West India Hill'. This is a rather strange name as there are no obvious links that would account for this. The house dates to before 1780 when the land-owner Thomas Chappell was paying tax on 'The West Indias'. There were no other buildings here at that time so the 'West India Hill' name appears to have been lost or contracted to the now-used 'Western Hill'.

In 1890 the house was sold to the RNLI for £100 and was known as the 'West India Hill Boat House Store Fort'. It was used as stables for the lifeboat horses - the stable door was where the window faces towards Badstep. Later it was used as the RNLI Committee Rooms and for lifeboat storage. It was turned into a private house in 1960.

WESTERN HILL:

'Western Hill' is the name given to this green area at the end of Irsha Street. Originally

an un-protected cliff edge, in 1904 there were calls for it to be made a place of attraction for residents and visitors, rails to be put up to keep people from falling over the edge and maybe a bandstand and a few seats. Today it is a great place to admire the grandeur of the scenery. A granite standing stone is being erected in 2009 to commemorate Appledore's connection with the Viking incursions of the 9th century and the part that men of North Devon played in defeating their chieftain Ubba and his army.

During the 2nd World War a pair of 4.7" naval artillery guns were installed on the green to provide a defence against enemy shipping entering the estuary. They were powerful guns sited one at each end of the green, and had breeze-block enclosures built around them disguised to look like houses.

On the day of testing a large number of people had gathered. Both guns were fired but the resulting noise was so huge that it shattered all the windows in Hillcliff Terrace. The shock-wave brought down a number of ceilings and made slates fall off the roofs. 9-year-old David Cable and his younger brother were playing on the rocks below at the time, and sixty years later when he described this to me he said that his ears had just stopped ringing!

After that the guns were only fired occasionally, and only after the Navy had given the householders enough notice to enable them to protect their windows! The

guns were kept on alert for the rest of the War, but after 1943 when the Navy unit left they were manned by the Appledore Home Guard.

BOMBS ON APPLEDORE:

The only Wartime bombs dropped near Appledore came from a German Aircraft which had apparently lost direction and jettisoned about a dozen bombs before trying to return to base. Coming over the hill from behind the church, the first bomb just missed the school and the others fell in a line across the estuary towards Instow. The plane was spotted from the Western Hill gun emplacements by 2nd gunner Billy Richards who immediately requested permission to open fire. *"Certainly not"*, replied his commanding officer *"that would give away our position!"*

Some houses in Instow were damaged by the falling bombs, but apart from that Appledore was otherwise unaffected by direct air or naval action.

Dog-fights were often seen in the skies of the Bristol Channel, and the North Devon Coast was considered by many to be on the front line of defence with H.M.S. Appledore at its strategic heart. A cage was set up on Appledore Quay to enable travellers to and from Lundy to be searched to ensure they weren't carrying concealed butter or cigarettes obtained from the Royal Navy's supplies to the Island.

The Home Guard had a base on Lundy, but their only contact with any Germans were five airmen captured when their plane crashed on the island. The prisoners were brought back to Appledore on the 'Lerina', but news of their capture had already spread round the village. Several hundred people gathered on the quay intent on giving the enemy summary justice. The situation was turning ugly, so it was decided to delay disembarking the men until after nightfall and when reinforcements had arrived. The first German to be landed screamed aloud as he believed they would all be shot as soon as they had arrived on the mainland.

HILLCLIFF TERRACE:

The sweeping curve of houses in Hillcliff Terrace face onto the green of Western Hill, the central one being slightly higher than the others. These thirteen houses were built in 1892 on land sold from the West Farm Estate by Oliver Heywood. Numbers 14 and 15 were added later in place of an old barn that stood at the end of the street.

These houses all took their water from four wells in the rear gardens of numbers 3, 7, 10 and 12. However, after just a few years the wells were all found to be contaminated with water from nearby sewers and cases of typhoid were breaking out. In 1902 the landlord John Tamlyn was arranging for daily casks of drinking water to be delivered by local haulier Charles Mills (bottled water is not new!), but one of the tenants felt that the charge of just over £1 per year was extortionate and refused to pay. The matter was settled in Court, but if only he knew what we would be

paying for water today.

THE ROPE PATH:

The Hillcliff Terrace houses were built on a parcel of land known as the 'North Rope Path Field'. A rope-path or rope-walk was a long straight track where ropes were twisted and made. Appledore had two of these, the other being on the land at Tomouth. This rope-path started at West Farm (opposite the Royal George pub) and ran along to this end of Irsha Street. It was in use as far back as 1780 when landowner Thomas Chappell was paying tax for it. When his descendant William Chappell died in 1846 the rope-path was described as being 624 feet long, with space to extend it to 180 fathoms (1,080 feet) if needed. The rope-path site also contained a tar-house, cellars, lofts, copper furnaces and other items needed for the rope-making trade.

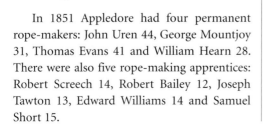

In 1851 Appledore had four permanent rope-makers: John Uren 44, George Mountjoy 31, Thomas Evans 41 and William Hearn 28. There were also five rope-making apprentices: Robert Screech 14, Robert Bailey 12, Joseph Tawton 13, Edward Williams 14 and Samuel Short 15.

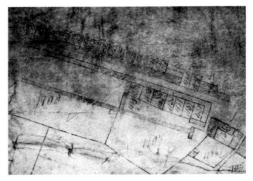

1840 Tithe map showing the Rope Path running behind the houses of Irsha Street. (Devon Record Office).

THE GRAVEL MINE:

If you had been standing on Western Hill a hundred years ago you would have witnessed the mining of gravel on a huge scale. The gravel bank in the centre of the estuary was known as the 'sprat ridge' and appeared to contain an inexhaustible supply of gravel for use in the road and construction industries. All you needed was a barge and some buckets and shovels.

In the early 1900s, about 300-400 men and more than 130 barges were regularly taking gravel from here. The barges would go out on high tide, anchor above the ridge and wait for the tide to go out. Then they had about eight hours in which to fill the barge with gravel before the tide floated them off and enabled the barges to be brought back to Appledore or Braunton. At its peak in 1905 it was calculated that about five-hundred tons of gravel was being removed every day from this ridge.

SEAWEED:

The river has long been a source of many other useful commodities. Whether shell-fish or salt, man will always use what he can from his surroundings. Seaweed was regularly gathered from the Skern Bay area as a foodstuff. Known as 'laver' it was rather like spinach, only

The men who worked the gravel barges had a hard back-breaking job. Gravel was shovelled into wicker baskets which could then be winched on board the barge and emptied. Once the barges had taken as much material as physically possible, they would make their slow way back to Appledore where they were unloaded in the same manner.

with a fishy taste. In 1899 it was reported as becoming scarce and was having to be brought from Hartland.

In 1890 John Cann aged 65 and Richard Taylor aged 28 were drowned in the river after having gathered seaweed near to Braunton. At the inquest it was found that their boat had been overloaded with so much seaweed (to be used as manure) that it was swamped, and sank like a stone. John Cann left a widow, seven children of his own, and three adopted children.

Nude bathing:

The river can also look inviting for a swim but don't be tempted. The currents are deceptive and very strong. However, boys will be boys and maybe this was the only bath that many of them got. In 1893 there were reports of a nuisance being reported at Appledore where bathers had been reported as being completely nude. The Parish Council confirmed that there was a by-law that covered this matter and that they would be 'putting this into force'.

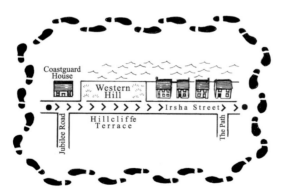

From Western Hill continue along the road into Irsha Street

What's in a name?:

I have often been asked where the name 'Irsha' comes from. The answer is 'I don't know', except to say that its origins do seem to be rather obscure.

Irsha is generally accepted as being the name of a separate hamlet next to Appledore, but it is never named as such on any old maps. Generally only the names of 'East Appledore' and 'West Appledore' describe the two parts of the village. Irsha Street is listed in the 1851 census when there were 103 households here, but there were another 63 households in what was called 'West Street'. The 'Irsha' name only seemed to apply to the street from West Quay back towards Appledore.

In the 1841 census the name of Irsha does not appear at all - it was all known as 'West Appledore'. Neither is Irsha mentioned on the 1840 tithe map schedule or in the Land Tax assessments for 1777, whilst some early 19th century deeds refer to it as 'Strand Street'. The definitive work on origins of place-names (Gover) does not mention 'Irsha' at all, presumably because it never been indicated on a map. This does suggest that this name might be an early Victorian invention.

However, the origin of place names can often be determined from the name itself. 'Irsha' is a strange-sounding word unlike anything else in the English language, sounding as though it has come from Celtic or Saxon origins. Place-names ending with the letter 'a' are rare, but in the Torridge area we also have the names: 'Bidna', 'Broada' and 'Wooda'.

The English Place-Name Society suggest that 'Irsha' probably came from the Old English 'ersc' meaning a ploughed field. However, given the sea-strand location it does seem an unlikely feature after which to name a settlement, especially as most farmland here is too steep to plough!

In dark-age times North Devon was also subject to Viking raids for a couple of centuries, sometimes with temporary settlements, which may have contributed some Viking genes into the local Devon gene-pool and possibly some Viking place names.

Further searching did however reveal some earlier examples of the Irsha name:

The Devon Record Office holds deeds for:
• *A house and garden in Irsha Street, Appledore (1839).*
• *A messuage, with cellar and garden, at Irsha, Northam (1835).*
• *A messuage with appurtenances at Irsha, Appledore (1830).*
• *A newly-erected house in Irsha in Appledore (1807).*
• *A messuage and cellar at Irsha, Northam (1795).*
• *A house etc. in Irsha (1746–1789).*

The Somerset Record Office holds deeds for:

• *Messuage at Irsha Appledore, Richard Melhuish to Thomas Elliott (1776).*
• *A deed for 'Passage Park' at Irsha Appledore, Melhuish family (1703).*

This takes the name back to almost 1700, but I was delighted to get the name back a further hundred years, from this endowed deed in the Devon Record Office:
• *1612 - Sale of land, cottages, etc, in Irsha, Northam, by George Willett to Thomas Docton, with thirty tenants names being listed.*

The 'Irsha' name appearing in a document from 1612.

This was obviously a major investment by the Docton family, and must have covered most of Irsha as it was then. The Willetts were the family who later owned the Manor of Tapeley and they seem to be selling Irsha hamlet to the Docton family, who were now making investments in Appledore. 1612 was just five years after the 1607 tsunami that did a lot of damage here. It is still strange that the 1607 tsunami report mentions damage to cliff-top houses at 'Appledore' (obviously Irsha), but doesn't mention the Irsha name.

However, it has been good to show that this name does go back at least four-hundred years, but that's as far as I can trace it. Can anyone else do any better?

One of the most desirable addresses in Appledore is Irsha Street, especially the water-side, however this was not always the case. It used to be a rough-and-ready place with reports during the 1860s of prostitution and witchcraft. Its salty reputation appealed to creative types. Henry Williamson, whose 'Tarka the Otter' was partly set in the estuary, was a regular at its pubs in the 1930s.

At first appearance Irsha Street appears to be an ancient street flanked by houses of diverse ages. This is indeed the case, but on closer examination they are not all as old as they first appear. There are many houses from the early 20th century (note the creamy-grey Petersmarland bricks). Others date from Victorian times, and some from the grander Georgian period (note the higher storey-heights for these houses, as opposed to earlier houses with more modest ceiling heights). All the houses are of different ages so it is clear that the site of each has been used a number of times. The oldest element is therefore the line of the street itself. The route that you take when you walk along it is one that the inhabitants of this self-contained and somewhat insular community have trodden for centuries. Soak in the memory of these people as you make your way along this ancient path.

PROSTITUTION:

Appledore 'ladies' had a bit of a reputation of being nice to sailors. A letter to the papers in 1884 complained of "Vice in its worst form on the open street, abuse in the most disgusting language possible to be uttered, and burning of objects endangering both life and property."

In 1860 three girls from Appledore were charged with 'obstructing the highway and annoying people passing by'. They were Ann Batten 20, Betsy Ross 21 and Fanny Keen 18. An enterprising man in Barnstaple used to run river trips on a Sunday morning when the tide was right. He filled two boats with men seeking the delights of the more liberal Appledore ladies down the river, calling them 'Trips down the Rhine'.

It worked the other way too. In 1858 John Fewings from Bideford brought two 'nymphs of the pave' to Appledore for the purpose of enticing some newly-arrived sailors back to his place at Bideford. It all went wrong though, he got drunk and had a physical argument with Samuel Bale and they were both arrested for disorderly conduct and assault.

SEA-GATES AND CELLARS:

For a community that tried to keep itself above water, it seems odd to hear so many stories of cellars and tunnels. Often a cellar was an area for storage in the lower part of the building rather than an actual underground room. However, we do find historical references to subterranean rooms, eg: *"House to let in West Appledore, with large underground cellar, adjoining workshops".* (North Devon Journal:

12th March 1868).

Other people have told me of tunnels that allegedly exist, although no-one could show me one. Quite what the need would be to construct such tunnels is puzzling. If they were for smuggling this does seem to imply considerable constructional effort and organisation, when all you really had to do was wait until dark and keep any Customs Officers busy elsewhere.

Occasionally Irsha Street residents do find a large void under their floors with water at the bottom. Where these appear on the river-side they were probably water-gates into which you could pull your boat and climb up a ladder into your house. The entrances to these chambers from the sea have now been closed off, to keep the sea-wall of Irsha Street more secure from the elements. It is probably these chambers that generate many stories about tunnels.

This house (now demolished) must have had a huge fireplace if the size of the chimney is anything to go by. Note how the house sticks out into the street, a sign that the street was even narrower previously.

WHICH HOUSE DID MY ANCESTOR LIVE IN?

I am often asked this question, but I'm afraid that it is often not easy to tell. The numbers that appear on the census returns were just the order in which the census enumerator went around his allotted district. They are not postal numbers, indeed postal numbers didn't exist in Appledore until the 1880s - if you were lucky enough to get any post then everyone knew where you lived. Houses have also been demolished since the censuses were taken and others built up. Sometimes more than one household was living in a property, and in Irsha Street itself the houses were re-numbered at some point in the 1930s. Even examining the deeds of a property doesn't always help. Many properties were let to tenants but only the (absent) owners' names appear in the deeds.

We therefore have various interesting snippets about Irsha Street residents, but can't exactly tell which house they lived in. However, these are some of the people that lived in the western end of the street:

- In 1897 Daniel Batten, Appledore's oldest resident, celebrated his 100th birthday. He took delight in spinning yarns for visitors and would talk to them for hours whilst smoking his pipe. He died three months later. (Actually that's a shame, because he had miscalculated his age, and was really only 98 – another good old Appledore yarn!).

- In 1863 Thomas Berry was thrown out of a pilot gig on the Bar, whilst trying to re-float a stranded ship called the 'Britannia' with her cargo of coal and iron. His body was eventually washed up at Saunton. He left seven children and a pregnant wife.

- In 1850 Bridget Keen celebrated her 104th birthday. Many of her relatives turned up to wish her well and it must have been quite an occasion. She was said to have had 7 children, 26 grand-children, 56 great-grand-children and 22 great-great-grand-children.

- Not to be out-done by such stories, a visitor to Appledore in 1867 reported that on the ferry-crossing the boatman told him about his father who married and had 11 children. When the ferryman's mother died, his father married again at the age of 64 and had 7 more children. He lived to be 108, saw the 5th generation, and by the time he died he had 300 descendants. Unfortunately no name was given to be able to check this, but it does sound like a yarn that has grown with the telling.

Mediaeval panelling in 41 Irsha Street.

OLDEST HOUSE IN IRSHA STREET?:

Number 41 is another house with a cockerel plate on the façade. It is probably the oldest house in this section of the street and potentially one of the oldest dwellings in Appledore. Note the off-centre front door indicating that the different halves were originally designed for living and scullery purposes – often the sign of an older property. Inside is a panelled wall dating back to the early 1500s when this would have been a grand merchant's house.

THE DOLLS HOUSE:

At number 55, the often photographed minuscule 'Dolls House' is cutely sandwiched between two larger buildings who appear to be trying hard to squeeze it even smaller. It is said that this used to be a slipway to the beach owned by Thomas Chanter. The story is that a cargo of stone was being unloaded here but that Chanter refused to pay for it. The boat owner unloaded the stone on the slipway layer upon layer until it reached a certain level, at which point he built a house on it. Whether this has any basis in truth is debatable. Certainly there was a slipway leading to the beach where number 59 Irsha Street now stands. This was called 'Ducks Alley' from which it was possible to get a view of any ships coming over the Bar.

ghost

A cleaner had a spooky experience in a house next to the Royal George. After finishing her cleaning at the top of the house she noticed a strong smell of tobacco smoke coming from downstairs. Fearing that someone had broken in she went down, and there sitting in a chair was an old man with a white beard and moustache tinged heavily with nicotine, smoking heavily. The man vanished (as did the cleaner!), but from his description he was identified as John Balfour, a sailor from the Channel Islands, who regularly used to stay in the house until he died here in 1957.

THE PATH:

'The Path' is a rather strange non-name for a street, but here we have three houses numbered: 1, 2 and 4 – evidence of two houses being knocked together.

The rope-path that stretched almost all the way to the other end of Irsha Street started from the top of this lane, so the name of 'The Path' probably derived from this.

The property at numbers 1 and 2 was a pub called the 'King's Head', which dates back to at least 1822 when the landlord was Samuel Sanders. In the 1870s Christopher Cobbledick became the landlord staying until the pub

closed in 1901. When the house was renovated in the 1970s Cobbledick's suit was discovered still hanging in a sealed chamber.

THE PASSAGE:

At the top of The Path was a little drang called 'The Passage', first mentioned in 1703. Living here in 1891 were John and Emma Evans with their four children: Thomas 15, Emmaline 11, Ellen 7 and John 5. They had a bedroom upstairs and a living room downstairs. When the house was inspected in March of that year the inspector described the floor as being in the filthiest condition. The smell was dreadful and the whole place causing serious injury to health. The children were flea-bitten all over, and although they were 'not clean' they were said to be 'not bad for Appledore children'. The boy (John) had only a thin cotton vest and knickerbockers and the girl (Ellen) only a thin cotton dress, a tiny shawl and no underclothing. The mother Emma had frequently been seen the worse for drink and was subsequently convicted of neglect and cruelty to her children. She was given fourteen-days hard labour.

The remains of the Evans family house can still be seen at the the back of number 56 facing onto the car park. Note the exposed cob-walling and the old joist-holes indicating the level of the upper floor.

RAINBOW CORNER:

In the 1970s the part of Irsha Street near to The Path became known as 'Rainbow Corner', due to the proliferation of fashionable colours that were chosen to grace its houses. A newspaper report in 1976 said that householders had fought a battle of striking hues and patterns over the last few years. At this time, the former grocery shop at number 56 became a clothes shop called 'Rainbow's End'.

CARNIVALS:

A word at this point about Appledore Carnivals, which always create a great attraction and focal point for village celebrations.

Carnivals first stated in 1903 when a fancy-dress parade and ball was held on the 28th October, although in later years this was moved to early September when it was realised that good weather was quite essential for an outdoor parade. Traditionally the procession gathered at Western Hill and made its way along Irsha Street, sometimes getting as far as Northam

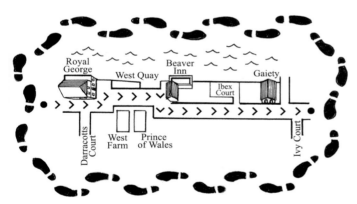

CONTINUE ALONG IRSHA STREET PAST WEST QUAY

DARRACOTTS COURT:

The 'Courts' are a unique feature of Appledore. The word is probably derived from 'courtyard', and each is a mini-community with all properties jointly owning the land in

DARRACOTTS COURT

the centre. Most of the Appledore Courts still retain their original cobbled surfaces, and in Darracott's Court you can still see the position of the capped-off well from which all the surrounding houses would have taken their water.

The Darracotts were a land-owning family in Appledore back as far as the 1580s, so at some point this Court has been named after them. Certainly some of these properties appear to date back to the early 1600s.

The deeds of number 3 refer back to 1770 when Elizabeth Docton (her ancestors having bought the land in 1612) is selling the house, part of the West Farm lands, to the Chappell family. At the far end of the Court there was an archway under number 4 through which horses were taken to the West Farm blacksmith's shop, where William Kelly the blacksmith would take care of them.

In 1856 this was the home of master mariner Thomas Williams who sailed from Appledore contracted to carry a cargo of iron rails on his brig 'Magic' from Newport to Alexandria, to be used for the construction of the Cairo to Suez Railway line.

THE FIRST BAPTIST CHAPEL:

In 1833 a Baptist Church was established in Appledore consisting of seven women and two men. They had split from the Independent Chapel in Meeting Street as they believed in the full adult baptism of believers. They were Ann Thomas, Mrs Mackworthy, Jane Bowden, Ann Soudan, Dorothy Chappell, Miss Hernaman, Mrs Bear, William Ross and Charles Vernon from Vernons Lane.

The 1906 carnival was marshalled by Harold Moody, and included numerous walking characters depicting: The Seasons, Flower girls, Married life a failure, Gypsies, Bears and keepers, Italians, Navies, Tired Tims, Monks, Niggers, and Ghosts. The Rev. Alfred Green produced an effective tableau showing an exact representation of a man-of-war with guns and lights.

Some typical carnival characters in Market Street in the early 1930s. Mary Ellen Fowler (left), Thirsa Dummett (right).

Elaborate carnival floats continue to the present day. This one was in 1979, seen in Tomouth Road before the procession. In the picture are Steve Bowden, Peter Cox, Kevin Conway, 'Grumpy' Drayton, 'Dinger' Bell, Allan Daniells, Ron le Mesurier, Paul Sussex, and Walter Fowler.

They rented a small sail-loft building from Mr and Mrs Bear in Darracott's Court which can still be seen today. As Chapels go it's not much, but would have just about been able to hold eight people at a squeeze. One of the men, Mr Vernon, was elected as the first Pastor and two of the women were appointed Deaconesses.

The first new baby was received into this Church in June 1834. She was Elizabeth Kingdon, and was my great-great grandmother, her parents William and Sarah having recently moved to Appledore from South Molton. This sail-loft was a temporary home for the Baptists whilst arrangements were made to build a permanent Chapel on land further along Irsha Street (more on this when we get to that point).

ATTEMPTED WIFE MURDER:

Near here in 1870, 43-year-old sailor Daniel Jenkins came home drunk and in a fit of jealousy attacked his wife Matilda with a large pocket-knife. He cut her throat in three places and chased her around the house threatening to kill her. Blood was pouring from her wounds but she managed to jump from a window where she was found and given assistance. Daniel was later caught by the Police and taken away for sentencing. It was incidents like this that sparked the temperance movements that were growing in popularity.

THE ROYAL GEORGE:

The 'Royal George' is a most historic public house which has stood here since the 1600s, although its early history is largely unknown and most of the features date to the early 1800s. It first appears by name in 1822 when the landlady is Elizabeth Smith. In 1826 William Chappell from West Farm is paying tax on the property, so it was presumably part of his lands. When sold in 1883 it was said that William Kelly had been its owner and occupier for more than forty years.

There are many stories of a tunnel leading across to West Farm (a short distance, so quite possible) although none has actually been found.

FIGHTING IN THE STREETS:

Street brawls were quite common outside pubs, but in 1867 a brawl took place outside the Royal George between two gangs of local women. It started with an abusive shouting match with the vile and obscene language quickly drawing a crowd of over a hundred people. After a short while a fight started and the women, who were described as 'bloodthirsty hags', were soon fighting like starved tigresses, tearing each others hair and trying to scoop each others eyes. Five sisters were particularly noted as being of the vilest character, and loathsome ghastly sights.

The Police were criticised for never being around when needed, not that they could have got through the cheering crowd. However, six women - Agnes Hocking 51, Betsey Johns 23, Louisa Taylor, Emma Youngston 25, Mary Ann Hocking 18 and Phillis Schillers 24, were all summoned for being riotous and using obscene language, and were fined forty shillings each. They all seem so different from the genteel-sounding 'collar-factory girls' employed in Appledore twenty years later.

Plan of the West Farm Estate and fields in 1890.

(Map showing: West India Hill Boathouse, Life Boat House, Customs House, North Rope Path Field, Lime Kiln, Gillhouse, Lovers Lane, South Rope Path Field, Rope Path, Garden Plot, Royal George, West Quay, West Farm, Lime Kiln Field, Meadow, Higher Style Field, Part Higher Style Field, Farm Close, Stable Close)

WEST FARM:

Opposite the Royal George sits West Farm. It doesn't look much like a farm now, but it used to control all the farmland from here as far as the lime kiln. There are no surviving old deeds for this house, but from previous research we can surmise that the West Farm lands were bought from the Willetts in 1612, passing to the Chappell family in 1770 (the Chappells are an Appledore family that go back to at least 1540 in parish records).

The oldest part of the West Farm building is the front, probably dating back to the late 1600s, but the original house has been extended further back over the course of subsequent generations.

When the house was sold in 1846 it was described as having: two parlours, a large kitchen, entrance hall, cellars, five bedrooms on the 1st floor, as well as attics, walled gardens, a stable, out-houses, fourteen adjacent cottages and fifteen fields.

ghost

The estate was acquired by Oliver Heywood in 1873 who ran a dairy at the back of the farm buildings. The dairy had a strange atmosphere and was thought to be haunted, although no-one admits to seeing anything specific. Other ghosts have been heard, smelt and seen in the house though, with a shadowy figure appearing in the downstairs rooms, the sound of doors banging and strong smells of tobacco, even when no-one was smoking. The building stopped being a farm in the early 1960s.

WEST QUAY:

"There was always keen rivalry between West and East Appledore. Over to Point, as the east side was sometimes called we thought ourselves far superior, and to show how inferior and uncivilised the other half was, we used to say that they ate the first missionary who landed there. For a few years before the 2nd World War, West Appledore decided to have a separate Regatta centred on the small 'quay' and slip-way between the Beaver Inn and the Royal George pub. Organised by Sammy Guard and John Dearing the programme was mainly filled with a greater emphasis on local rowing and sailing races; the West of England Rowing Clubs did not compete."

(*Appledore Boyhood Memories*, by E R Carter).

The sea wall has many times been damaged by the pounding tide. In 1904 sixty feet of the West Quay wall was washed away during a severe gale and had to be hastily patched and repaired. This happened again in 1925 and

The remains of Irsha Street houses washed away by the sea after a storm in 1909.

A collapse of part of Appledore Quay near the Seagate Hotel.

A further breach of the sea wall happened in 1925, and it was all hands to the pumps to make it secure again before the next high tide.

1974 and you can make out various repairs that have taken place in the quay wall here over the years. To keep the water out of the joints these sea-walls were often painted with wood-tar, also used for coating ships.

SMUGGLING:

Smuggling has gone on ever since there were customs duties, and these were first levied by the Romans – so that's something else that the Romans did for us! In 1602 the Bishop of Exeter took action against the fishermen of Appledore who hadn't been paying their due tithes for the landing of herring. John Davie, William Bennet, Richard Jewell, Richard Whitstone, Richard Bishop and William Jefferies were all fined for non-payment.

However, we only ever really hear about smuggling in romantic novels or when it goes wrong and someone gets caught. The earliest mention of smuggling appears in 1718, when there were reports of French vessels being seen in the Bristol Channel waiting to unload brandy onto the limestone ships crossing from South Wales.

In 1763 the naval sloop 'Dispatch' arrived at Appledore, the first preventative vessel to be stationed here. Within a year it was reported that smuggling had decreased dramatically, however there were still some dramatic seizures:

In 1780 the lugger 'Swallow' was brought into Appledore. She was found to be carrying nearly 27,000 lbs of black tea, plus brandy and casks of wine all in small containers for easy unloading.

In 1800 the Bideford skiff 'Endeavour' tried to take advantage of the temporary absence of the customs vessels which had been called away into service near France. However Navy cutters were still patrolling and inspected this vessel. Instead of hiding contraband under the rest of her cargo, her entire cargo was found to contain 1,076 gallons of brandy, 225 gallons of rum,

500 gallons of gin and 4 cwt of salt.

In 1804 the Navy cutter 'Shark' captured the sloop 'Betsy' which was carrying 500 kegs of spirit and casks of wine. The prize was brought into Appledore and a guard stationed on board the ship overnight. The next day customs officers boarded the ship but found the guard missing - he was later found dead floating in the river.

Once the goods were seized they were still not safe from pilfering. In 1811 salvaged wine was being held in a warehouse at Appledore. It was broken into overnight and an intruder fixed a tap in a cask, but fled on the approach of officers. The £20 reward has still not been claimed, so if you feel like ratting on one of your ancestors please write to H.M. Customs & Excise - and don't forget to ask for interest on the reward money!

THE PRINCE OF WALES:

West Quay certainly had plenty of pubs. Apart from the 'Beaver' and the 'Royal George' there was also the 'Prince of Wales' at number 72, and in the early 1930s the 'Barnstaple Inn' traded from what is now called 'West Quay House'.

The Prince of Wales first appears with that name in 1822 when Thomas Penhorwood was the landlord, although the style of the building suggests that it must have been fairly new at that time.

In 1869 when the pub was being sold it contained a parlour, smoking room, bar, tap room, kitchen, pantry, cellar, brew-house, stable for 2 horses, skittle alley, 5 bedrooms on the middle floor and 5 bedrooms on the top floor.

In 1865 an argument was started in the pub by John Williams, who boasted that he was the best steersman the 'Ocean Queen' had ever had. William Marshall, Thomas Marshall, Joseph Boon, William Boon and Joseph Bennett felt inclined to disagree with him on that matter, and a fight ensued which the landlord was unable to stop. The Policeman was called, who then became the focus of the fight. P.C. Trewin received a black eye and a cast-iron spittoon was thrown at him. The fight spilled onto the pavement and eventually all were persuaded to go home. Later they were all fined ten shillings for disorderly conduct.

For the record, other licensees up to the 2nd World War have been: Francis Screech, David Nicholls, John Rees, Mrs Richardson, John Seaman, Stephen Hare, William Baker, William Gabriel, Clark Swift, Sidney Bennet, John Bolt, Adela Tedray, Mary Ann Smith, George and Florence Eastman and Ernest Pitcher. The Prince of Wales closed as a pub in about 1985.

THE THATCHED HOUSE:

73 Irsha Street represents Appledore's last remaining thatched house. Many houses would have originally been thatched, with just higher-status properties having stone or slate roofs. However, thatch is not a good material to use next to a salt-laden environment. The cottage here probably dates back to the 1700s with cob or stone walls, and is a remnant of how the frontage at West Quay would have looked a couple of hundred years ago.

THE BEAVER INN:

The 'Beaver Inn' is one of Appledore's traditional pubs. It is woven into a novel written in 1920 by J Weare Giffard called 'Lure of Contraband', which tells the story of smugglers in 19th Century Appledore. A landlord about thirty years ago is reported to have had a sale document for this pub dating back to about 1450, but no-one appears to know anything about this now. The age of the pub is uncertain, as is the origin of its name. Beavers used to live in the Torridge but became extinct here in the 16th century. Does that mean the name of this pub goes back over 500 years?

We can only date the 'Beaver' name back to 1822 when pub names were first recorded along with the name of the licensee.

In 1873 Robert Hocking was arrested in the Beaver by the wonderfully-named P.C.Bastard for being drunk and trying to engage the landlord in a fight. Spirits of the ghostly kind are sometimes experienced here, many staff have seen glasses fall off the shelves all by themselves and a shadowy figure appearing by the fireplace.

EUCHRE:

On some nights you might see the card-game 'Euchre' being played here. This game is localised to parts of Devon and Cornwall, and is virtually unknown in the rest of the country. It is also popular in eastern Canada and the USA where it is first mentioned in 1829 as 'Uker'. This was the time when Appledore

Ignore the 2 boys in the foreground, and look at the background. The building on
the right hand side is the Beaver Inn shown here in the late 1890s.
In the centre can be seen the roof of the Gaiety (built 1893).

Landlord Jack Dawson outside the Beaver Inn in about 1935, proudly showing the new frontage.

The young people of Appledore formed their own ragtime band, seen here in 1912 at West Quay.
The girl on the left with the collecting tin is 12-year-old Alice Vaggers.

A coronation party celebration in Irsha Street in June 1953.
Amongst the people in the photo are: Ellis Blackmore, Ruth Evans, Gladys Portlock, Billy Bowden,
Lena Fishwick, AnnMarshall, Danny Ingrouville, Gerald Cawsey, Mona Pike, Marjorie Evans, Marjorie Evans,
Diane Fishwick, Pam Houston, Vera Ford, Gertrude Eastman, Annie Moss, Elsie Eastman, Hettie Rendle,
Barry Vincent, Brian Rendle, June Pike, Tom Ford, Adrian Hitchcock, Nathie Sharrock, Julie Harris, Pam Rowe,
Brian Sharrock, Margaret Rendle, Tom Harris, Roger Harris, Diane Eastman,
Pat Clements, Mona Branch and Gillian Cole.

sailors were regularly trading to this part of the world, so it is quite likely to have been spread by sea-faring men. The fact that it is also very popular in the U.S. Navy also reinforces this link. Euchre is derived from an ancient European game called 'Jucker', possibly from Germany, and was the original game for which the Joker was introduced to the pack, hence its name.

PRESS GANGS:

Impressment, or the 'Press Gang' as it was more usually known, was generally an occupational hazard for sailors and Appledore was no exception. This method of enforcing men to join the crew of military warships started in 1653 and ended in 1814 with the defeat of Napoleon. Anyone between the age of 18 and 55 could be taken, provided they were not under 5'4" tall, were without shoes, or known to be a Catholic. Whilst impressment seems archaic to us today there was no military conscription, so other means had to be found to provide sailors for His Majesty's Navy in times of war. In 1799 a captain, two lieutenants and two squads of men were stationed in Appledore and Bideford keeping a watch on the incoming ships. However about half of the men that they 'recruited' were considered as volunteers, possibly because volunteers earned a bonus on top of the 24 shillings a month normally paid to pressed men.

Here the Admiralty appointed a gang captain, and he was given the tools to do the job: a fast rowing boat was obviously vital, also his warrant card and weapons to provide enforcement. He could also claim expenses – indeed one gang captain managed to put in a claim for an umbrella to be used in rainy weather - cost 12s 6d. The men were not immediately put onto Navy vessels. Appledore men were often transported overland to Plymouth, thereby avoiding a long and sometimes dangerous sea passage.

ROAD WIDENING SCHEME:

Irsha Street at the corner by the Beaver Inn, was originally very narrow and tortuous - but then it wasn't built for cars. The corner by the Beaver was particularly constricted so in 1876 several houses were purchased and demolished by the Council in order that the street could be widened. Mrs Fisher and Susan Stapledon were re-housed for the benefit of this scheme. Further houses were demolished in 1910, as shown on the page opposite.

Later on number 78 was Bowden's fish and chip shop until 1906. Number 76 then became Bowden's grocery stores until the late 1960s.

VICTORIA CRESCENT:

Through an archway can be found the four houses of Victoria Crescent. These were built in 1897 by Robert Moody. A testimony to the historic site can be gained from a small trade-token unearthed near the top of this terrace.

Dated 1672, these tokens were produced by local shopkeepers faced with a shortage of halfpennies or farthings to give their customers.

Ibex Court is one of Appledore larger Courts. Its narrow passageways seem to lend themselves perfectly to smuggling, leading Customs Officers on a hide-and-seek hunt looking for contraband which locals were much better at hiding than officers were at finding.

This was also a good place for mischievous boys to carry out the practice of 'baiting' the local policeman. After having made sure that he would chase them they would run into Ibex Court, only for him to find out too late that the boys had fixed an ankle-height rope across the narrow alley, the boys having already jumped over it knowing where it was.

Before and after photos showing the houses that were demolished to widen the road by the Beaver Inn.

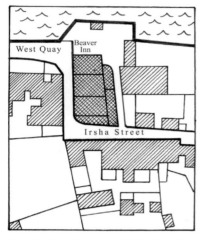

Map showing the corner of Irsha Street by the Beaver Inn around 1890.

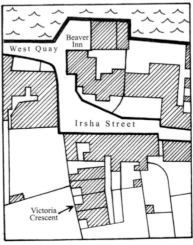

Map showing the widened Irsha Street today.

The houses all appear to huddle together here as if to keep warm. At one time it was said that Appledore was such a close community, that if you kicked an Appledore man they would all limp. Living in the confinement of these Courts this is easy to understand.

"There can be but little domestic privacy in West Appledore. A man must be either friend or foe with his neighbour. Relations are necessarily too intimate to admit of half-measures." (Lure of Contraband, J Weare-Giffard).

At the bottom of Ibex Court stands the former boat-building yard of the Waters family which operated from 1890. Known as the 'Kelpy Yard' it was named after a boat of the same name.

For 40 years prior to that it was the boatyard of George Parkin whose gig-boat 'Wildfly' was demonstrated with great success at Swansea Regatta in 1859, handsomely beating all opposition. From this he won various contracts to built pilot boats for Cardiff and Swansea.
We will hear more of these waterside boatyards shortly.

At the top of Ibex Court stands 'Webber's Cottage'. Named after John 'Webber' Craner who lived here, it is clearly the oldest building in this section of Irsha Street probably dating back about 400 years.

ISLAND COTTAGE:

Have you always wondered why the surname 'Carter' is so prolific – well here's the reason…

At number 101 stands 'Island Cottage', so named because you can walk around all four sides of it, although it used to be two cottages. This was the home of my great great grandparents John and Janie Carter, and now bears the name 'Gran Carter's'. Large families were quite common in Appledore but John and Janie had <u>fifteen</u> children between 1868 and 1893 - which certainly shows considerable dedication in keeping the Carter line going.

As well as bringing up her own family, Janie helped to raise some of her sister's children, a daughter's family and also four of her son's children. On Sunday evenings the whole family gathered and had musical evenings, which (of course) spilled over into Irsha Street itself.

"At mealtimes there could be up to 24 hungry humans to feed. Two sittings were needed for each meal, some perched on the stairs with plates balanced on their knees. The door of her house was never locked, and any tramp or stranded person was welcome to take shelter by the fireplace for the night, and they frequently did."
(Appledore Boyhood Memories, by E R Carter).

Despite this oversized family the house had no toilet and everyone had to cross the path at the rear to use a neighbour's facilities until the 1920s, when with great excitement their own personal indoor lavatory was fitted.

One of John and Janie Carter's children was William Lawrence Carter, born in 1876 and known as 'Billy'. Although disabled, he used an upstairs room as a hairdressers.

"Uncle Billy was crippled as a baby with infantile paralysis and was always in a hand-propelled wheel chair. He would frequently be seen occupying a regular place on the Quay at the bottom of Bude Street 'Ope'. His handicap did not stop him learning a tailor's trade with Mr Beara; cutting hair also augmented his income."
(Appledore Boyhood Memories, by E R Carter).

This ramshackle collection of buildings was home to the boatbuilding yard of George Parkin (1817-1900).

Cobbled Irsha Street around 1900. The old thatched cottages on the right hand side (numbers 98 to 104) have now been replaced with newer houses, built in the early 1960s.

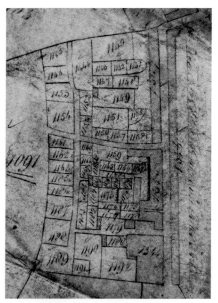

1840 Tithe map showing the houses and garden plots in this part of Irsha Street. (Devon Record Office).

THE GAY ADVENTURE CAFÉ:

In the 1950s at number 108 Irsha Street was the wonderfully-named 'Gay Adventure Café' run by Sid Lamden. Prior to that in the early 20th century it was a grocery shop run by the Lawday family, and subsequently by Eliza Evans.

THE GAIETY CINEMA:

The Gay Adventure Café probably took its name from the cinema just opposite. Still known as 'The Gaiety' this was Appledore's cinema between 1920 and 1960. However it was not built as a cinema, it was built in 1893 as a Public Hall by Harold Robert Moody whose initials still appear in one of the keystones on the frontage.

Harold Moody was a bit of a philanthropist, son of a Civil Engineer who had studied under Brunel. He owned a number of properties in Appledore, augmented with money inherited from his wife's family. Called 'Sabina', she owned three cottages on the site of the Gaiety

which Moody knocked down in order to build a hall where theatrical and musical events could be staged. He also widened the slipway at the side of the building which is still known as 'Moody's Slip'.

The resulting hall was 65 feet long, 29 feet wide, 21 feet high and could hold 500 people. It had dressing rooms, a green room, and a 'commodious' stage. In fact this was the first secular hall to be provided for Appledore, all the others belonged to the Church or the Chapels.

It is rumoured that Moody was friendly with a professional pianist in London but there was nowhere in Appledore for the pianist to come and play, so Moody built a private hall for his use. Whether that is true or not Appledore certainly made good use of this wonderful facility.

In 1895 the 'Appledore Minstrels & Variety Entertainers' gave a concert. The hall was decorated with flags and flowers. The Appledore band played and there were songs by William Short and John Braund, such as 'Ally Soper's Party' and the 'Whistling Coon'.

Alfie Green's Variety Company produced many popular entertainments, including some benefit concerts for Billy Carter. In 1902 it was announced that enough money had been raised to buy a 'machine' - just the mode of transport for a cripple, it could be halted on the steepest hill.

William Lawrence (Billy) Carter in his 'machine' on Appledore Quay.

By 1904 the village schools had more pupils than could be accommodated so the infant classes were moved into this Public Hall. Within a couple of years they were looking after 128 youngsters here in the capable hands of 26-year-old Matilda Kelly from Alpha Place. She was to devote forty years of her life to the teaching of Appledore's children.

From 1914 it became known as the 'Gaiety Theatre' in which school children sometimes performed full-length operettas. It also showing occasional films, but it was not until after Harold Moody's death in 1923 and the building was taken over by Samuel Hawkins that it became known as the 'Gaiety Cinema'.

Older Appledore residents remember being smuggled in under granny's long skirts to see the latest releases. The early films were silent, and live piano accompaniment was provided by Kathleen Mary May Wilkinson Marshall (born as Kathleen Williams). Her mother was a musician and her father a travelling actor. Indeed Kathleen had starred in some of his shows as a bare-back rider.

Kathleen Marshall, pianist for the silent films.

"If the scheduled film failed to arrive, the reserve standby was 'The Hound of the Baskervilles', and we must have seen it about 20 times. Very popular on Saturday mornings were the epic serials such as 'Perils of Pauline' where our heroine was usually left in dire straits such as being bound to the rails while the express thundered down on her. We were supposed to bite our finger nails for a whole week." (Appledore Boyhood Memories, by E R Carter).

The cinema closed in about 1960. One of the last films shown was 'Ice Cold in Alex' – set in a stifling hot desert landscape. The Rising Sun Inn immediately opposite did a roaring trade afterwards with everyone quenching their thirst.

THE RISING SUN INN:

Although a plaque indicates that 110 Irsha Street was built in 1664, there is no obvious evidence to support this apart from the fact that the building appears to date from the 17th century and a 1690s coin being found in the grounds. However, the 'Rising Sun' name does not appear until 1878, although the landlord at that time, John Scobling (he was also a shoemaker) was summoned for serving out of hours drinks in 1865, so this may have previously been a small pub.

In 1891 it was bought by Harold Moody (who built the Gaiety), although the following year he was described as being landlord of the 'Angel Inn'. When he died in 1923 Moody left six other houses In Irsha Street, four in Victoria Crescent and various other pieces of land. The film star Pat Kirkwood often stayed here in the 1930s. The Rising Sun Inn closed around 1963.

It is alleged that there is an underground tunnel leading from the Rising Sun down Irsha Street to Island Cottage, and from there down to the Beaver Inn. However this is all rumour, no evidence has actually been found – by me at least.

An elderly resident in the 1960s recorded a story of smugglers. He remembered being a child in the 1890s and helping his father and uncle roll some heavy barrels up the steep slipway, across the cobbled Irsha Street and into the Rising Sun. The women and children kept watch for the Revenue men, who if they appeared were led on a tortuous route through the inn before being cornered and knocked on the head. It was said that their uniforms were burnt and their bodies taken at night outside the Bar and thrown overboard on the ebb tide. Their horses were ridden inland and sold to farmers.

WHITE HORSE LANE:

The small lane leading up from Irsha Street to Torridge Road is called 'White Horse Lane'. Apart from the fact that a white horse used to live in the stables at the top of this lane, there seems no other reason to call it this. Locals often called it 'Stinky Lane' because of the smell from the gas regulator housed in a structure at the bottom of the lane.

BIBLE CHRISTIAN CHAPEL:

On the site of the modern 'Admiral's Lodge' house at number 116a once stood a Chapel. It was built by the Baptists, who had until then been meeting in a sail-loft in Darracotts Court. Richard Vernon whose son Charles had helped to found the Church here three years previously, donated the land, and the Chapel opened in March 1835.

Apparently it wasn't always used for religious purposes. In 1843 after storms had wrecked a number of vessels on the Bar, an outbreak of plundering was reported and orders were issued to search various properties for evidence. In a vault underneath the pulpit various items from one of wrecks were found, including some sails and oars.

Over the next few years the Baptist membership grew, and as most of the members were from East Appledore it was agreed that a new church should be built nearer to them in the centre of the village. In 1858 the Chapel was sold to the Bible Christian Sect and was demolished in 1908. Some lock-up garages were then built on the site.

THE CROWN AND SCEPTRE:

Next to the Bible Christian Chapel was the 'Crown and Sceptre' pub. It first appears in 1856 run by James Hooper, although he was described as a 'boat builder and beer retailer' almost twenty years before then. It closed as a pub in about 1880. There are 3 other pubs known to be in Irsha Street, but whose location has not been determined. These are:

- *The 'Shipwright's Arms' (disappears around 1858).*
- *The 'Mariners' Inn' (disappears in the 1860s).*
- *The 'Anchor Inn' (mentioned in 1867).*

From 1830 the Beer Act allowed any householder to sell ale and porter from their house, with a two-guinea licence, so these would just have been front-room drinking dens.

This courtyard of cottages dating back to the 1600s used to contain a common well used by all the surrounding householders. Its position can just be made out in the paving at the top of this Court. It was partly sunken and had some steps to get down to it. The water was eventually found to be contaminated, and as soon as mains water arrived it was paved over.

WILLIAM REARDON SMITH:

At number 3 Ivy Court (demolished in the 1950s and turned into the yard of number 4), William Smith was born in 1856. He was the youngest of eight children. His mother was widowed and found it difficult to cope so he was brought up by his grandmother. This wouldn't normally be the best start in life but he went on to become a millionaire and one of Appledore's greatest benefactors.

William Reardon Smith (Amgueddfa Cymru – National Maritime Museum Wales).

His full name was William Reardon Smith, grandson of Daniel O'Riordean an immigrant from Ireland. He first went to sea aged 12 and took his first command at the age of 25, eventually becoming employed by William Tatem in Cardiff (another Appledore boy-made-good). He 'retired' from the sea in 1900 and started up his own shipping line. Initially this was called the 'Instow Steamship Co Ltd', but by 1928 it was called the 'Reardon Smith Line' and operated a fleet of nine modern tramp steamers, most of which were Bideford registered even though they operated from Cardiff. In 1920 he became a Baronet in recognition of his contribution to the War effort. By the time of his death in 1935 he had

been knighted, and the firm was a multi-national business which continued its success well into the second half of the 20th century. The firm was eventually wound up in 1985.

Sir William never forgot Appledore and stipulated that when he died his ashes should be scattered on Bideford Bar. This was duly done from the lifeboat.

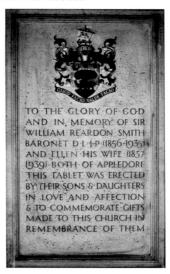

Memorial to William Reardon Smith formerly on display in Appledore Baptist Church.

APPLEDORE WOMEN DON'T GET OUT MUCH!

There was certainly a big difference between the lives of men and the lives of women in times past. Men went to sea and earned a living in the only way known to them, whilst women stayed at home and looked after the house and children. Sailors from Appledore are known to have visited such far-flung places as the Mediterranean, Buenos Aires, Bombay, Rio de Janeiro, Singapore, Leningrad, New York, New Zealand, China, Australia and many other places in between. Women on the other hand hardly went anywhere. However, Appledore was an insular place in those days and self-sufficient in most respects.

In 1891 Ellen Slade was living at 5 Ivy Court. She had married mariner Philip Williams in 1892. Although Ellen lived to be 89 she was proud of the fact that she had never once left the village, not even to visit Northam.

Even more extreme was the case of Louisa Powe. From the date she married in 1900 to the time she died, it is said that she didn't even venture beyond Ibex Court, not even to Irsha Street. Most supplies were delivered direct to the doorstep on a daily or weekly basis. Delivery-men would not expect to find a door locked. They would march straight into the house and leave the goods on the kitchen table. If it wasn't delivered you could always send the 'cheil' (child) over to Point.

Have it delivered:

In the 1920s and 1930s all suppliers made house-deliveries direct to the customer. There were plenty to choose from:

Bakers:
- *Kivell's (previously Reed's Bakery) in Bude Street.*
- *Popham's, in Marine Parade.*
- *Mitchell's, from Bideford.*
- *Friendship, from Bideford.*
- *Coles, the Old Bakehouse in Irsha Street.*

Butchers:
- *Jewell's, in Odun Road.*
- *Clement's, in Market Street.*
- *Bradford's, in Northam.*
- *Watt's, in Northam.*
- *Tucker's, in Westward Ho!*

Dairies:
- *Vaggers, in New Quay Street.*
- *Moore, from Wooda Farm.*
- *Withecombe, in Hubbastone Road.*
- *Griffey, from West Farm.*

Newsagents:
- *Dickie Fishwick, in Market Street.*

Coal Merchants:
- *Mills, who were joined by Harris on Appledore Quay.*
- *Littlejohn's, from Bideford.*
- *Also Paraffin from Mr Bartlett, in Pitt.*
- *Oil from William Taylor.*

Grocers:
- *Boyle's, in Market Street.*
- *Francie Bowden, opposite the Beaver.*
- *World Stores, in Bideford.*

Vegetables:
- *Cork, from Odun Farm*
- *Leslie Evans, from Northam.*

Mary Ellen Fowler seen here in the doorway of her home at 1 Myra Court in the 1930s.

MYRA COURT:

Another of Appledore's attractive Courts, but it was not always considered so attractive. In 1970 the Northam Council Conservation Area Report concluded that the houses here were not the most interesting and as they were unfit for human habitation, they should be demolished and replaced with a block of ten flats and a row of garages. (Yes, that should enhance the character of this lovely old Court!).

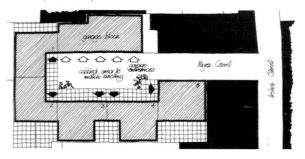

Plan showing the proposed flats and garages to replace Myra Court.

Farmer Ernie Cork from Odun Farm delivering vegetables to the ladies of
Irsha Street in 1953, from his cart usually pulled by his horse 'Dolly'. The ladies are (left to right): Mary Scobling,
Connie Harris, Hettie Rendall, Lizzie Young, Thirza Waters and Anita Edwards. (North Devon Athenaeum).

In 1891 Sarah Pile was living at No 5 Myra Court. She is seen here gathering seaweed, cockles, timber or anything
else available from the sea-shore.

DANIEL FARSON'S HOUSE:

Number 129 was the home of author and TV broadcaster Daniel Farson. After his more wide-spread fame on Rediffusion TV in the 1950s and 1960s, he lived here in alcoholic obscurity until his death in 1997. A friend of Henry Williamson, he wrote about 22 books including a biography of his great uncle Bram Stoker.

Daniel Farson's book called simply 'Curse' (published 1980), is the story of a West-Country fishing village with a long-standing curse over it. This village has rival east and west parts, a quayside, quaint narrow streets and cobbled drangs, historic links with Prince Edward Island and a nearby muddy bay called 'Skern' – sound familiar?

The conclusion of this tale describes a huge wave destroying much of the village - a sinister echo of the tsunami of 1607, even though that historic event was only really recognised as such after this book was written. However, his description of this destruction does seem to be frighteningly accurate:

"The waves rose against the village, fell and rose again, seizing and sucking back the nearest cottages. Rapidly the repeated onslaught of the water hit the hillside, which started to collapse. As it did so, the waves poured through to join forces with the water attacking the quayside. Gradually the whole village began to break apart. Buildings were pounded to rubble and floating planks. Uprooted trees joined the tide of the onslaught, boats were smashed into floating debris. With a terrible shudder the entire quay tumbled into the river. In one horrendous hour of destruction the entire landscape was altered." (Curse, by Daniel Farson).

THE BOATYARDS OF IRSHA STREET:

Although you can't tell as you walk along Irsha Street this used to be a thriving boat-building area. Behind the waterside houses and facing onto the river were a number of small boatyards. Materials were delivered from the river and when finished the boats were launched over the sea-wall.

At the side of number 129 you can see steps leading down to a lower level. These led down to Teddy Harris's boatyard.

HINKS YARD:

Further along behind numbers 135 to 139 Irsha Street was a boatyard belonging to the Hinks family. This was established in 1844 by Henry Hinks who later won a major prize for lifeboat design at the Great Exhibition of 1851. Henry's son John took over in 1878. The yard was still in production in 1952 when a visitor described it as follows:

"Almost hidden under a mountain of assorted junk and timber, is a relic of the past. It is a wooden wheel some six feet in diameter which, worked manually with a handle and connected to a belt, used to provide the power for turning a

lathe. Installed by the founders of the firm, it still works, and the present principal of the firm recalls spending many hours of his youth providing the motive power."
(*The North Devon Story, by Eric R Delderfield*

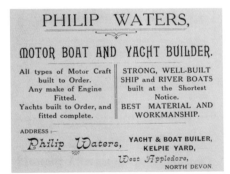

WATERS YARD:

The Waters boatyard (at the bottom of Ibex Court) was started by Philip Waters, who began his apprenticeship in 1877 at the age of 14. His master was Thomas Williams, but conditions were hard and he was the only apprentice to complete his seven years. His wages were 2s 6d a week, increasing to 7 shillings a week at the end of his training.

The working day ended at 8:30pm in the summer and 7:30pm in the winter. Often the time for starting work would be as early as 5:00

or 5:30am, particularly if there was a tide to catch or to bring timber down from Bideford. Philip Waters was still working the yard in 1950, and had never been without a day's work during this period.

FORD'S YARD:

Ford's boatyard, sometimes known as the 'Park Yard', was at the end of Irsha Street where three modern riverside houses now stand. Started in about 1930 by Horace Ford it operated until the 1970s.

IRSHA STREET SHOPS:

Like most Appledore streets there were many front-room shops in Irsha Street, the exact locations of which are often unclear. However in the first part of the 20th century all of the following were listed as shopkeepers in Irsha Street:

Helen Oatway, Lily Jeffery, Florence Marshall, John Stribling, Beatrice Hutchings, Elizabeth Taylor, Agnes Rendle, Mary Ann Hutchings, Mary Daniel, Frederick Willis, Margaret Smallridge, Harold Hulme, Janie Hinks and Mary Trick, most of them supplying general provisions.

At the end of Irsha Street, number 142 was the grocery shop belonging to the Down family. This was one of the last grocery shops serving this community. Started in about 1900 by William Down it survived until the 1980s, by which time the Bideford supermarkets were attracting most of the trade. When he died in 1985 Freddie Down requested that his ashes be placed in the antique lamp-post that still stands outside the shop here so that he could still keep an eye on who was coming and going. Say 'hello' to him as you pass this point.

CANNS COURT:

One of Appledore's Courts that didn't escape demolition was Canns Court. Standing next to Irsha Court at the southern end of Irsha Street it survived until 1938, when the conditions of its houses had become too bad to permit further use. The area has now been grassed over.

Canns Court first appears by name in 1890, however there have been various Cann families living here since ship's carpenter Richard Cann moved from Braunton in 1825 and married an Appledore girl called Elizabeth Hancock. The Cann family continued to live in this Court until his great grandson Richard Cann was the last Cann to leave in 1921. This family gave their name to the Court and created a dynasty of Canns in Appledore which continues to this day.

In the early 1800s Canns Court contained a pub called the 'Woolpack', supposed to have been the inspiration for the smuggler's den in Kingsley's Westward Ho! The Woolpack was run by John 'Jacker' Hancock, and it is after him that the adjacent slipway (known as the 'Jackeran slipway' or 'Hancock's Slip') was named.

Apparently there were also rather a lot of pigs around here. In 1858 there were many complaints about the intolerable stench from the pigsties. In 1877 Dr Pratt recommended that the pigs near to the National School be done away with as typhoid fever resulted from such creatures. In 1777 tax records show that land tax was being paid on 'Pigs Court'. Was this an earlier name for this Court?

The condition of the houses was pretty awful though. An Appledore resident still alive today remembers being brought up in a two-roomed house here in the 1930s. It had one cold water tap from which the water flowed out in a channel under the front door, and it had just a ladder to get upstairs. How much worse was it in Victorian times?

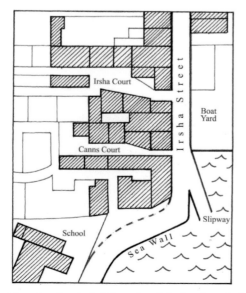

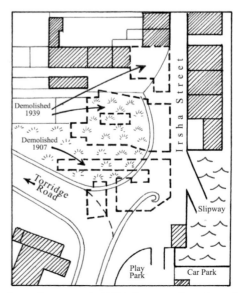

Maps showing the buildings demolished at the end of Irsha Street. Some went in 1907 when a road was formed to the Station, and the rest in 1938 to clear uninhabitable houses.

View of the estuary in the mid 1930s. The buildings just left of centre are Canns Court, now demolished.

The Jackeran slipway and the houses of Canns Court, seen from the beach below.

In 1891 Thomas and Elizabeth Keen of Canns Court were charged with neglect and cruelty to their seven children. (Actually they had nine children at this time, but as the eldest two were over twelve they were no longer classed as children). All eleven of them were reported as sleeping in one room.

In 1895 James and Hannah Evans were charged with failing to look after their two children properly. The bedroom was in a filthy state with a broken iron bedstead, a nasty mattress and greasy pillows covered with vermin. Downstairs there were sickening things in the pantry. The children were thinly-clad, flea-bitten, with dirty matted hair and over-run with nits. The father was violent and the mother a confirmed drunkard. The couple were given 14-days hard labour and the children taken into the workhouse at Bideford where their ragged clothes were immediately burned.

CONVICTED BY TATTOO:

In 1897 in Irsha Court 19-year-old Elizabeth Cox was 'courted' by her neighbour Thomas Curtis, a 21-year-old sailmaker. She became pregnant and demanded maintenance money. In Court he said that he had not promised to marry her, but he was found to have her name tattooed on his arm and admitted to have stated "now you are mine forever". The case was proved and the couple later married.

HOW TO GET RID OF A LODGER:

In 1908 Maria Cann pleaded guilty to having a chimney fire. She told the Court that she had put petroleum on the fire because she was annoyed with her nephew who was lodging with her and it was the only way she could drive him from the house!

TRAGIC ROAD ACCIDENT:

Appledore's first fatal road accident happened here at the entrance to Irsha Street in May 1938, just before the Canns Court properties were demolished. The bend was very tight and restricted, but early motor buses still came down here. Little Betty Carter was visiting her grandfather in Canns Court and ran out from a blind corner just as Walter Cook drove round the corner in one of Sammy Guard's 'Pride of the West' buses. Just 3½ years old she was killed instantly. Shortly afterwards the corner was improved when Canns Court was demolished, but Sammy Guard never forgave himself even though the driver was exonerated. Sammy Guard gave up the bus business after the War.

THE WATER PROBLEM:

The conditions in Canns Court serve well to illustrate that having a clean and plentiful supply of water is essential for good health.

A public health report in 1866 found that Appledore had cess-pits next to wells, blocked drains, open privies, dung heaps and filthy water. One house was examined and found to contain pigs in the back garden, rabbits in the house, and twelve people living in two rooms. Unless the drainage system and water supplies were completely overhauled then Appledore would remain permanently unhealthy. Thirty years later nothing much had been done. The well in Irsha Court was found to be badly contaminated and was closed. Residents were forced to gather rainwater from butt pitchers or walk half a mile to a useable well.

An old Appledore well, now capped off in a back garden.

It was not until 1901 that Appledore was fitted with a network of mains water pipes so that clean water could be brought straight into people's houses. Three years later the good water and vastly improved sanitation was described as a great blessing to the town.

but on average the level of water was about four feet down.

A builder in the 1970s admitted that when starting any renovations the first thing they would do would be to take the floorboards up to find the well. They could then use this as somewhere to throw all the rubbish and not have to pay for skip hire.

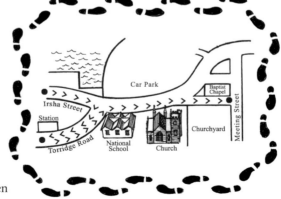

A ghostly apparition was frequently seen near to this slipway in the 1930s calling out to sailors on their boats, urgently asking for a lift across the river. He was a man wearing a hat but he vanished as soon as anyone put a boat in to help him. Known as 'Old White Hat' he hasn't been seen for some time – maybe he eventually got his lift!

WELLS:

All properties in Appledore originally had access to a well. There are very few signs of these now, although a few houses do have glassed-over wells as a feature in their kitchens.

Most wells were placed close to the back door or in the centre of a shared courtyard. Many residents report finding a well in the back kitchen which probably indicates that the original house had been extended over that area. Digging a well is a challenging process, but at Appledore the underlying layers of shillet bedrock face vertically, allowing water to percolate into any hole driven deep enough. The well walls were generally lined with large pebbles and simply wedged into the surrounding clay or soil. Generally the water level would rise and fall by about twelve feet over the course of the seasons,

GO UP TO TORRIDGE ROAD AND THEN ALONG PAST ST MARY'S CHURCH

The opening of the railway to Appledore was celebrated in style. There were bands, speeches and a grand public tea.

Station Master Harold Moody standing proudly over his new station opened in May 1908.

THE BIDEFORD, WESTWARD HO! AND APPLEDORE RAILWAY:

Appledore seems an unlikely place to have its own Station. It's not on the way to anywhere and only had between two and three thousand inhabitants, most of whom could travel by boat to anywhere they wanted to go.

In 1875 a steam tramway was proposed to link Appledore with Westward Ho! along the Northam Burrows, but this never came to anything. Then in 1896 a scheme was approved taking a round-about route from Bideford through Westward Ho! and ending up at Appledore. A company was formed and by 1901 the first section of the line was ready for use. Unfortunately this only went as far as Westward Ho! where wrangling caused a halt in construction for six years before work started again, and it was eventually completed to the original plan. The railway had arrived and Appledore was no longer isolated.

APPLEDORE STATION:

It was a single-track line but the station at Appledore had a 300-foot long platform. The building consisted of a booking office, general waiting room, ladies waiting room and toilets for both sexes. On the platform were weighing machines, timetable boards and seats for passengers. There was an engine shed, water tower, signal box, two railway cottages (which can still be seen) and a footbridge that linked Irsha Street with the nearby allotment gardens further up the hillside.

The opening day on 1st May 1908 was celebrated in style. There were speeches and a grand public tea. The first train was received by the Station Master Harold Moody and the whole area was crowded with people. Confidence was high that this new service would bring a huge influx of visitors and wealth to the village.

Each carriage could carry 10 first-class passengers and 40 third-class passengers. A 3rd class return ticket from Appledore to Bideford cost 8d. There was also a set-price charge for various other items: bicycles were 6d, dogs (accompanied by passengers) were 3d and harps were 2s 6d.

However whilst everyone was celebrating the completion of this long-awaited project, no-one seemed to have noticed that it wasn't really needed. The road journey to Bideford was about two miles, and even if you walked this it would take you about the same length of time as the train journey – about half an hour. Holidaymakers arriving at Appledore were far more likely to use the road for the last part of their journey, and for Appledore people working in Bideford the first train didn't arrive until nearly 9:00am, long after they needed to be at their place of work. At an average speed of 14 m.p.h, the railway catered only as a curiosity for tourists or golfers and was therefore doomed to failure from the start.

The custom-made steam engines 'Kingsley', 'Grenville', and 'Torridge' soldiered on into the 1st World War, but closure finally came when the engines were taken away for War duties. On the 27th March 1917 the last train pulled out of the Station, and silence fell over this ill-fated venture.

Only the back wall of the station building now survives with the fireplaces visible that served the waiting room and station office. The level of the pavement shows where the platform once stood. The nearby gardens all have very black soil caused by the waste coal from the engines being spread over them.

The tracks were taken up, the grass grew up and the route was forgotten. Then in 1935 the 'old lines' were turned into Torridge Road - named after one of the steam engines. In 2006 a commemorative plaque was unveiled here produced by local ceramic artist Maggie Curtis.

BLACKIES:

The sloping grassland opposite the old Station used to be known as 'Blackmore's Field' but is now known as 'Blackies'. Mr Blackmore was a lamp-lighter who worked the land here, and the name 'Blackies' took root amongst the numerous small children that he had to chase off his property. During the 2nd World War a shed on the land housed guns and armaments belonging to H.M.S. Appledore. The area was landscaped in 2005 as an open-space for the people of Appledore.

APPLEDORE SCHOOL:

There had been numerous private schools run by individuals in their houses for many years. In 1708 Robert Kees was said to have taught school in the village for over twenty years. There were many others plus a number of parish charity schools, but no formal education existed. The 'National Schools' were started in 1811, the aim being to have a Church School in every parish in the Country, but Appledore did not benefit from this until over 30 years later.

The land for the school was provided from a corner of the churchyard and the school opened its doors in 1844. There were two classrooms: one for boys taught by 30-year-old George Baker, and one for girls taught by George's wife Emily Baker. They both lived in the accommodation provided as part of the building. Within a year the school had 213 pupils each paying 1d per week to attend. The numbers continued to grow, swelling the school, helped by the Bakers' seven children. In 1898 the school had to be extended – the front 'wing' being added at this time.

Original facade of Appledore School (Devon Record Office).

A MOMENTOUS FIRST:

A momentous and historic event happened in the school on 30th May 1902. At precisely ten minutes to three-o-clock on a Friday afternoon with the whole school waiting keenly, the first toilet was flushed. Works had been going on for the last nine months laying a network of water mains around the village, and the school was one of the first places to benefit from mains water. Until then water from wells or pumps had to be obtained for all purposes in Appledore. However, it was another four years before mains water served the Methodist School in Richmond Road.

In 1914 a 'Roll of Honour' was put up in the classroom listing over 120 Old Boys who

The Appledore National School class of 1936:
Back Row: Norman Ford, Billy Cook, Dennis Lesslie, Jimmy Harris, Dennis Job.
Middle row: Sissy Mitchell, Dorothy Jewell, Joan Cann, Pauline Whitaker, Rona Moyce, Renne Cane,
Betty Brennan, Hilda Osborne, Yvonne Jewell, Joyce Hallett. Front row: Jackie Bale, John Smale, Billy Powe, Edwin
Harding, Billy Cawsey, Bobby White, Terence Raymond, Clifford Short.

The Appledore National School class of 1951:
Back row: Dilys Owen, Sheila Cox, Jillian Cole, Valerie Magee, Jean Hayward, Dawn Williams, Ann Williams, Ann
Symons. Next row: Tessa Harris, Sheila Walsh, Jillian Peak, Glenda Cox, Josephine Evans, Joyce Griffey,
Renne Tucker. Next row down: Larry Bignell, Michael Walsh, Brian Rendel, Walter Fowler, Alec Craner, Richard
Harris, Michael Cawsey, Ronald Griffey. Front row: Bobby Cann, Michael Lamey, Eric Hocking, Michael
Wetherden, Leslie Pyke, Jack Whitaker, Cyril Day.

A large turn-out for a jumble sale in Appledore School Hall in 1913.
Amongst the people in the photograph (working from front to back) are: Freddie Jenkins, Vera Braund, Mabel Ross,
Rita Bowden, Don Tucker, Bertie Heard, Tommy Bassett, Sydney Cann, Helen Hinks (the lady with the hat),
William Heard, Dolly Cox, Vicky Lobbett, Grace Seborg, Hubert Brooks, Jane Vaggers, Frances Lobbett,
Mrs Hammett, Prince Keen, Jack Evans, Eva Evans, John Williams, Bert Blackmore, Ethel Down, ~?~ Cobbledick,
Mrs Lobbett, MrsGriffiths, Mrs Fisher, Ben Blackmore, Belle Richards, Grace Evans, Maud
Robey, Charlie Day, Gertie Vivian, Belle Gorrell, Ada Brend, Eunice Short, Mrs Short, Sally Harding, Matilda Slade,
Florrie Cole, Mrs Youngson, Mrs Carter, Mrs Hare, and Mrs Taylor.

The roadway being constructed below St Mary's Church in the late 1930s

were currently on HM Service. At the end of the War another amazing sight caused many children to be late from school when a huge airship passed over the village.

The school was a great success and many generations of Appledore's children were educated here. However once the Council School had opened in 1909 the numbers slowly started to drop and the buildings gradually deteriorated until it was no longer viable to continue. The school finally closed on 18th Dec 1969 after 125 years of schooling, when the last 34 remaining Primary pupils were transferred to the County School up the road. The hall reverted to church ownership and is now well-used as a Community Church Hall hosting many events such as exhibitions, plays, social clubs, play schools, fairs, meetings, etc. and so still provides a valuable space for all the village to use.

The production of amateur village plays is not new though. In 1884 a Mr Garvice from Boathyde presented three evening performances of his play 'The Fisherman's Daughter' – described as a laughable farce, acted by well-known amateurs, and presented in a thoroughly professional manner. His successor Tommy Waters is continuing this tradition by providing similar amateur plays for the village today.

APPLEDORE CHURCH:

No history of Appledore would be complete without a history of its church set on steeply-sloping wooded ground next to the river, but St Mary's isn't that old compared with the rest of Appledore's history, only appearing here in 1838. Prior to that the land had a religious history stretching back to 1564 when Queen Elizabeth I gave the Appledore church and manor lands to the Dean of Windsor. There was already a Catholic Chapel on the site dating back to at least the 14th century when many private chapels were built. A church is first known to be here in 1575 when it appears on a map produced by Christopher Saxton.

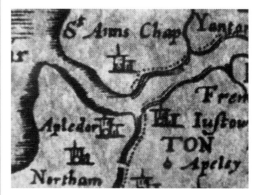

John Speed's map of 1610, showing church buildings either side of the estuary.

The prior use of this site as a religious place could date back to Dark-Age or pre-Christian times, and the need for offerings or prayers to be made before making a treacherous river crossing. For pilgrims and traders this was a matter of course, and we know that small Chapels appeared on both sides of the river. The old Chapel at Appledore was demolished when St Mary's was built, but the one on the Braunton side of the river survived in its wilderness of sand - indeed its foundations still exist, buried under the Braunton Burrows.

1841 Braunton tithe map showing location of St Anne's Chapel. (North Devon Record Office).

THE CHAPEL OF THE SANDS:

The Chapel on Braunton Burrows was known as the '*Chapel of the Sands*' and is also indicated on the map of 1575 as '*St Anne's Chapel*'. It is interesting to us as it would have been the twin of the Chapel at Appledore which is also believed to have been dedicated to St Anne. This building survived until about 1820 when it was pulled down and the stones used in a farm-building. However, we have a description of it as being 14'6" long x 12'0" wide, walls built of rubble stone and with a sandstone arch. Its font has survived and is now in St Anne's Church at Saunton.

THE OLD CHAPEL AT APPLEDORE:

The old chapel of St Anne at Appledore would have been very similar to the one at Braunton, although at 40 feet by 20 feet Appledore's was quite a bit larger. It had four windows, two doors, a turret containing two bells, and a well at the east end. It was sited near to the western end of the present church but all trace of it has now vanished.

Non-conformist worship came to Appledore in the late 1600s pushing aside the old religious ways in favour of more understandable worship for the people, so the old chapel became used less and less. In 1718 it was described as being 'continually in want of repair' and by 1754 it was no longer in use. In 1812 these Glebe Lands were still owned by the Dean of Windsor but were let to tenants and the Chapel was being used as a cow-shed. At this time old Mrs Hammett remembered a service being held there in her childhood and a burial taking place in the church grounds, so we can assume that it was still used until the 1730s. By the 1830s the lower part of the land was described as a cliff continually being washed away by the sea, and concern was raised about the lack of religion in Appledore as wrestling matches and donkey races were taking place on the Sabbath.

Interestingly when the chapel was demolished in 1836 a roof timber was discovered to have "Daniel D. 1121" carved into it. Could this possibly mean that the Chapel dated back to the period not long after the Norman Conquest?

THE BUILDING GOES AHEAD:

In 1836 the foundation stone for Appledore's new Chapel-of-Ease was laid, apparently witnessed by a crowd of over 2,000 people. A coin was traditionally placed under this stone. During the digging of the foundations a great number of human remains were discovered

The original interior of St Mary's Chapel of Ease - there is no rood screen or organ and the pews are laid out with 2 side aisles, not the central aisle which is there today.

Commemorative photo following the completion of the church tower in 1909. The men in the picture are: William Down. Jack Richards, 'Lambeth' Richards, Tom Pyke, Mr Heard, Tommy Parsons (headmaster C.of E. school). Front row: John Harris, Jack Tawton, Rev George Scholey, Jack Gorrell, William Heard. With the exception of the vicar, John Harris and Mr Parsons, the others were key workers involved in the project.

confirming that this land had been used as a burial ground for hundreds of years. Bones had also been found whilst digging near the site for Appledore Station so the burial ground must have been quite extensive.

Appledore Church as it originally looked, without a tower. This was added in 1909.

In 1838 the church was finished and opened to great delight. The building was described as 'chaste and handsome' with high-back pews arranged with two side aisles, but no font, as this was just a Chapel-of-Ease and Appledore didn't get its own vicar until six years later. The Chapel did have half a tower though (unfortunately the money ran out and this tower wasn't completed until much later).

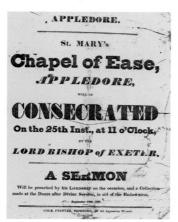

Some timber from the old demolished Chapel was built into the pulpit steps but was later removed, as it was considered too Catholic.

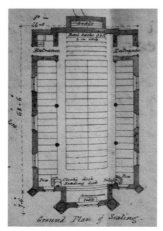

The original plan of Appledore Church in 1838. (North Devon Record Office)

In 1876 gas lighting was installed, and in 1898 the old pews were replaced with lower ones and a central aisle. Major alterations were carried out in 1909 when the stump of the tower was demolished and its Welsh stone used to extend the church, the rear gallery being removed to achieve this. Local stone was then used to build a new tower containing a clock previously belonging to the United Services College at Westward Ho! and a peal of bells presented by William Tatem (Lord Glanely). Electric lights were installed in 1932.

The Rood Screen was presented by the late P.K. Harris and erected in 1912. It is crafted from timber taken from the sailing ship 'Marco Polo' which in 1852 sailed from Liverpool to Australia with 930 passengers, taking only 68 days to complete the journey. At that time the journey usually took anything up to 150 days.

The building has had its architectural critics though. In 1923 a writer stated that *"The building exhibits all that lack of architectural merit, characteristic of the date of its erection"* and in 1954 a guide-book stated that *"The*

Enough boys here for a football competition, not just a single team. They were all organised as part of a church group. Rev. Muller can be seen on the right of this photo, taken in 1922.

Rev. Muller with his confirmation class pictured outside the front of the vicarage in 1924.
Back row: Belle Richards, Lizzie Hutchings, Billy Eastman, Sarah Eastman, ~?~ Cann, George Clark, Blanche Tatem, Polly Lamey, Claude Woodlock, Beatrice Ley, Lizzie McCullum, ~?~ Guard, Hilda McCarthy.
Second row: Claude Hammond, ~?~ Screech, Jack Hammond, Sally Eastman, Sally Down, Billy Marshall, ~?~ Beer, Fanny Fisher, Ruby Jennings. Third row: Annie Bilton, Helen Gorrell, Minnie Ross, Eveline Powe, Mrs Muller, Rev Muller, Mrs Stevens, ~?~ Hookway, Alice Heard. Front row: Bert Heard, 'Happy' Lamey, Kelly Eastman, Jimmy Heard, Reg Taylor, [unknown], Walter Lesslie, [unknown].

Church of St Mary (built 1838) is dull, however everything else about Appledore is fascinating." The description of the Church in the Listed Buildings Register is perhaps somewhat kinder by not saying anything at all, apart from *"Parish Church 1838, in Gothic style; tower and west additions 1909"* (hardly a glowing endorsement of its design!).

APPLEDORE'S VICARS:

Church histories can often be rather dry and dull, but the same certainly can't be said of Appledore's vicars. We've certainly had some interesting and eccentric ministers in our time, to which I am sure our present incumbent John Ewington will feel happy to be included. Here are just a few of the ones who have spent their lives doing God's work in this parish:

REV. EDWARD REYNOLDS:

Appledore's first vicar was previously a curate at Northam. Appointed in 1845 at the age of 27 he remained as vicar at Appledore for 51 years until his death in 1896 at the age of 78. He is buried at the top of the churchyard by the gate leading to the vicarage. He dedicated his

life to the people of Appledore, and in his long tenure he must have buried just about everyone he knew when he first came to the village.

REV. ALFRED GURNEY GOLDSMITH:

Served from 1896 to 1905. His previous posting was working with Missions to Seamen at Hong Kong. After Appledore he went to Melbourne and eventually died in Japan.

REV. HUGH CHRISTIAN ANDREAS SIGVALD MULLER:

Served from 1921 to 1953. Related to the Royal Family of Denmark he was a gifted linguist, speaking seven languages fluently - very useful with many foreign sailors visiting Appledore. He always got into couple's wedding photographs and their reception, whether he was invited or not. When he died there was a minute's silence at the Bideford Football match and his widow received over 550 letters of condolence from around the world.

"It is very hard, well nigh impossible to describe this fascinating, eccentric, unique character, who will always be a local, living legend. Rev. Muller was certainly unlike any other vicar you or I have ever encountered. He seemed to be a sort of reverse Scarlet Pimpernel. There was no need to seek him, because he was here, there and everywhere, involved in everything appertaining to the village and the district. Visiting the sick at all hours of the day or night; attending every wedding (Church or Chapel), going with the lifeboat whenever she was called out; even knocking on doors on wet nights asking owners to let their cats in."
(*Appledore Boyhood Memories, by E R Carter*).

REV. DONALD LEWIS PEYTON-JONES:

Served from 1973 to 1978 and was born in Australia. A founder member of the Royal Marines Special Boat Service. He often wore a green Marines beret, white cassock and

sandals. When he found that he could get fined for parking his car on double yellow lines he took to riding his piebald horse 'Magpie' to all pastoral visits – *"let them try and put a ticket on that!"* He also found that he could not be breathalised when on a horse (not sure if this still applies). He brought his dogs to church for communion services and he loved spending time on Lundy where he was also chaplain for the island. Although the island was in regular radio contact with the mainland, Peyton-Jones preferred a more reliable means of communication – homing pigeons. He used to send messages back to the mainland using carrier pigeons, and had a network of children in Appledore called 'Post-Angels' who collected the messages and delivered them to the right people.

He was a hopeless time-keeper, his services often starting late because he was off swimming or sailing. However upon his arrival back at the church, he would hoist his towel and swimsuit up the flagpole so that everyone would know that he was back - *"If my towel is flying, you'll know I'm here!"*

Just so the others don't feel left out, all the Appledore vicars (with their dates of service) have been:
Rev. Edward Reynolds: 1845 to 1896.
Rev. Alfred Gurney Goldsmith: 1896 to 1905.
Rev. George Scholey: 1905 to 1921.
Rev. Hugh Muller: 1921 to 1953.
Rev. Royston Dixon: 1953-1972.
Rev. Donald Peyton-Jones: 1973 to 1978.
Rev. Keith Feltham: 1979 to 1982.
Rev. Lester John Yeo: 1983 to 1989.
Rev. Robert Varty: 1989 to 1995.
Rev. John Ewington: from 1996.

APPLEDORE CHURCHYARD:

No excursion into Appledore's history would be complete without a walk round the churchyard looking at the graves of all the mariners who are buried here. It would be impossible to mention just one or two - so I won't even try. However there many more sailors who died in foreign places or who were lost at sea who have no memorial here.

Representing these others I will mention just one: sailmaker Stephen Slader, who in 1855 was on a voyage in the Mediterranean. He died shortly after contracting an unknown illness and was buried at sea near Majorca - latitude 38'10" north, longitude 3'10" east. All his effects were listed in the ship's log and auctioned off to the crew. The money raised was sent home to his widow Grace who survived without him in Appledore for a further 53 years. Their son (John Thomas Slader) never knew his father, and he later became Parish Clerk in Appledore, a position that he held for fifty years.

Not all bodies in the graveyard were human. In 1899 a workman was passing the graveyard when he heard groans coming from amongst the graves. He ran to fetch the sexton and they both heard the groans becoming more rapid. In trepidation they went to investigate, and by the dim light they saw that a donkey had fallen into one of the vaults. Together they helped the poor creature from his uncomfortable position and the animal appeared none the worse for its adventure.

Daniel Fowler: the first Appledore man to be killed in the 1st World War. He was 32 and was serving on HMS 'Swiftsure'.

An engraved view of Appledore in 1830. The Seagate Hotel is on the far right. Top left is Staddon House, and below that is the Independent Chapel in Meeting Street. The other building towards the right is the ancient chapel of St Anne on the site of the present church of St Mary. Evidence from a wooden beam taken from this old Chapel suggests that it might have dated back to the year 1121.

The Appledore 'swimming pool' wasn't too good for bathing but it was a great place for little boys to sail their boats - as I can personally testify. This beach was also somewhere to collect unusual rocks. Any geologist wandering along here would have been amazed to see: basalt, exotic corals and other strange rocks from all around the world littering this beach. They had all been brought in by vessels as ballast and were then dumped overboard at the end of their voyage.

The War Memorial:

Outside the Churchyard stands the War Memorial, erected in 1930 to remember the Appledore men lost in the 1st World War – their names are listed on the central section. On the lower section were later added names from the 2nd World War. 104 names are included here in total to commemorate all the men from the armed services and merchant ships who lost their lives in these conflicts. Many of these have no service grave so this is our only reminder of their sacrifice.

Exotic coral taken from the beach below the church, these rocks were brought in as ballast on the sailing ships.

Appledore Swimming Pool:

The land below the church originally sloped down to the beach, and although a track ran round here this was not formed into a proper road until the late 1930s. A children's play park was formed below the road and you could get down the beach via a ladder where a sea-water-filled swimming pool was constructed. Unfortunately it was never very clean and was used more by trapped fish than swimmers. In 1954 a trial to grow mussels for human consumption was undertaken here but this failed to take off. The swimming pool gradually fell apart and what remained of it was finally covered by the Churchfields Car Park in 1990.

Anyone going onto the beach here in the 1960s will remember these paintings on the sea wall. They were respectively painted by Jimmy Cox and Johnny Fowler.

The Anchor:

The anchor now displayed as a focal point to the end of Appledore Quay was discovered buried in the river mud during the construction of the car park in 1990. It is believed to have come from a 500-ton sailing ship dating from the 1850s.

Tavern Shipbuilding Yard:

On the beach just past the Seagate Hotel (formerly known as the Tavern) was the 'Tavern Yard', also sometimes known as the 'Churchfield Yard'. It was an exposed place to undertake shipbuilding so a breakwater of rocks was formed to protect it from the worst of the storms. The yard was established in 1853 by 23-year-old William Cock, but when he died of cholera the following year his father James Cock took over. Within a few years James was employing seventeen people on the site which contained offices, blacksmiths, sail-makers, block-making shop, saw-pits, etc. Eighteen ships were built here before the Cock family moved to the Richmond Dry-Dock in 1882 and the site fell into disuse. The Cocks appear to have been boat builders in Appledore for a very long time. In 1617 a 36-ton vessel brought back 16,000 fish from Newfoundland. The master and owner was John Cock, son of shipbuilder Philip Cock.

BLACKMORE'S SHIPBUILDING YARD:

In about 1910 Mathew Blackmore took part of the site as a boat-building yard, although his site was a little further north roughly where the play-park is today. Sheds were built and this area again rang with the sound of boat-building activity. It became a successful business and by 1928 had expanded sufficiently to warrant a move to a new site further up the river at Boathyde. The site here again became redundant and was shortly afterwards made into a promenade and children's play park.

CHURCHFIELDS:

This is the name of the little street leading through to Meeting Street. 'Churchfields' or 'Chapel Fields' also denoted the lands belonging to the original Chapel at Appledore, the lands having been given to the Dean of Windsor in 1564. These included the two blocks of dwellings from the Seagate Hotel to the Baptist Church, and the land between the Church and the river.

There were shops here: Henry Lang bootmaker and his father Peter Lang a baker had businesses in Churchfields in the 1840s, and in the 1930s Joshua King ran a greengrocer's shop. In the yard at the back of the Seagate Hotel was a blacksmith's shop. In 1899 Mr Beer's forge set the nearby thatched roofs alight and threatened to destroy all the neighbouring roofs, but luckily the fire was able to be put out, before it spread further.

HIGHER ROAD:

From the War Memorial, take the narrow cobbled path towards Meeting Street. This path was known as the 'Higher Road' as it was higher than Churchfield Road.

BAPTIST CHAPEL:

The Baptists moved here in 1858 from their former Chapel in Irsha Street. Their benefactor was John Darracott, a prominent member of a local Teetotal Society and a devout Christian who gave the land and also a considerable amount of money towards the construction of the building. The Chapel opened on 7th July 1858 and the 350 seats were crowded to excess. It had high-backed pews and a box pulpit, although these were removed in 1900 during renovation works.

At the rear was a schoolroom and squeezed between the two was a house for the minister given in 1880, but this was not in a very good condition and was demolished fourteen years later. An enlarged schoolroom for 400 pupils was built on the site in 1897 which is the building you see today facing Churchfields. Electric lights were fitted in 1929.

In 1928 Lady Reardon-Smith came over from Cardiff especially to dedicate the new £500 organ, partly donated by her husband. However the weather on the Bar was too bad and their boat had to put into Ilfracombe instead so she missed the ceremony. The organ was removed in 2005 as part of modernisation work, sadly along with the marble wall memorials which are now in storage.

Photos showing the shipbuilding yards located where the main car park is today.
Above is a view from the river showing the Tavern Yard, and below is Blackmore's yard in the 1920s.

The Baptist Church celebrated their 100th anniversary in 1933. They did it in style – this was just the tea committee. Back row: Katie Cooksley, Lottie Jenkins, Kate Fishwick, Olive Ford, May Lamey, Nellie Cobbledick, Maud May, Helen Varley. Second row: May Gale, Alice Vaggers, Ivy Harris, Doris Slade, Lydia Lunn. Third row: 'Bimbo' Hocking, Beryl Ford, Marjorie Cooksley, Florence Kearon, Graham Vaggers, Violet Lunn, May Cann, Mary Slade, Pauline Webber. Front row: Eileen Lunn, Johnny Lunn.

Bartlett's grocery shop at the corner of Market Street and Meeting Street around 1920. Sisters Elsie and Clara Bartlett can be seen in the doorway.

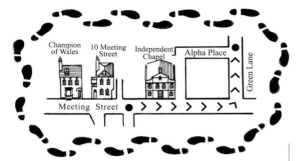

TURN RIGHT UP MEETING STREET AND LEFT INTO GREEN LANE

We now enter Meeting Street, probably the oldest route down the hill to the river-front even though the appearance of its houses does not reflect the age of this ancient track.

The bottom of Meeting Street has been home to a number of shops over the years, these early 19th century buildings replacing others that previously stood in this location. At number 2 on the junction with Market Street was Bartlett's grocery shop, which traded until after the 2nd World War.

On the opposite corner at number 3 (now Sylvester's Fish and Chips) was a watchmaker's in 1906 (Hubert Lemon) and a newsagents until the 2nd World War (Husband's, then Bailey's). After the war it became Harris's shoe-repairers and then a ceramics and novelties shop. Most Appledore shops have continually changed use and owners and this continues to this present day.

FLOODING:

In 1859 flooding occurred in Meeting Street, but not as you might expect from the sea. The North Devon Journal reported: "*A thunderstorm burst with a fury that beat everything ever seen before. A torrent poured down Meeting Street, carrying with it large quantities of stone & shingle, which accumulated near the Tavern. It formed an embankment, causing the waters to rush right and left, into the adjacent houses, filling the rooms to two or three feet. It put out the kitchen fires, and the occupants took refuge on the chairs, and then on the tables. In St Mary's Church, the cushions, prayer books and footstools were found floating about.*"

THE THREE TUNS:

At number 4 Meeting Street were the blacksmith's premises belonging to the Lemon family. The Lemons were a family that went back to the 17th century in Appledore, many of whom have been coopers and smiths who provided Appledore with its metalwork for many generations.

Prior to that this building was a coaching inn called the 'Three Tuns' tavern, upon which Peter Benson was paying land tax in 1777, part of the former Melhuish lands. In 1782 Thomas Headon was appointed landlord in place of Christopher Bassett. The inn was still there in 1797, but by 1826 the building was referred to as 'formerly the Three Tuns'. The ground floor level used to have a large archway leading through to the back where horses could be stabled.

Champion of Wales:

Another ancient inn and malt house stood next to the Three Tuns – the 'Champion of Wales'. This name first appears in the 1822 register of licensees when Robert Day was granted permission to sell beer here. Quite where the inn's name comes from, no-one seems to know.

In 1871 John Fishwick 38 and his son Emmanuel 16 from Vernon's Lane, were charged with being drunk and riotous at a late hour of the night in the Champion of Wales. They used threatening language to the Police constable, broke a table, were disorderly and assaulted and knocked down the landlord's wife Mary Jane Day. A typical Saturday night out!

For the record the known landlords up to the 2nd World War have been:

Robert Day, William Cox, Daniel Lovering, Daniel and Mary Ann Lovering, Elizabeth Cann, Mary McCulllum, William Stapledon, William Day, John Day, Joseph Cox, Robert Stevens, Elizabeth Oatway, Joshua King, Lewin Uglow, and Gomer Trevor Jones.

The pub closed its doors on 8th September 2008.

The Man who built Appledore:

At number 10 Meeting Street lived John Lambates Richards, generally known as 'Lambeth' Richards. Born in 1864, son of a mariner whose family came originally from Hanover, he became a stonemason and in 1896 set up his own building business. For the next thirty years or more he had a hand in almost every building job in Appledore, from whitewashing a wall to building a row of houses – he was the man that did it. He built the row of houses at the bottom of Vernons Lane, all of which were occupied by members of his family. He also built 'Shalimar' in Pitt for himself, and the adjacent row of houses which was often referred to as 'Lambeth Terrace'. He married three times and his son took over the business after his death.

'Lambeth' Richards workbook, detailing the work undertaken throughout Appledore from 1896. This page shows the bill for the construction of the houses in Victoria Crescent.

This massive construction spanning the road near the Champion of Wales was erected to celebrate the Diamond Jubilee of Queen Victoria in 1897. The 60th anniversary of the start of her reign was celebrated by the giving of money to the poor, and there was also a grand public tea on the Burrows with a music band. Children and old people, gentry and workers, all joined in the festivities together. (Roy Cann Collection at North Devon Museum Trust).

John 'Lambeth' Richards (centre) and his workers in 1899.

THE DRANG WITH NO NAME:

Next to number 12 Meeting Street is a small covered drang leading through to Vernons Lane, although it appears to have no known name so maybe I can suggest 'Richards Court'. This is not for Lambeth Richards, but for Thomas and Ann Richards (no relation) who lost four of their children in the cholera outbreak of 1866. They lived here in this little enclosed court but it is not surprising that the cholera spread given the inspector's subsequent report on this area:

"This narrow drang-way leads into a small open space, three sides of a square, in the centre of which, under the very windows of their house, stands the privy used by the whole of the houses. The stench emitted from this nuisance was described by the neighbours as insufferable. Higher up the street we found an open drain which carried off the sewerage from the higher part of the town, and the nuisance was flowing over the soil, close to a well which had recently been sunk, and which was the only water in the whole street that was not fetid."

MEETING STREET HOUSES:

The houses in Meeting Street were all sited on the Melhuish lands which stretched across to Bude Street. The highest shop in Meeting Street was at number 18 where Eliza and Doris Slade ran an over-the-counter grocery store between 1927 and 1954. There were no more shops up the Street, although the house a couple of doors up from here did have a reputation as being a 'shop of ill-repute'!

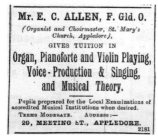

Mr. E. C. ALLEN, F. Gld. O.
(Organist and Choirmaster, St. Mary's Church, Appledore),
GIVES TUITION IN
Organ, Pianoforte and Violin Playing, Voice - Production & Singing, and Musical Theory.
Pupils prepared for the Local Examinations of accredited Musical Institutions when desired.
TERMS MODERATE. ADDRESS:—
29, MEETING ST., APPLEDORE.
2181

(Bideford Gazette: 29th April 1902).

THE RUNAWAY CAR:

Make sure your car has good brakes before driving down this hill. In 1981, 49-year-old Staddon resident Hazel Langbridge lost control of her car on this hill early on Sunday morning, when her accelerator stuck. The car gathered speed down the hill, went across the quay, over the pavement and somersaulted through the railings into the river. Unfortunately no-one witnessed the incident and it was a quarter of an hour before her car was spotted under the water, too late to save her and her dog. Her body was eventually recovered by a diver and the RNLI.

The runaway car being retrieved from the river in 1981.

INDEPENDENT CHAPEL:

Non-conformist worship has always been

Two views of Meeting Street. The upper picture shows a large group of children gathering for this photograph in about 1900, probably from the Baptist Sunday School.
The lower picture shows the view looking the other way in about 1930. On the right, the bowed window shows the location of Slade's grocery shop.

strong in Appledore largely due to the village not having its own parish church until 1838. In 1662 after the Civil War and the Act of Uniformity a Puritan preacher called Anthony Down was ejected from the church at Northam when he refused to use the Book of Common Prayer. He came to Appledore and started holding services in a barn belonging to Thomas Gribble. The barn became licensed for worship and was eventually replaced by a purpose built Chapel or Meeting House after which Meeting Street is named.

The Chapel was built in 1699 and could hold 350 people. A hundred years later the members found that it was not big enough so they decided to build a new one. The Meeting House Chapel was demolished and rebuilt in 1816 as the Independent Chapel seating about 500 people, and this is the building you can see today. It subsequently became the Congregational Chapel and then the United Reformed Chapel, but was closed in 1996 when the members dwindled ending 334 years of worship on the site. It has now been converted into a private residence called 'Bell Tower House'.

ENTERTAINMENTS:

The Independent Chapel hall was used for many evening entertainments. In 1868 the Appledore 'Amateur Madrigal and Glee Society'

performed songs in the hall, and in 1895 there was an entertainment with a phonograph. John Tamlyn's singing was recorded and played back to the audience who found the ghostly applause at the end sounding very strange. Maybe if you listen hard enough you can still hear it!

The church bought a new organ in 1910, half the cost of which was met by Andrew Carnegie the millionaire philanthropist, described at the time as the richest man in the world. This was probably arranged by his cousin Claude Carnegie who conveniently lived in Northam.

APPLEDORE VICARAGE:

Appledore's current vicar now lives in a three-bedroomed bungalow on the corner of the churchyard site. The original purpose-built vicarage was much grander. Planned after the death of Appledore's first vicar Edward Reynolds (who lived in Staddon House), it was certainly a grand rambling house which suited a late-Victorian vicar and his family. It was built on property owned by the church and had its own well, coach-house and stables. It was first occupied at the end of 1897 and was used as Appledore vicarage until 1983. It later became a residential home for the elderly and has now been converted into flats.

In 1984 the vicarage was being renovated by a new owner who was sleeping in one of the guest bedrooms. Rudely awakened in the middle of the night by the sound of a radio playing loudly downstairs, even though this had been turned off, she called the police who searched the house and grounds without finding anything suspicious. Two hours later she was woken again by the sound of two young girls standing at the end of her bed, laughing. They were dressed in Edwardian clothes with lace collars and seemed to be amused that the police had been called earlier by their little prank. When challenged they vanished into thin air and were never seen again.

DIRTY DICK'S BOYS CLUB:

You couldn't get away with a name like this today, but in the 1920s and 1930s a club for boys was run in the old vicarage coach-house known as 'Dirty Dicks'. The coach-house still exists at the top of the hill on the right and the name is thought to have come from a warehouse of the same name in London which inspired Charles Dickens, as it had a reputation for never having been cleaned out. I guess the coach-house had the same appearance - and the name stuck.

The land below the old vicarage was known as 'Mills Field'. It was used as allotments before the churchyard was extended in 1959 and the new vicarage bungalow built in 1983.

THE GALLOWS:

A gallows is believed to have been sited at the top of Meeting Street roughly where the old vicarage now stands. Although there is no written evidence about this it is supposed to have been used in the 1700s at a time when Meeting Street was said to be full of robbers and thieves, and that when convicted the condemned didn't have far to walk to be hanged. On dark and windy nights you could apparently still hear the sound of the gallows creaking and chains rattling, and the young people ran past the spot as quickly as they could down Meeting Street. Ah the imagination of youth – but wait a moment, what's that creaking noise…?

BONDS MILL LANE:

The deeds for 30 Meeting Street show that in 1797 the lands from the Independent Chapel upwards were called 'Molford's Ground' and were leased to James Chappell. He was permitted to use the stone from the stables, shippen and barn on the site to build some of these houses. The documents indicate that Green Lane was then apparently known as 'Bond's Mill Lane', and that a mill existed on the corner with Meeting Street. This would probably have been animal-powered producing corn from a grist mill for the local bakers.

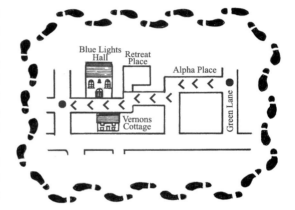

TURN LEFT DOWN ALPHA PLACE AND THEN RIGHT DOWN VERNONS LANE

ALPHA PLACE:

Appledore's longest surviving cobbled street. Note how the cobbles get rougher the further you go down the street. The terrace of houses in Alpha Place was built around 1866. Number 7 was used as the Manse for the Baptist Church between 1894 and 1910. Originally a double-sided terrace was planned

These 3 photos show the changing views of number 1 Alpha Place. Top left shows the house in 1897 with John Lang and his mother Mary. Subsequent generations of the Lang family lived here. The view below was taken in 1927.

for Alpha Place with a similar row of houses on the other side of the street, but thankfully this has still not happened. The allotments facing Alpha Place still contain some North American apple trees brought to England by William Yeo.

The row of houses in Alpha Place.

MOLFORD'S LAND:

The land in this part of Appledore was known as 'Molford's Land', named after a William Molford who owned the land here in the early 1600s. This was long before the Melhuishes became landowners, although these two noble families do appear to have earlier links in other parts of Devon. The Molfords came from South Molton and William Molford first appears as a landowner in Appledore in 1612. By 1630 has built himself a grand house which still exists in Vernons Lane, however the family disappear from Appledore shortly afterwards only to re-appear living on Long Island, New York. This was the height of the Puritan migration to America, so the Molfords probably emigrated for religious reasons.

VERNONS . LANE

The Vernon family appear in parish records as far back as 1610, and a Richard Vernon seems to have been a landowner around this part of the village in the late 1700s.

In the 1841 census Vernons Lane is known as 'Point Lane' and has just eleven dwellings,

one of which is occupied by a Vernon family so it is likely the lane was subsequently named after them, ie: 'the lane where the Vernons live'.

However in the 1871 and 1881 censuses part of Vernons Lane also appears as 'Darts Lane', apparently named after chandler and ironmonger Richard Dart who lived at the bottom of the lane and who died in 1864.

In addition the lower part of the street adjacent to the Quay is not part of Vernons Lane and was known as 'Bethel Ope', but is now known as 'Quayside' (confused? – hmmm, me too!).

VERNONS COTTAGE:

Half-way down the lane and set in its own grounds stands Vernons Cottage. Originally a grand house that fronted onto Meeting Street, the back part now faces Vernons Lane. Its deeds indicate that the newly-appointed Lord-of-the-Manor Thomas Melhuish leased the land to mariner George Limbery in 1685, upon which Philip Gribble built this house. Apart from the annual rent an interesting clause was put in the lease. This stated that whenever George Limbery visited a wine-producing Country he was to bring back a 10-gallon barrel of wine for the use of Thomas Melhuish, for which he would be reimbursed the cost price (just like today, popping over to France on a wine-run). The arrangement obviously worked well for the Melhuishes because sixty years later the deeds state that the new owner George Berrill still had to bring back 10-gallons of wine from each voyage for Roger Melhuish (son of Thomas Melhuish).

Originally it must have been a grand house as in 1768 it was split into four separate dwellings, of which two now form this cottage and the other two front onto Meeting Street.

RETREAT PLACE:

Behind a gate opposite Vernons Cottage is Retreat Place, in which there are a handful of dwellings. One of these is a 400-year-old house with a grand plastered ceiling, probably built by William Molford in the 1620s who managed his estate 'Molfords Land' from here.

Part of the ornate plastered ceiling in a house at Retreat Place.

The house was later bought by Jerome Clapp during his stay here as Independent Chapel minister, although he never lived in it and seems to have taken all the deeds with him when he left Appledore in 1855.

 The ghost of a girl with her hair in ringlets has occasionally been seen in this house. She is believed to be the ghost of 10-year-old Martha Ley whose family were living in Retreat Place at the time. She died in the influenza epidemic of 1918 which claimed more lives than the whole of the 1st World War. During two weeks in October 1918 there were about twenty burials in Appledore, ten-times the normal number. The schools were closed for five weeks to stem the epidemic and there was scarcely a family in Appledore who were unaffected. Many of Martha's school friends attended her funeral in the Church.

BLUE LIGHTS HALL:

Near the bottom of Vernons Lane stands the 'Blue Lights Hall'. Originally built as a Chapel for the Plymouth Brethren in 1868 it now serves as a Public Hall. It was bought by William Anderson (who lived at Wooda) at an

auction in 1922, and after his death it was left to the people of Appledore in 1959 to use for social gatherings.

The 'Blue Lights' name allegedly comes from the time of the Plymouth Brethren, who placed lamps inside the front windows so that people could see their way up the awkward steps in the dark. Unfortunately the glass that the lamps were behind was red. Not wishing to get a reputation that they didn't deserve they moved the lamps behind glass of a different colour – blue. And so blue light shone from the hall and the name stuck. However, the first record of the name 'Blue Lights' does not seem to appear until 1955 so this could be just a 'colourful' story.

UNFIT FOR HABITATION:

In 1970 it was suggested that numbers 2 to 10 Vernons Lane were unfit for human habitation as the narrowness of the street prevented sunlight from reaching them. These houses were to be demolished and replaced with a modern block of flats with garages underneath, set back five feet from the street and the frontage paved with concrete slabs.

Thankfully the people of Appledore fought to prevent such an outrage happening. Unfortunately it's a battle that continues to this day, and we are still fighting to prevent our history being eroded piece by piece.

The wedding party of Beatrice Ley outside her house in Retreat Place in 1930.

A view of Vernons Lane, showing the houses on the right scheduled for demolition in 1970.

The grocery shop of Douglas Austin at 48 Market Street in the 1940s. Prior to that it was a bakery belonging to the Evans family. In 1911 Mary Ann Evans, baker and confectioner of Market Street, won 1st prize for bread-baking in the old-fashioned way.

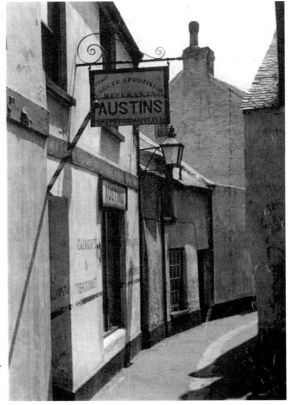

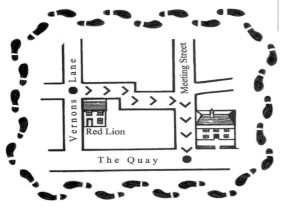

AT THE BOTTOM OF VERNONS LANE TURN LEFT INTO MARKET STREET AND RIGHT TO THE QUAY

THE RED LION:

It doesn't look much like a pub now but number 36 Market Street on the north corner of Quayside and Market Street used to be the 'Red Lion' Inn. It is first mentioned by name in the pub licences of 1822 when the Fishwick family are the owners, and continues as a rough drinking establishment until it is closed for a while in 1874 – the temperance movement claim this as a victory. It re-opened, but in 1882 gained further notoriety when 16-year-old William Tatem and a young lady from Appledore were found drinking on the premises after hours (this was the William Tatem who later became Lord Glanely). The landlord James Braund was found guilty of breaking licensing rules and the pub closed shortly afterwards, never to re-open.

APPLEDORE, DEVON.
TO BE LET, AT CHRISTMAS, THE
'RED LION INN,'
An old established Beer and Spirit House.
☞ Apply to Mr. T. Cook, Appledore. ⌈933

(North Devon Journal: 26th July 1860).

DEATH ON A ROYAL WEDDING DAY:

Next door to the Red Lion at number 38 Market Street, lived the Cox family. In 1893 a tragic event was to hit them which shocked the whole village. 36-year-old Nathaniel Cox and his wife Henrietta had produced seven children and were expecting an eighth. It was a Royal wedding day (the Duke of York was getting married in St James's Palace in London) and Appledore was preparing to celebrate the occasion with a grand sports day and celebration tea in a field on Staddon Hill. As part of the celebrations a small cannon was brought up the hill so that the Royal couple could be given a special salute. Nathaniel Cox was to fire the cannon and at 6:00pm he applied a light to the fuse. What happened next was a noise that left people's ears ringing, but when the smoke cleared it was found that the children's best clothes were spattered with blood and Nathaniel was lying dead on the grass.

Screams rang out and the men rushed to see what had happened. They found that the cannon had exploded and Nathaniel Cox standing behind it had not stood a chance. The shrapnel from the shattered barrel hit him in the head, and he died instantly, the force throwing him 28 feet from the gun. The day's celebrations came to an abrupt halt, Nathaniel's body was covered with the Union Jack and taken back to his house in Market Street using a gate as a stretcher. No-one who was there forgot the horror of that day for the rest of their lives, especially his widow Henrietta who lived in Appledore for another 45 years.

At the inquest into Nathaniel's death it was found that the cannon had been fired several times already that day, but on this occasion Nathaniel Cox tried three times to fire it without success. Another man then tried and failed, following which Nathaniel tried again and the cannon exploded. The gun was blown into about a dozen pieces, with one 6-lb portion being hurled nearly 600 yards down the hill into Chapel Fields. The other man who tried to fire the gun was John Carter – my great great grandfather – who by a twist of fate escaped having his head blown off by the narrowest of margins. If he had, then you wouldn't be reading this book today.

Nathaniel Cox in 1890.

Five days later another explosion was heard at Appledore. Some dynamite cartridges were pulled from the river in a salmon net by George Evans. These had probably been used by Trinity House when blowing up the wreck of a ship a few years earlier on Braunton Sands.

Unfortunately some children got hold of these and put them on a bonfire on the beach below the Beaver Inn. The explosion broke several windows in the pub and cut through an iron chain and an oak mooring post, but fortunately no-one was hurt.

A REMARKABLE VOYAGE:

Across the street at number 39 lived the Stoneman family. John Henry Stoneman grew up here in the 1880s, but in 1893 at the age of 21 he took part in a remarkable voyage to Siberia. With him were William Labbett and Alexander Ross from Vernon's Lane, John Marshall from Darracotts Court and John Carter from Irsha Street. Together they made an extraordinary journey around the northern arctic coast of Tsarist Russia, contracted to carry 1,600 tons of rails for the Trans-Siberian Railway, then under construction. They had three vessels but all of the Appledore men sailed together on the 'Blencathra', a vessel that was specially strengthened in the Richmond Dock to prepare her for the ice-packed waters of the northern ocean. She took provisions for three years, the crew not knowing how long they would be gone. As it happened their voyage lasted just four months, but covered 6,000 miles and many strange sights were encountered, including the aurora borealis, ice falling from the encrusted rigging, the whaling factories of Vardo, the convict stevedores unloading cargo at Golchika and the local people living in eskimo-like dwellings.

John Carter's discharge papers from the 'Blencathra' after his unique voyage along the northern coast of Russia in 1893.

ADOLPHUS HOCKING:

At number 40 Market Street lived Adolphus St.David Hocking. He was brought up in a two-room house in Ibex Court, but he wasn't born there - he was actually born in a much lowlier place. In fact his middle name (St. David) gives us a clue as to his birth place. No, not St David's in Wales – the 1891 census records that he was born "in the train near Exeter" and was therefore named after the Station where his mother finally embarked – Exeter St David's. He's the only person I know to have been named after a railway station!

END OF THE TOUR:

Turn right to take yourself back to the Quay. Sadly we've now reached the end of our tour around historical Appledore. I hope you have enjoyed the literary journey and have learnt some fascinating new things about this magical place.

We finish at the same point we started, overlooking the car-park and new concrete slipway - both rather incongruous in this historical setting – but I'll leave you puzzling over some final strange events....

THE

END

Appledore Quay around 1925, with the ketch 'Francis Beddoe' in the centre of the picture.
The boys: Billy Fishwick, Frederick Vanstone and Billy Down are jostling for the best position in the photo.

STRANGE PHENOMENA:

In a village which always keeps one eye on the sea it is not surprising that tide-related matters are a topic of conversation, but these are rather stranger than most:

- An odd event was observed in 1859 when the level of the river suddenly rose about four feet, and just as suddenly receded. This effect was reported in other places around Cornwall and Somerset and was attributed to under-sea volcanic activity. A fisherman who was on the river at the time found himself lifted high and dry on the beach.

- In 1903 the outgoing tide suddenly started flowing back in again - in fact it poured up the river in a three-foot high wave. No damage was reported, just some rather puzzled looks on the faces of the sailors.

meant that someone needed a ferryman to bring them across the river. A couple of the sailors took a boat out to investigate and it was a stiff row against the incoming tide. When they arrived they found an immaculately dressed gentleman waiting for them, all in evening dress wearing a silk top hat, a black silk cape lined with red and carrying a silver cane. The sailors thought of the generous tip that they would receive after bringing this man across the river, so they were very deferential to him, and politely rowed him to Appledore where he was helped out of the boat at the Bethel slip. A small crowd had gathered to see who this important gentleman was, curious sailors and women carrying babies in shawls. The gentleman was carefully helped out of the boat but the rowers didn't quite get the tip they were expecting. Instead the man smiled, tapped his cane on the ground and immediately turned into a ball of fire which rolled up the slip-way and away out of Appledore up Meeting Street.

The women were too afraid to sleep for some nights and the two boatmen's hair turned white with shock. Appledore people still talk of the night the Devil paid them a visit.

THE DAY THE DEVIL CAME TO APPLEDORE:

Even more puzzled faces were observed on the sailors who often gathered at the end of the quay here, during this factual event recorded in the memoirs of Philip John Bailey (1912-1997).

Some of the men gathered on the Quay noticed a light burning at Crow Point, lit to attract attention, which generally

Do you speak Appledorian?

Many English regions developed their own words and dialect, some of which have spread into common usage. Appledore is an insular place and many phrases used by Appledore people were unheard in other places. You may still hear a few of them being used in the village, but most have fallen into disuse. Fifty years ago however you would be quite likely to have overheard the following conversation on the Quay:

Ahoy *me 'anse* [my handsome], *Ow be knacking?* [How are you?].

Weest [poorly] Davvy, me *heed is bullbaiting* [got a thumping headache]. That *hanging chain* [up to no good] son of mine be the death of me, *gert yard o' pump water* [thin]. He's lately been a bit *zim-zam* [off his food] and is now as *fat as Hammet's cat* [a scrawny creature].

Wo be too? [Where is he?].

Gone abroad [left the house] this morning to see some *Westby Stranner* [someone born at the Western end of Appledore] he be *mazed as a brish* [completely mad] about, an' he's never got more than *toodree shillings* [two or three shillings] to 'is name. I said *"Wo be gwain* [Where are you going] *sal hatch* [dressed funny] *in this scat?* [light rain]. *E be fleating* [You'll be wet through] *afore e run a cable length* [before you get 200 yards]", I says.

"Appledore maid" [girl born in Appledore] says he, as if I didn't know his *missledraft* [small thing] *dipper* [bucket for baling out a boat] is on the *thwarts* [a seat running across a boat] so that he can't tell sliced *cuckumbers* [cucumbers] from *'eel taps* [thin sliced potatoes].

So with me so-wester set against the *scat* [light rain], I gave stern chase, *dapping on* [hurrying along], and as I takes a bearing on the Quay here, him be a *traipsing along* [wandering aimlessly] yard-arm a yard-arm, *all oory-tory.* [pretentiously grand].

Efty wench [large young woman] *'er be* [she is], as big as he, an' proud with it, *put in the orben* [oven] *with the loaves, an' taken out with the cakes* [an over-rated person].
Married afore too, I reckon. Never *seed nort like it* [seen nothing like it]. Not that I would care for some *zamboid* [overcooked/spoilt food] *boily-bake* [boiled up mixture of meat & vegetables] *orts* [leftovers] from another man's *trencher* [wooden platter] myself. It's all too *cawch* [unfamiliar food] for me.

Only *a fleating* [wet through] *dough-bake* [simpleton] like 'e, would be interested in holding hands with some *Hanna McDonald* [someone all dressed up*] out in *scat* [light rain], if she thinks herself the *cat's mother* [thinks a lot of herself].

So *there'm be* [there they are], and being the old *rug* [rogue] that I am, not wanting any *nimming & namming* [hesitating], I walks up, an' introduces me'self, in case there's been any *akum for squakum* [misunderstanding]. Looking down from her great nose, as though I was a load of *shozens* [sheep droppings] she says *"Dunnum talk funny"* [Doesn't he talk strange].

The cheek of 'er! If she were mine, I'd have given her a right *dough-dap [a smack]* to *set her jib aright* [straighten her up], so I would.

And then I starts to have me doubts. It ain't that I would expect a maid her age to come into the wind with *cleared decks* [tidied up] *all like minter* [spotlessly clean], but I could see that her top-hamper an running rigging was all *fraped up* [improvised job] with oakum, she weren't a *chiel* [young girl] at all.

Trust my boy to get himself *luffed up* [messed up] *and mazed as a gawk* [completely mad] over some *widdershins* [perverse] *rug* [rogue], flying false colours with his trousers *backsy-fore* [back-to-front]. And she's only useful as an *ornament* [someone whose use is only decorative].

An' I told him to his face I did, *Tid'n* [It isn't] natural, *t'wad'n* [It wasn't] right, an' told 'er not to see my boy again, and leave 'e alone.

"Well me hanse," she says over her shoulder as she minces up the *drang* [alleyway], "You're a *bitter weed* [never say anything good], but if *he can't have hake, he shall have to have herring* [make do with something cheaper]". ~

And if you can follow that, without resort to the translations, then consider yourself a true Appledorian.

* refers to the old Appledore lifeboat of that name.

BIBLIOGRAPHY:

Victoria County History of Devon, Vol.1.
New Maritime History of Devon, Vol.2.
Appledore Baptist Church History, 2005.
A Book of Remembrance, Baptist Churches in North Devon, 1885.
Devon & Exeter in the Civil War, Eugine Andriette.
Maid of Sker, R D Blackmore.
Disappeaing Devon, Pauline & Robert Brain.
Devon Reflections, Jilly Carter.
Devon Tales of Mystery and Murder, Judy Chard.
Rev Jerome Clapp in Appledore, Peter Christie, Devonshire Association 2007.
A Living from the Sea, Devon's Fishing Industry and its Fishermen, edited by M G Dickenson.
Smuggling Survey, North Devon, Graham Farr (NDRO Athenaeum ref: D364 Far).
Curse, Daniel Farson.
Queen of the Estuary, Harry C Finn, 1967.
Follies Journal, Number 5, 2005. the Folly Fellowship.
Lundy's War, compiled by Mary Gade & Michael Harman.
Trial of the Bideford Witches, Frank Gent, 1982.
Old Bideford & District, Muriel Goaman.
Lost Devon, Felicity Goodall.
Salmon Netting in North Devon, Alison Grant & Philip Waters.
Devon and the Slave Trade, Todd Gray.
Tudor and Stuart Devon, edited by Todd Gray, Margery Rowe & Anthony Erskine.
Westcountrymen in Prince Edward's Isle, Basil Greenhill & Ann Giffard.
1607 coastal flood in the Bristol Channel, Simon Haslett & Edward Bryant.
The Press-Gang Afloat and Ashore, John R. Hutchinson.
Yankee Jack Sails Again, Tony James.
Bideford, Westward Ho! & Appledore Railway, Stanley C Jenkins.
Lundy, Island without Equal, Lois Lamplugh.
Two Rivers Meeting, Lois Lampugh.
Estuary & River Ferries of South West England, Martin Langley & Edwina Small.
Shipwrecks of the Devon Coast, Richard Larn.
Shipwreck Index of the British Isles, Richard & Bridget Larn.
I Remember, Lottie Hetty Linstead.
Haunted Places in Devon, Rupert Matthews.
North-East Passage to Muscovy - Stephen Borough & the first Tudor Explorations, Kit Mayers.
m.s. Oldenburg, Stanley Newman.
Tales of Old Devon, Sally Norris.
The Making of the Novelist by Nikolai Tolstoy, Patrick O'Brian.
Tiger Bay and the Docks, Dan O'Neill.
SBS, The inside Story of the Special Boat Service, John Parker.
Life in Nelson's Navy, Dudley Pope.
A Field Guide to the Archaeology of the Taw and Torridge Estuaries, Chris Preece.
The English Resistance - the Underground War against the Normans, Peter Rex.
Trinity House Petitions, Society of Genealogists 1987.
Looking Back, Muriel Stanton.
Loyalty and Locality, Popular Allegiance in Devon during the Civil War, Mark Stoyle.
Lives of the Queens of England Vol 1, Agnes Strickland.
Strong's Industries of North Devon, 1889 & 1971.
The Nightingale Scandal, Stanley Thomas, 1979.
Northam Burrows, Philip Waters.
The Pathway, Henry Williamson.

ACKNOWLEDGEMENTS:

This book is dedicated to the people of Appledore – past and present.

Many people have helped me with this – far too many to acknowledge individually, but I couldn't have done it without you. So thanks to everyone who showed me your photo albums, personal documents, and provided me with stories and artifacts – you know who you are, and my thanks go out to you all.

I will specifically acknowledge the following for their special help:

· Bill Wright for his excellent illustrations.

· Warren Collum for his graphic design work.

· North Devon Record Office at Barnstaple,
· Devon Record Office at Exeter,
· North Devon Journal Collection at North Devon Athenaeum,
· Northam Community Archive,
· Exeter Local Studies Library,
· Somerset Record Office,
· National Monuments Record Centre, Swindon,
· National Archives, Kew,
· UK Hydrographic Office, Taunton,
· and not least the Appledore Library.

· Tommy Waters, Mark Woolaway and Des Cole for their local knowledge and assistance.

· Jim Jackson, for the Appledorian story.

· Julia and Zoe for their proof-reading, and telling me where to stick my commas and apostrophes!

· Last but not least: Jenny for her un-ending tolerance of living with a reclusive author, and allowing me the time to work on this over the past few years.

There's a lot more history out there, in documents which haven't made it into the public domain. We can still add to our pot of knowledge about Appledore, so I would be pleased for more people to share these with me. There might even be enough for another book!

I hope you have enjoyed reading this, as much as I enjoyed writing it. If it has at least sparked your interest about Appledore's past, then it's all been worth it.

Surname Index: